Contents

Introduction

If you are new to Ashton-Tate's *dBASE* family of products, this book will make it possible for you to start working immediately with the newest member: *dBASE IV*. If you are already familiar with *dBASE*, this book will acquaint you with the many new features of *dBASE IV*.

In keeping with the times, *dBASE IV* is a relational database. It incorporates SQL, the Structured Query Language originated by IBM, in both the interactive form (where you need no knowledge of programming or the internal structure of *dBASE*), and the embedded form (which you can use to run a program containing SQL commands).

dBASE IV also supports QBE (Query By Example), another IBM creation, as well as many other new features to make your database management tasks simpler and faster. At the same time, it retains the efficiency and easy-to-learn characteristics of the *dBASE* language.

dBASE IV will cover a wide range of database management needs, from the small, single-user operation on a microcomputer, all the way to large installations with many work stations. In addition to supplying you with an efficient system for storing and retrieving data, it will simplify your report writing, form design for on-screen use, and customized label design and printing.

Since *dBASE IV* is designed to cover the needs of a wide range of computer sophistication, this text is also directed to both the casual user who has no knowledge of programming and the professional programmer who writes application programs. The chapter descriptions that follow indicate which portions the nonprogrammer may skip and still have a working knowledge of *dBASE IV*.

The contents of this book, chapter by chapter, are as follows:

Chapter 1 gives an overview of the functions of *dBASE IV* with a brief explanation of the various features. It also lists those features that are new or modified compared with previous *dBASE* products.

If you have used previous versions of *dBASE*, you will be especially interested in Chapter 2, which shows the new commands and functions appearing in *dBASE IV*, as well as the modifications that have been made to preexisting *dBASE* commands and functions. If you are new to *dBASE*, you might want to only scan Chapter 2, rather than to go through it thoroughly at first reading.

Chapter 3 opens the door to *dBASE IV* by describing the Control Center—the core of the Non-Procedural Interface. The next four chapters discuss the functions of the six main panels of the Control Center.

Chapter 4 explains how to set up and use database files, which can be reached through the Control Center (for nonprocedural use) or through the dot prompt for procedural work with the files.

Chapter 5 explains and illustrates how to use the new QBE facility. This feature is especially useful to users who are not familiar with programming and who need to work with the database.

Chapter 6 explains the many possibilities for creating and using forms, reports, and labels. The way you customize your output is limited only by your own imagination and hardware, since *dBASE IV* offers a wide variety of colors, border designs, print styles, and possible formats for these purposes.

In Chapter 7, the *dBASE IV* applications generator (APGEN) is explained. You can use APGEN to help generate applications to modify your database files. For example, if someone else is entering data into one of your database files, you can set up menus and screens to be used specifically for this task. These menus and screens will make it unnecessary for the data entry personnel to know anything about the *dBASE* language.

Chapter 8 gives an overview of the Procedural Interface (PI) to *dBASE IV*. PI allows you to run programs and procedures that you have written into .PRG or .PRS files (where .PRG denotes *dBASE* programs and .PRS denotes SQL programs) to be used with your database. The difference between using APGEN to write programs and writing your own programs is that APGEN helps you set up your applications, whereas you do your own coding with PI. (If, however, you use APGEN, you will still have to embed some codes in your applications.) The choice of doing all your own coding via PI or using APGEN is yours. PI is where you run programs using the DO command.

Chapter 9 contains a description of the security and integrity system built into *dBASE IV*. The software provides for a range of security measures you can institute according to your own needs for confidentiality of different parts of your database. The security system, called PROTECT, allows you to take advantage of your security needs through a system of passwords, data encryption, and restricted access wherever your operation requires these measures. To maintain the integrity of your system, *dBASE IV* has a system of catalogs, mostly with automatic updating, which, in conjunction with a system of locks for multiuser situations, keep data current and valid.

Chapter 10 starts the explanation of SQL (pronounced "sequel"), the Structured Query Language that has been built into *dBASE IV*. In this chapter, the syntax for setting up the database objects (tables, synonyms, indices) is illustrated.

Chapter 11 shows how to manipulate your data within the SQL framework. It covers queries and subqueries, aggregate functions, comparison operators, clauses, and expressions.

Chapter 12 explains how to create views, load and unload data, update the database, and use joins, all in the SQL language.

Chapter 13 explains how to embed SQL within the *dBASE* language so you can write programs that include SQL statements. In previous versions of *dBASE*, before *dBASE* included SQL, you had to write programs to be included in .PRG files. With embedded SQL, you write programs that include SQL statements to be performed in SQL mode and included in .PRS files.

Chapter 14 discusses the use of *dBASE IV* in a local area network (LAN) environment.

Appendix A contains a list of *dBASE IV* SQL error messages. Appendix B lists all of the *dBASE* commands used in *dBASE IV*, and shows which commands can be used in SQL statements. Appendix C lists all of the *dBASE* functions used in *dBASE IV* and shows which functions can be used in SQL statements.

The glossary defines the specific terms used in this book. It should be especially helpful if you are new to *dBASE* or new to the field of database management systems.

The index has been heavily cross-referenced and made as complete as possible to aid you in quickly locating the information you need while working at your computer.

1

What Is dBASE IV?

dBASE IV is the newest member of Ashton-Tate's *dBASE* family of database management programs. It incorporates vast changes from previous *dBASE* products. Some of these changes are entirely new, and some are enhancements of previous facilities. At the same time, it retains the simplicity and ease of use of the *dBASE* language. If you are already a user of *dBASE*, you will find many enhancements to the commands that you have been using.

Everything you used in previous versions of *dBASE* is in *dBASE IV*, but there are also many additions that will make your job easier. Therefore you can continue to work with the familiar aspects of *dBASE IV* and add the new features at your leisure. You will find that your database files, forms, reports, and application programs from the previous versions are upwardly compatible with *dBASE IV*.

If you are new to *dBASE*, you need to know that *dBASE IV* is a relational database system with many ways of doing anything you would ever want to do with a database management system. You can create databases containing multiple files (called *tables* in relational database terminology). Once you have set up your files, you can insert data into them, update the data, create and run forms and reports, design and print labels, query the database for information, and create and run application programs.

Features of dBASE IV

One of the principal new features of *dBASE IV* that makes it easy for you to learn to do these things is the Control Center. The Control Center is a screen with six panels, each corresponding to a different kind of operation on your database. If you are not an accomplished programmer, you probably will work mainly from the Control Center at first.

Everything that you do from the Control Center is organized and recorded in a Catalog file. The name of the catalog and the path to the catalog are prominently displayed on the Control Center screen.

If you decide not to take advantage of the Control Center, you can do everything you could do from the Control Center from the dot prompt. At the dot prompt, you can issue *dBASE* commands; for interactive work with your database, however, it is much easier to work from the Control Center. The main function of the dot prompt is to allow you to start programs and applications and enter SQL (pronounced ''sequel''), the Structured Query Language.

The addition of SQL is a very important new feature of *dBASE IV*. This simplified approach to querying a database is now available within the *dBASE* structure, both as an interactive feature and as an embedded capability. Facility with interactive SQL can easily be acquired by even the casual user who does not want or need to learn a programming language. Chapters 10 through 12 describe the SQL language as it is used in *dBASE IV*. For the programmer, Chapter 13 shows how to embed SQL in the *dBASE* language.

You can reach interactive SQL from the dot prompt. After executing the command SET SQL ON at the dot prompt, you can use the full power of the SQL query language to create and manipulate your database. Programs using embedded SQL can be started at the dot prompt.

As an alternative to using SQL at the dot prompt, you might want to use QBE (Query By Example) through the Control Center. QBE is another new feature. Instead of having to be concerned with the syntax of formulating queries, with QBE you merely show *dBASE IV* "by example" what you want from the database.

Appendix B contains a brief description of all of the *dBASE* commands, and indicates whether they are new or modified in *dBASE IV*, and whether or not they can be used in SQL.

Appendix C does the same thing for *dBASE* functions that Appendix B does for *dBASE* commands.

For the benefit of previous *dBASE* users, the following is a list of the differences between *dBASE IV* and its predecessor, *dBASE III Plus*. These are in addition to the new features mentioned previously.

- ☐ Aliases supported: Instead of SELECTing a work area, you can now use the alias name in your commands.
- ☐ Applications generator supported.
- ☐ Array support: Memory variable arrays are a new feature, and there are now commands to take advantage of arrays.
- ☐ Command line error handling improved.
- ☐ Command line length is increased.
- ☐ Critical error handling enhanced.
- ☐ Database structures extended.
- ☐ Date delimiters: Braces ("curly brackets") can now be substituted for the character-to-date (CTOD) conversion function.
- ☐ Debugger enhanced.
- ☐ Disk space available checked automatically.
- ☐ DXREF Utility: Now provides Control structure checking, cross-referencing, flow-chart capability, and automatic indenting.
- ☐ Financial functions supported.
- ☐ Fixed/floating point numeric support.
- ☐ Foreign-file support enhanced.
- ☐ Help System enhanced (is now context-sensitive).
- ☐ Indexing method improved.
- ☐ Interface enhanced: Control Center provides easy user interface.

☐ Mathematical functions added.

☐ Memo field improved.

☐ Memory variables increased: You can now have up to 2048 memory variables.

☐ Menus now user-definable.

☐ MODIFY COMMAND/MODIFY LABEL editor enhanced.

☐ Multiple child relations supported.

☐ Multiuser automatic locks provided for files and records.

☐ Number of open files increased.

☐ Printed output quality enhanced.

☐ Procedures enhanced.

☐ PROTECT utility now available from dot prompt.

☐ Pseudocompiler included.

☐ Read-only DOS files now allowed.

☐ Statistical functions added.

☐ Transaction logging now supported.

☐ Transform file (for quick searches of memo and nonmemo fields) now supported.

☐ User-defined functions now supported.

☐ Windowing supported.

Conventions Used in This Book

The use of conventions and notation in this text coincides with those used in your Ashton-Tate documentation. You will find it is easy to use this text in conjunction with the manuals provided to you with *dBASE IV.* Following is a list of notations used.

ANGLE BRACKETS INDICATE WHAT YOU FILL IN. Angle brackets enclose a general term describing the specific term that you must fill in. For example, <*filename*> means that you will fill in the name of a file in your database. (You do not put the angle brackets around the file name when you do fill it in.)

SQUARE BRACKETS INDICATE AN OPTIONAL TERM. Square brackets indicate that the term inside them is optional; you may choose to include it or not. For example,

```
SELECT <target list>
FROM <clause>
[WHERE <clause>];
```

means that you have the option of adding a WHERE clause to the commands listed. Do not put the square brackets around the enclosed term if you do choose to use it in a SQL statement.

ELLIPSES INDICATE CONTINUATION. An ellipsis means that the same item continues. For example, *column 1, column 2, . . ., column N* means that the numbered columns continue, no matter how many there are, until the last numbered column (N) appears.

COMMANDS AND FUNCTIONS ARE IN ALL CAPS. All dBASE IV commands and functions are shown in ALL CAPS. You do not have to enter them that way when you use them. You may enter them in uppercase letters (i.e., all caps), lowercase letters, or a combination of upper- and lowercase letters. Thus, you may enter the command SELECT as select, SELECT, or Select.

INITIAL CAPS INDICATE FILE AND TABLE NAMES; LOWERCASE LETTERS INDICATE COLUMN AND FIELD NAMES. In this book, file and table names are entered with an initial capital letter, and column and field names are entered in all lowercase letters:

Employee Table

   containing columns or fields: name, address, salary.

In many cases the names also will be in a sans-serif type face. (Occasionally this convention will change for a specific reason; when this happens, the change will be explained in the text.)

   You may use your own conventions regarding the upper and lower cases for table and column names.

SLASHES INDICATE THAT YOU HAVE A CHOICE. A slash within an expression is used to indicate that you have a choice among two or more possibilities. For example, the notation (ALL/SOME/ANY) means that you may choose one of the terms ALL or SOME or ANY.

SEMICOLONS ARE TERMINATORS FOR SQL STATEMENTS. The semicolon is used to terminate all *dBASE IV* SQL statements. (Note that it is not used to terminate *dBASE IV* statements that are not SQL statements.) In *dBASE*, the semicolon means that the command continues on the following line.

Database Objects

The individual databases within your database management system—as well as the tables, views, indices, synonyms, aliases, columns, and rows that you can create—are called *database objects*. When this term appears, it will refer to one or more of these entities, with its exact meaning made clear by the context.

Summary

In addition to being compatible with previous versions of the program, *dBASE IV* contains the following new features:

- ☐ A new user interface called the Control Center
- ☐ The Structured Query Language (SQL) both in its interactive and embedded form.
- ☐ An alternative query language, Query By Example (QBE), allows you to simply place the components of your query in appropriate boxes rather than adhering to the semantic rules of querying.

For the benefit of previous *dBASE* users, the major differences between *dBASE III PLUS* and *dBASE IV* are listed.
The conventions and notations used throughout this book are listed and illustrated.

2

New and Modified dBASE Commands and Functions

Compared to *dBASE III PLUS*, *dBASE IV* provides a greatly increased set of commands and functions. Most of the *III PLUS* commands and functions still exist, but many have been modified to be more functional, and others have been replaced by new commands or functions. In this chapter, we will survey what has been modified and what is new. Since complete details on every change made in *dBASE III PLUS* to produce *dBASE IV* is beyond the scope of this book, you will occasionally be referred to *dBASE IV* documentation.

Modified Commands and Functions

This section lists those *dBASE III PLUS* commands and functions that have been modified in *dBASE IV* and shows what modifications have occurred.

The @ Command

The @ command has been greatly extended to include many

optional clauses that will allow you to trap data-entry errors and display your own error and help messages. The format for the modified @ command is:

```
@ <row,col>
  [SAY <expression>
    [PICTURE <clause>]
    [FUNCTION <function list>]
  ]
  [GET <variable>
    [[OPEN] WINDOW <window name>]
    [PICTURE <clause>]
    [FUNCTION <function list>]
    [RANGE <exp>,<exp>]
    [VALID <condition>]
    [ERROR <expC>]
    [WHEN <condition>]
    [DEFAULT <exp>]
    [MESSAGE <expC>]
  ]
  [COLOR [<standard>],[<enhanced>]]]
```

where:

- □ <row,col> are the screen position coordinates.

- □ [PICTURE <clause>] [FUNCTION <function list>] now allows four new picture functions:

  L Displays leading zeros.

  $ Displays a currency symbol immediately before the amount, and a separator symbol between the thousands. (See also SET SEPARATOR, SET CURRENCY, and SET POINT.)

  ^ Indicates exponential format.

  M Enumerated data types. The format of this function is:

  ```
  PICTURE '@M <list of valid values>'
  ```

  where the *list of valid values* can be either strings or numbers separated by commas. You can toggle through the list either by using the space bar, or by typing the first character of the desired value. The value is selected by striking the enter key or one of the cursor keys.

☐ [[OPEN] WINDOW <*window name*>] is used to specify the name of a previously defined window. (See the DEFINE WINDOW command following.) If OPEN is specified, the window will display with the memo field open; otherwise, the window will be closed and the field will be displayed with the name. This clause only works if the variable of the GET clause is a memo field. When the cursor is advanced to the memo field you must press Ctrl-Home before the memo field can be edited. When you press Ctrl-Home, the window is activated and the variable is edited within the window.

☐ VALID <*condition*> is any logical expression, e.g.:] GET pay VALID pay > 0.

☐ ERROR <*expC*> is an error message to be displayed if VALID <*condition*> is not satisfied.

☐ WHEN <*condition*> is any valid logical expression. The condition must be satisfied before you are allowed to edit the GET variable. If the condition is false, the cursor will skip the field and go to the next field.

☐ DEFAULT <*exp*> is an expression that must match the data type of the GET variable; <*exp*> specifies a DE-FAULT value for the GET variable.

☐ MESSAGE <*expC*> displays a character string centered on the bottom line of the screen if STATUS is on.

☐ COLOR is of the same form as in the SET COLOR command:

[foreground color code [/background color code]

The @ . . . TO . . . command, which draws a box on the screen, has been extended to have the following format:

@ <row1>,<col1> TO *<row2>,<col2>* COLOR*<color attribute>*[DOUBLE/PANEL/NONE/*<border string>*]

where:

-   ☐ *<color attribute>* follows the same rules as the SET COLOR command.
-   ☐ [DOUBLE/PANEL/NONE/*<border string>*] overrides the SET BORDER command.

The new @ . . . FILL TO . . . command allows you to fill a rectangular region of the screen with a specified color attribute. The format of this command is:

   @ *<coordinates>* FILL TO *<coordinates>* COLOR *<color attribute>*

APPEND

Some new features have been added to the APPEND command. One of them is to APPEND from an array of memory variables declared with the new ARRAY command. The format for this is:

   APPEND FROM ARRAY *<array name>* [FOR *<condition>*]

The elements are appended one row at a time when the condition (if the optional FOR clause is used) is evaluated as true. Of course, the data types must match.

Another modification to the APPEND command allows a memo field to be appended from a text file (usually having the file extension .TXT). The format for this is:

   APPEND MEMO *<memo field name>* FROM *<filename>* [OVERWRITE]

The new text is appended to the existing text unless the OVERWRITE option is used.

The APPEND FROM *<filename>* command has been modified to allow three more file types:

-   ☐ dBASE II   dBASE II files (file extension must be .DB2).

☐ FW2   *Framework* spreadsheet and database types
☐ RPD   *Rapidfile.*

The MODIFY COMMAND Command

Included in *dBASE IV* is a new editor capable of editing files of unlimited size with lines up to and including 1024 characters. In addition, the new editor is able to work within a named window. (See DEFINE WINDOW.) To accommodate working within windows, the new format of the MODIFY COMMAND command is:

MODIFY COMMAND *<filename>* [WINDOW *<window name>*]

The new editor is also invoked when you attempt to edit a memo field.

If you use the TEDIT= option in the Config.DB file, the WINDOW option will be ignored.

BROWSE

The complete syntax for the modified BROWSE command is:

BROWSE [NOINIT] [NOFOLLOW] [NOAPPEND] [NOMENU] [NOEDIT]
  [NODELETE] [NOCLEAR] [COMPRESS] [FORMAT]
  [LOCK *<expN>*] [WIDTH *<expN>*] [FREEZE *<field name>*]
  [WINDOW *<window name>*]
  [FIELDS *<field name>* [/R][/*<n>*] /*<calculated field id>*
   [,*<field name>* [/R][/*<n>*] /*<calculated field id>*
  . . .] . . .]

where:

☐ [NOINIT] is an option to call up the previously defined BROWSE or EDIT configuration. For example, BROWSE NOINIT will use the table of the previous BROWSE.

☐ [NOEDIT] puts the BROWSE table in a read-only state.

☐ [NODELETE] prevents deletion of records.

☐ [NOCLEAR] will cause the table to remain on the screen when you exit BROWSE.

☐ [COMPRESS] compresses the table slightly to allow two more lines of data on the screen.

☐ [FORMAT] allows BROWSE to use the current format file if there is one. If not, BROWSE will create its own.

☐ [WINDOW <*window name*>] will cause BROWSE to work within a window defined by the DEFINE WINDOW command.

☐ [FIELDS] has been modified as follows:

/R   is the optional read-only flag.

<n>   is the width of the column in which the field is displayed.

<*calculated field id*> is of the form:
<*calculated field name*> = <*expression*>.

EDIT

EDIT has been modified to support the BROWSE features so that you can flip back and forth between BROWSE and EDIT. The format for the modified EDIT command is:

EDIT [FIELDS <*field list*>] [<*scope*>] [FOR <*condition*>]
[WHILE <*condition*>] [NOFOLLOW] [NOINIT] [NOMENU]
[NOCLEAR] [NOAPPEND] [NODELETE] [NOEDIT]

You should compare this new format with the BROWSE command in order to understand the new options.

SET CARRY

A new version of SET CARRY has been added to make it

possible to specify the fields that will be carried forward:

SET CARRY TO [<*field list*>] [ADDITIVE]

The ADDITIVE option is allowed to add the list to those fields already specified with SET CARRY TO.

The SET CARRY ON/OFF command still exists, but if you use it without the SET CARRY TO, all fields will be carried.

CHANGE

The CHANGE command has been modified to support EDIT features, including the NOEDIT, NODELETE, NOAPPEND, NOFOLLOW, NOINIT, NOMENU, and NOCLEAR options. (See BROWSE.) The new format for CHANGE is:

CHANGE [NOFOLLOW] [NOINIT] [NOMENU]
 [NOCLEAR] [NOAPPEND] [NODELETE] [NOEDIT] [<*expN*>]
 [FIELDS <*field list*>] [<*scope*>] [FOR <*condition*>]
 [WHILE <*condition*>]

CREATE/MODIFY

CREATE/MODIFY QUERY/VIEW <*filename*>/? will now invoke QBE (see Chapter 5 for details on QBE). The ? will Query the current catalog for files.

CREATE/MODIFY SCREEN/REPORT/LABEL will be upwardly compatible with *dBASE III PLUS* (see also Chapter 3).

CREATE/MODIFY APPLICATION <*filename*>/? will invoke APGEN (see Chapter 7 for details on APGEN).

SET FORMAT

SET FORMAT TO [<*format filename*>/?] will enable you to use .FMT files from *dBASE III PLUS* or forms designed using the *dBASE IV* forms designer. SET FORMAT TO begins by trying to find a .FMO file. If it can't find one, it tries to find a .FMT file and compile it into an .FMO file. A format file can now contain DEFINE WINDOW commands in the initialization portion.

If a format file is active and an EDIT, READ, INSERT, APPEND, or BROWSE command occurs, the initialization part of the format file will be executed. Then the command will be performed using the forms control portion of the format file.

GOTO and SKIP

The GOTO and SKIP commands have been modified so that the work area can be identified in the command. The formats are:

GO/GOTO TOP/BOTTOM/[RECORD] <expN> [IN <alias name>]

SKIP [<expN>] [IN <alias name>]

INDEX

Now *dBASE IV* allows descending as well as ascending indexes. Many indexes can be kept in one file, each with a *tag* name. The new files will have a .MDX file extension. Old *dBASE III PLUS* .NDX files are upwardly compatible. The new format for the INDEX command is:

INDEX [ON <key expression>] TO <index file>]/[TAG <MDXtag> OF <MDXname>]] [UNIQUE] [DESCENDING] [DISTINCT]

If the TAG clause is missing, an NDX index file will be created. If the TAG clause is included, an MDX index is created and placed in the target MDX file. Each MDX file can have a maximum of 47 index tags.

dBASE IV has a command to convert NDX files to MDX. The format is:

COPY INDEXES/TAG <taglist> [TO <MDXfilename>]

If the optional TO clause is missing, the production MDX file will be assumed. There will be a default production MDX file for each database file. It will have the same name as the database file with an MDX file extension.

TAG names have the same naming conventions as memory variable names. As a result of the changes in indexing, the SET ORDER TO command has the following format:

SET ORDER TO [<expN>] / [TAG <MDXtag> [OF <MDXname>]]

where:

☐ < *expN* > is limited to seven open NDX files and cannot be used if the active database has an associated MDX file.

☐ TAG < MDX*tag* > specifies the MDX TAG of the index.

☐ OF < MDX*name* > is optional if there is a production MDX file in use.

The named index becomes the new MASTER index.

SET ORDER TO 0 and SET ORDER TO < *cr* > return the database to its natural order and all indexes continue to be updated. The REINDEX command will REINDEX all open MDX and NDX files.

Tags may be removed from MDX files by the new DELETE TAG command:

DELETE TAG < MDX*tag1* > [OF < MDX*name* >] / < NDX*tag1* >
[, < MDX*tag2* > [OF < MDX*name* >] / < NDX*tag2* > . . .]

where:

☐ < NDX*tag* > provides a convenient way to close NDX files.

☐ < MDX*tag* > actually deletes the index TAG. If all MDX TAGs are deleted from an MDX file, the file will be deleted.

DISPLAY STATUS

DISPLAY STATUS will now display index information. All NDX files and MDX files active in each work area will be listed along with their key expressions.

LIST and DISPLAY

All list commands in *dBASE IV* are able to send output to a file. The DISPLAY STRUCTURE command can designate an alias work area. The new formats for these commands are:

```
LIST [OFF] [<scope>] [ [FIELDS] <field list>] [<expression list>]
   [WHILE <condition>] [FOR <condition>]
   [TO FILE <filename>/TO PRINTER]

LIST FILES [LIKE <skeleton>] [TO FILE <filename>/TO PRINTER]

LIST HISTORY [LAST <expN>] [TO FILE <filename>/TO PRINTER]

LIST MEMORY [TO FILE <filename>/TO PRINTER]

LIST STATUS [TO FILE <filename>/TO PRINTER]

LIST STRUCTURE [IN <alias name>]
   [TO FILE <filename>/TO PRINTER]

DISPLAY STRUCTURE [IN <alias name>]
   [TO PRINTER]/TO FILE <filename>]
```

If the TO FILE option is used, output will be to both the screen and the disk file. After the DISPLAY STRUCTURE command is performed, the original work area is automatically reselected.

DISPLAY MEMORY and LIST MEMORY

The DISPLAY MEMORY and LIST MEMORY commands have been modified to allow output to a file and to give information about user-defined menus and windows. The new formats are:

```
DISPLAY MEMORY [TO FILE <filename>/TO PRINTER]

LIST MEMORY [TO FILE <filename>/TO PRINTER]
```

MIN and MAX

The MIN and MAX functions can take date arguments in dBASE IV.

SET ALTERNATE

An ADDITIVE clause has been added to SET ALTERNATE to allow for the addition of output to the alternate file without erasing it. The new format is:

```
SET ALTERNATE TO [<file name>] [ADDITIVE]
```

USE

The format for the USE command in *dBASE IV* is:

```
USE [<DBFname> [IN <work area number>]
    [INDEX <NDXfile1>/<MDXfile1> ... ]
    [ORDER <NDXtag>/<MDXtag> [OF <MDXname>]]
    [ALIAS <alias name>/EXCLUSIVE]]
```

where *<work area number>* is a number from 1 to 10, telling the number of the work area where the file will be.

SET RELATION

In *dBASE IV* there can be multiple child relations. Therefore, the format of SET RELATION TO has been modified as follows:

```
SET RELATION TO <exp1> INTO <alias1>
    [, <exp2> INTO <alias2> ... ]
```

SET VIEW

The SET VIEW TO command has been changed to coordinate with the catalog. If a catalog is in use and SET CATALOG is ON, each file opened with the SET VIEW command will be added to the catalog.

SET FIELDS

The SET FIELDS command has been modified to set a read-only flag for fields and calculated fields and to support LIKE with wild cards. The new format is:

```
SET FIELDS TO <field> [/R]/<calculated field id>
    [<field> [/R]/<calculated field id> ... ] ...
    /ALL [LIKE/EXCEPT <skeleton>]
```

where each calculated field has the form:

$$<calculated\ field\ name> = <expression>$$

SET FUNCTION

SET FUNCTION has been modified to provide programmable function keys. The format is:

SET FUNCTION <exp> TO <expC>

where:

☐ <exp> must be Shift-F1 through Shift-F9 or Ctrl-F1 through Ctrl-F10.

☐ <expC> is a character expression.

SET DEVICE

The SET DEVICE command has been modified for output to a file. The new format is:

SET DEVICE TO SCREEN/PRINTER/FILE <filename>

SET BELL

The SET BELL command has been modified to allow the user to set the frequency and duration of the bell tone. The format is:

SET BELL TO [<frequency>,<duration>]

where:

☐ <frequency> must be between 18 and 10,001 cycles per second.

☐ <duration> must be greater than 0 and less than 20 ticks. A tick is about 0.0549 seconds.

If you perform SET BELL TO without the optional frequency and duration, the frequency and duration will be set to the defaults, which are 512 cycles per second and 2 ticks, respectively.

Locking

The locking and unlocking capabilities have been extensively modified; see Chapter 9 for details.

REPLACE

REPLACE now causes the system to attempt either a record or file lock before it is performed, provided a lock has not already occurred. The locks remain until another command is executed.

ON KEY

The ON KEY command has been modified to trap specific keys. The new format is:

ON KEY [<*key label*>] [<*command*>]

The ON KEY command takes precedence over the SET FUNCTION command. The key names and key labels are shown in Table 2-1.

Table 2-1. dBASE IV Key Names and Key Labels.

Key Name	*Key Label*
F1 – F10	F1 – F10
Alt F1 – Alt F10	Alt-F1 – Alt-F10
Ctrl F1 – Ctrl F10	Ctrl-F1 – Ctrl-F10
Ctrl A – Ctrl Z	Ctrl-A – Ctrl-Z
Shift F1 – Shift F10	Shift-F1 – Shift-F10
Alt 0 – Alt 9	Alt-0 – Alt-9
Alt A – Alt Z	Alt-A – Alt-Z
Left Arrow	LEFTARROW
Right Arrow	RIGHTARROW
Up Arrow	UPARROW
Down Arrow	DNARROW
Home	Home

(Table 2-1 Continues.)

Key Name	*Key Label*
End	End
Page Up	PgUp
Page Down	PgDn
Delete	Del
Backspace	BACKSPACE
Ctrl Left Arrow	Ctrl-Leftarrow
Ctrl Right Arrow	Ctrl-Rightarrow
Ctrl Home	Ctrl-Home
Ctrl End	Ctrl-End
Ctrl Page Up	Ctrl-PgUp
Ctrl Page Down	Ctrl-PgDn
Insert	INS
Tab	TAB
Backtab	BACKTAB

(Table 2-1 Ends.)

SET DATE

The SET DATE [TO] command has been modified by adding two new options: JAPAN and USA. The JAPAN format is YY/MM/DD and the USA format is MM-DD-YY.

New Commands and Functions

In addition to the modifications to the old *dBASE III PLUS* commands, *dBASE IV* has a set of new commands to make working with your database easier.

ALIAS

This new function returns the alias name, in uppercase, of work area *expN*:

```
ALIAS([<expN>])
```

CALCULATE and the Statistical Functions

The new CALCULATE command has the format:

CALCULATE [<*scope*>] [FOR <*condition*>] [WHILE <*condition*>]
<*option list*> [TO <*memvar list*>/TO ARRAY <*array name*>]

where <*option list*> can be any of the following:

- ☐ NPV(<*rate*>, <*flows*>, <*initial*>), where NPV stands for net present value, *rate* is the discount rate as a decimal, and *flows* is a series of periodic cash flow values. Flows will normally be the name of a field. *Initial* is a numeric value to represent initial investment, in which case it should have a negative sign.
- ☐ STD(<*expN*>),where STD stands for standard deviation, and *expN* is a numeric expression, normally the name of a field.
- ☐ VAR(<*expN*>), where VAR stands for variance, and *expN* is an expression that normally will be the name of a field.
- ☐ MIN(<*expN*>), where MIN stands for minimum, and *expN* is an expression that normally will be the name of a field.
- ☐ MAX(<*expN*>), where MAX stands for maximum, and *expN* is an expression that normally will be the name of a field.
- ☐ AVG(<*expN*>), where AVG stands for average, and *expN* is an expression that normally will be the name of a field.
- ☐ SUM(<*expN*>), where SUM stands for sum, and *expN* is an expression that normally will be the name of a field.
- ☐ CNT( ), where CNT stands for count.

SCAN

SCAN is a command that combines the properties of DO WHILE with the LOCATE, FIND, and SEEK group of commands. The full format of the SCAN command is:

```
SCAN [<scope>] [WHILE <condition>] [FOR <condition>]
   <commands>
   [LOOP]
   <commands>
   [EXIT]
   <commands>
ENDSCAN
```

where:

- □ <scope> limits the number of records processed. For example, if a scope of NEXT <n> is used, the SCAN begins at the current record. The default is all records in the file.

- □ WHILE <condition> limits the scope just as in a DO WHILE.

- □ FOR <condition> must be satisfied by each record within the scope. Only those records that satisfy the condition will be processed.

- □ LOOP and EXIT are the same as for the DO WHILE.

- □ ENDSCAN ends the SCAN loop just as ENDDO ends the DO WHILE loop.

SET SKIP

The new command SET SKIP controls the way the record pointer is updated when processing related files

```
SET SKIP TO [<alias1> [,<alias2> . . . ]]
```

It is effective only if the SET RELATION command has been used to link the files involved. The relation chain and the alias list specified by SET SKIP together determine the order in which records are skipped. First the record pointer in the last database file in the relation chain in the SET SKIP list advances. Then the record pointer in the next to last file in the relation chain that is in the SET SKIP list advances, and so on.

LINENO, PROGRAM, and MEMORY

LINENO( ) returns the line number of a command that is about to be executed in a command or procedure file.

PROGRAM( ) returns a string that is the name of a program or procedure that is being executed or is suspended when an error occurs.

MEMORY( ) returns the amount of memory available in kilobytes (K).

LOOKUP

The new *dBASE IV* provides a function to look up values in alias work areas. Its format is:

LOOKUP(<return expression>, <look for>, <field>)

where:

- ☐ <return expression> is any valid expression. For example, Employee→name. Fields outside the active work area must be aliased.
- ☐ <look for> is any valid expression that will determine the record to be found.
- ☐ <field> is the field that is checked for the <look for> search expression.

For example, LOOKUP(Employee→name, "1104", Employee number) will try to find the employee number 1104 in the employee number field in the employee work area, and return the employee's name. The record pointer will be repositioned in the lookup work area, and the FOUND( ) flag will be reset in that work area to either true or false, depending on whether the value being looked up was found.

Menu, Window, and Popup Commands

A collection of new commands in *dBASE IV* allows you to control the screen and to make selections from menus and popups.

The window commands allow you to draw windows on the screen within which subsequent events will occur, such as selections from menus. Menu commands allow you to put menus on the screen from which you may select what you want to do next. The prompts in the menus are called *pads*. You can allow your users to make choices by moving the highlight to the pad and selecting it with a carriage return. Another choice is to activate a popup at the prompt, which has its own prompts called *bars*.

When you select a prompt, a command is performed (usually a DO) to activate a program. Within the program, you can determine what prompt was selected by using the new PROMPT( ), PAD( ), and BAR( ) functions. The format for the DEFINE POPUP command is:

```
DEFINE POPUP <popup name> FROM <coords> TO <coords>
  [PROMPT FIELD <field name>/
  PROMPT FILES [LIKE <skeleton>]/
  PROMPT STRUCTURE]
  [MESSAGE <expC>]

DEFINE BAR <expN> OF <popup name> PROMPT <expC>
  [MESSAGE <expC>] [SKIP [FOR <condition>]]
```

where:

- ☐ <expN> designates the line number, starting with 1, in the popup. The selection highlight is moved up and down between the bars using the up and down arrow keys.

- ☐ SKIP makes the bar a nonselectable option. If the optional FOR occurs, the prompt is skipped only when the condition is true.

DEFINE BAR cannot be used with a popup that was defined with a PROMPT.

The format for the DEFINE WINDOW command is:

```
DEFINE WINDOW <window name> FROM <coords> TO
  <coords>
    [DOUBLE/PANEL/NONE/<border definition string>]
    [COLOR [<standard>] [,<enhanced>] [,<frame>]]
```

The [DOUBLE/PANEL/NONE/<*border definition string*>] option is the same as in the SET BORDER command. The [COLOR . . . .] option is the same as in the SET COLOR command:

[*foreground color code* [/*background color code*]]

ACTIVATE WINDOW <*window name list*>/ALL displays all the windows named in the list and makes the last window named the active window.

DEACTIVATE WINDOW <*window name list*>/ALL deactivates currently displayed windows by erasing them from the screen. Anything on the screen that was covered by the window is restored.

CLEAR WINDOW releases all windows from memory and erases them from the screen.

RELEASE WINDOWS [<*window name list*>] erases windows from the screen and releases them from memory.

SAVE WINDOW <*window name list*>/ALL TO <*file name*> saves the named windows to a file with added file extension .WIN unless <*file name*> has a different file extension.

RESTORE WINDOW <*window name list*>/ALL FROM <*file name*> restores windows in the name list to memory. The window in the list that was active when it was stored will again be the active window.

MOVE WINDOW <*window name*> TO <*coords*>/BY <*change in coords*> moves a window to a new location on the screen.

The format for the DEFINE MENU command is:

DEFINE MENU <*menu name*> [MESSAGE <*expC*>]

If MESSAGE is included, it will appear centered on the bottom line of the screen.

The prompts for the menu must be defined individually using the DEFINE PAD command. The format for the DEFINE PAD command is:

DEFINE PAD <*prompt pad name*> OF <*menu name*>
PROMPT <*expC*>

[AT <*coords*>] [MESSAGE <*expC*>]

ACTIVATE MENU <*menu name*> [PAD <*prompt pad name*>] displays the named menu on the screen so that its prompt pads can be accessed in the order in which they were defined.

SHOW MENU <*menu name*> [PAD <*prompt pad name*>] displays the named menu and highlights the named prompt pad without activating it.

DEACTIVATE MENU deactivates the named menu and erases it from the screen. Any text covered by the menu when it was activated is restored.

RELEASE MENUS [<*menu name list*>] releases menus not in use and erases them from the screen.

CLEAR MENUS erases all menus not in use and clears them from memory.

ON PAD <*prompt pad name*> OF <*menu name*>
[ACTIVATE POPUP <*popup name*>]

This command causes the named popup to be activated when the selection bar is moved to the named prompt pad. With this command, you can activate popups while moving the selection bar using the Right- and Left-Arrow keys. If the optional ACTIVATE POPUP is not used, no action will occur at that particular menu prompt.

ON SELECTION PAD <*prompt pad name*> OF <*menu name*> <*command*> causes <*command*> (usually a DO) to be performed when you press Return while the selection bar is positioned to the prompt pad given by <*prompt pad name*>. All menus are temporarily deactivated, but remain on the screen. Either the ON PAD or the ON SELECTION PAD should be used; otherwise, an error will occur.

MENU( ) returns a character string, which is the name of the active menu. PAD( ) returns a character string, which is the name of the most recently selected pad. Those two functions are used in a program file that is being performed as the result of a DO command.

ACTIVATE POPUP <*popup name*>

Only one popup (the most recently activated) can be active

at any given time. A popup has prompt bars in contrast to a menu, which has prompt pads.

SHOW POPUP <*popup name*> displays a popup without activating it. DEACTIVATE POPUP deactivates the active popup and erases it from the screen, returning control to the menu bar if the popup was activated by ON PAD. CLEAR POPUPS erases all popups not in use and releases them from memory.

RELEASE POPUPS [<*popup name list*>] erases the named popups not in use from the screen and clears them from memory.

ON SELECTION POPUP <*popup name*>/ALL <*command*> causes <*command*> to be performed if the popup named by <*popup name*> is selected.

A selection in a popup is made by moving to any of the bars and pressing Return. The command (usually a DO) will be performed upon selection. The ALL option means that the ON SELECTION POPUP refers to any popup. If a DO command is executed, the program decides what to do using the PROMPT( ), POPUP( ), and BAR( ) functions.

PROMPT( ) returns a character string that represents the most recent selection in either a popup or a menu. POPUP( ) returns a character string that represents the name of the most recently activated popup. BAR( ) gives the bar number of the most recently selected popup option.

SET WINDOW OF MEMO TO

The new SET WINDOW OF MEMO TO <*window name*> command sets the default window for editing a memo field in EDIT or BROWSE.

NDX, MDX, ORDER, TAG, and KEY

NDX(<*expN*>[, <*alias name*>]) returns the names of active NDX files in the work area specified by <*alias name*>.

MDX(<*expN*> [, <*alias name*>]) gives the name of the index file in the *expN*'th position of a previously issued SET INDEX TO <*index file list*> or USE . . . INDEX <*index file list*> command.

ORDER([<*alias name*>]) returns the index file name of the index that is controlling the order in the work area designated by the alias name.

TAG([<MDX*file*>,]<*expN*>[,<*alias name*>]) returns the tag name in the expN'th position of the index file for the work area <*alias name*>.

KEY([<MDX*file*>,] <*expN*> [,<*alias name*>]) returns the key expression of an index.

COPY INDEXES/TAG

COPY INDEXES/TAG <*tag list*> TO <NDX*filename*> creates an NDX file from the first tag in the tag list, where <*tag list*> consists of up to 10 clauses of the form:

<*tagname*> [OF MDX*spec*]

CONVERT

CONVERT [TO <*expN*>] adds to the active database file a field named __DBASELOCK required for multiuser lock detection and for automatic refresh for BROWSE and EDIT.

CHANGE

CHANGE( ) will return true if a record has been changed since it was opened.

NETWORK

NETWORK( ) returns true if the system is running under a network, false if otherwise.

LASTKEY

LASTKEY( ) returns the ASCII equivalent of the last key pressed.

ON READERROR and READVAR

To help you validate data and check for input errors, the

command ON READERROR and the function READVAR( ) have been added to *dBASE IV*. The format is:

ON READERROR <*command*>

so that a command (usually a DO) is performed if an invalid date is entered or if the RANGE or VALID criteria are not met in an @ command. READVAR( ) returns in uppercase the name of the field or memory variable that is being edited. READVAR( ) works with APPEND, CHANGE, EDIT, INSERT, and READ.

PLAY MACRO, SAVE MACROS, and RESTORE MACROS

The new commands PLAY MACRO, SAVE MACROS, and RESTORE MACROS, work with macros created by the NPI macro creator (see Chapter 3). The format for PLAY MACRO is:

PLAY MACRO <*macro name*>

where <*macro name*> is either Alt-F1 through Alt-F9 or Alt-F10 followed by a character a through z. The keystrokes saved in the macro definition are performed as though they had been entered by the user.

The macros can be stored to a file and restored from a file by the commands:

SAVE MACROS TO <*macro file*>

and

RESTORE MACROS FROM <*macro file*>

PRINTSTATUS

The new function PRINTSTATUS( ) returns a true if the printer is ready to accept output; otherwise, PRINTSTATUS( ) returns a false.

SEEK

The new SEEK(<exp> [,<alias name>])function attempts to find <exp> in the master index of the work area given by <alias name>. If it succeeds, it returns a true; otherwise, it returns a false. Also, the record pointer in the <alias name> work area is repositioned.

SET

The new SET(<expC>)function returns ON or OFF, depending on whether the SET option <expC> is ON or OFF. For example, SET(Bell) will return ON if SET BELL is ON.

SET AUTOSAVE

The SET AUTOSAVE command is an important new feature of dBASE IV that allows you to make sure that any record changes will be saved immediately on disk. The format is:

SET AUTOSAVE ON/OFF

The default is OFF.

SET DISPLAY TO and SET COLOR OF

SET COLOR TO and SET COLOR ON/OFF have not been changed, but two new commands, SET DISPLAY TO and SET COLOR OF, have been added to enhance screen-display control. The formats of these two commands are:

SET DISPLAY TO [MONO43/EGA43/EGA25/MONO/COLOR]

where:

- ☐ MONO43 switches to a 43-mono-line display on EGA monitors.
- ☐ EGA43 switches to a 43-color-line display on EGA monitors.

☐ EGA25 or MONO switches back to the standard 25-line display.

☐ COLOR switches to the standard color display.

and

SET COLOR OF [<*name*>] TO <*attribute*>

where:

<*name*>   is TEXT, HEADING, STATUS, BOX, or FIELD.

<*attribute*> sets the foreground/background as in *dBASE III PLUS.*

SET CLOCK

SET CLOCK ON displays the system clock in the upper right-hand corner of the screen SET CLOCK TO <*row*>, <*column*> automatically SETs the CLOCK ON and displays it at the coordinates given. The display format depends on SET HOURS and is either *hh:mm:ss am/pm* for SET HOURS TO 12, or *tt:mm:ss* for SET HOURS TO 24.

SET INSTRUCT

Information boxes are provided in *dBASE IV* to aid novice users. These boxes do not appear until two seconds after the command is activated. If you press a key before the two seconds are up, the information box will not appear. The command that controls the appearance of the information boxes is:

SET INSTRUCT ON/OFF

SET SPACE

The new SET SPACE ON/OFF generates a space between the two expressions for the ? and ?? commands. The default is ON.

DTOS

The new DTOS(<*expD*>) function converts a date expression into a character-string expression that can be concatenated with a character-string expression for indexing. The date is converted to a character string of the form CCYYMMDD where C is century, Y is year, M is month, and D is day.

LIKE

The new LIKE(<*pattern*>,<*expC*>) function, where <*pattern*> contains wild cards and expC is a character expression, returns a true if the comparison is a match. For example, LIKE(a*b*c,string) will return a true if the string starts with an a, contains a b, and ends with a c, and returns a false otherwise.

SELECT

SELECT( ) returns a number representing the highest unused work area.

SET BORDER

The new SET BORDER command has the format:

SET BORDER TO [SINGLE/DOUBLE/PANEL/NONE/
<*border definition string*>]

where:

- ☐ SINGLE stands for a single-lined box.
- ☐ DOUBLE stands for a double-lined box.
- ☐ PANEL uses the ASCII character denoted by 219.
- ☐ NONE eliminates the border.
- ☐ <*border definition string*> is a list of ASCII numbers for the top, the left, the right, the bottom, the top left corner,

the top right corner, the bottom left corner, and the bottom right corner, respectively.

For example, SET BORDER TO PANEL is equivalent to SET BORDER TO 219. SET BORDER TO 55, 56, 57, 58, 59, 60, 61 would set the top to 7's, the bottom to 8's, the left to 9's, the right to :'s, leave the top left corner unchanged, set the top right corner to ;, set the bottom left corner to <, and set the bottom right corner to =.

SET DESIGN

SET DESIGN OFF prevents users from switching from the nonprocedural interface to design mode.

SET DEVELOPMENT

For developers who are using an external editor, such as *WordStar*, the new SET DEVELOPMENT ON/OFF command will activate a code to compare creation times of .PRG files and .DBO files, and recompile the .PRG file if the .DBO file is older than the .PRG file.

SET NEAR

The new SET NEAR ON/OFF, when ON, will cause a SEEK or FIND to position the record pointer to the record whose key value would immediately follow the sought-after value key in the event of a sort. FOUND( ) will only return a true for actual finds. If the sought-after value is greater than any in the file, the EOF( ) function will be set to true and the record pointer positioned after the last record.

Other New Set Commands

One new command is SET POINT TO [<expC>]. For example, SET POINT TO "," determines the symbol to be used for the decimal point.

SET SEPARATOR TO [<*expC*>] determines the separator for numeric expressions. Normally the separator is the comma as in 123,456. However, SET SEPARATOR TO ":", for example, would cause this code:

```
Any = 55555
@ 1,1 SAY Any PICTURE "999,999"
```

to result in 55:555 being displayed on the screen.

SET CURRENCY TO [<*expC*>] changes the currency sign to be displayed with numbers using the "@$" PICTURE clause. The default is the $ (dollar) sign.

BEGIN/END TRANSACTION, ISMARKED, and RESET

The new transaction processing commands are described in the section on transaction processing in Chapter 8. During a transaction, a tag is set in the database file header. A new function, ISMARKED( ), has been added to *dBASE IV* to check if the transaction tag is set. If it is, ISMARKED( ) returns a true; otherwise, ISMARKED( ) returns a false. The format for ISMARKED( ) is:

```
ISMARKED([<alias>])
```

where <*alias*> specifies the work area of the database file to be checked.

The tag checked by ISMARKED( ) can be removed with the new command:

```
RESET [IN <alias name>]
```

LKSYS

The new function LKSYS(n) lets you find out who has locked a record or file and when it was locked. The argument n of the function can have the values 0, 1, and 2. LKSYS(0) returns the time, LKSYS(1) returns the date, and LKSYS(2) returns the user identification (ID). The output is in the form of a character string. LKSYS( ) depends on the __DBASELOCK field. (See the preceding CONVERT command.)

SET LOCK

The new SET LOCK ON/OFF command enables or disables locking for the commands AVERAGE, SUM, CALCULATE, COPY [STRUCTURE], COUNT, JOIN, REPORT, LABEL, TOTAL, SORT, and INDEX. For those commands that both read and write, SET LOCK affects only the reading portion of the command.

SET REFRESH

The new SET REFRESH TO < *expN* > command determines the length of time that *dBASE IV* waits (after the last keyboard input) before checking to see if a record has been changed and the screen updated. The integer < *expN* > is the time in seconds, which must be between 1 and 3600.

SET SQL

The new SET SQL ON/OFF command controls the availability of the new SQL function. See Chapters 10 through 13 and Appendices A, D, and E. When SQL is SET to ON, many *dBASE* commands do not work; and when SQL is SET to OFF, SQL commands do not work.

SQL program files have a .PRS file extension—unlike *dBASE* program files, which have a .PRG file extension. When a program file with a .PRS file extension is activated with the DO command, SQL is automatically SET to ON; and when a program file with a .PRG file extension is activated with a DO command, SQL is automatically set to OFF.

USER

The new USER( ) function returns the name of the user logged into PROTECT. If no name is registered in the Dbsystem.DB file, the function returns a null string.

Fixed-Point Numbers

dBASE IV has implemented a binary-coded decimal (BCD) package that supports fixed-point numbers to supplement the old floating-point arithmetic. Fixed-point numbers have a data type of N, and floating-point numbers have a data type of F. Numeric constants always have a data type of N. The data types of memory variables will depend on how they are created. For example, if created from a logarithm function or square root function, they will have data type F.

When an expression uses both fixed- and floating-point numbers, all fixed-point numbers are converted to floating points for the calculation. For output, all floating-point numbers are converted to fixed-point. The maximum floating point number is $0.9e + 308$, and the smallest is $0.1e - 307$.

SET PRECISION

The BCD package in *dBASE IV* has a variable precision. The SET PRECISION TO [<expN>] command is used to set the precision, which can be between 10 and 20. The default is 16.

FLOAT and FIXED

The new functions FLOAT(<expN>) and FIXED(<expF>) allow you to convert numeric data to floating-point data and vice versa.

Memory Variables

Memory variables in *dBASE IV* have been modified in two ways. First, the default maximum number of memory variables has been increased from 256 to 500. Second, one- and two-dimensional arrays of memory variables can be declared with the new DECLARE command.

The Config.DB file controls the maximum number of memory variables that can be used by means of the parameters MVMAXBLKS and MVBLKSIZE. MVMAXBLKS has a minimum value of 1, a default value of 10, and a maximum value of 25. MVBLKSIZE has a minimum value of 25, a default value of 50, and a maximum value of 1000. If you put the lines MVMAXBLKS = 25 and MVBLKSIZE = 25 in your Config.DB file, you will increase the maximum number of memory variables to 625.

All memory variables require a basic 56 bytes from a memory variable block. Character memory variables require an additional 2 bytes plus as many bytes as the length of the character string.

ARRAY

Two new commands are used to declare one- and two-dimensional arrays of memory variables:

DECLARE *<array definition list>*
PUBLIC ARRAY *<array definition list>*

where *<array definition list>* is a list of array names, each with its dimensions in square brackets, e.g., ARRAY A[5,12],B[56]. The number of elements in an ARRAY is limited to 1024.

When an array is declared, it is allocated one "slot" from a block. A special array block is allocated to hold all members of the array. Each element of the array requires the same number of bytes as a memory variable of the same type.

AVERAGE and SUM

The AVERAGE and SUM commands have been modified to support arrays of memory variables. The new format for these commands is:

AVERAGE [*<expN list>*] [*<scope>*] [FOR *<condition>*]
  [WHILE *<condition>*]
  [TO *<memvar list>*/TO ARRAY *<array name>*]

SUM [*<scope>*] [*<expN list>*]
  [TO *<memvar list>*/TO ARRAY *<array name>*]
  [FOR *<condition>*]
  [WHILE *<condition>*]

COPY

The COPY command has been modified to take advantage of arrays. The new format is:

COPY TO ARRAY <*array name*> [FIELDS <*field list*>] [<*scope*>]
[FOR <*condition*>] [WHILE <*condition*>]

APPEND

The APPEND command has been modified to add records from an existing array. The format is:

APPEND FROM ARRAY <*array name*> [FOR <*condition*>]

Input/Output

Up to 99 files may be open in *dBASE IV*. The maximum number can be set in the Config.DB file by the command FILES = <Nexp>, where *Nexp* can be from 20 to 99 inclusive. The same database file can be open in more than one work area. This is accomplished by using different alias names in different work areas (see the USE command.)

The Compiler and Linker

dBASE IV has a new compiler and linker. The new compiler converts source code into an intermediate format called ''dCODE,'' which is subsequently executed, depending on the command issued. Table 2-2 lists the compilation commands and their input and output file extensions.

The new DBLINK <*input filename*> [/L] command links a .DBO file and all object files that it references into a large .DBO file. The input filename must be the name of a .DBO file. If you

Table 2-2. Compiler Input and Output.

Command	*Input*	*Output*
COMPILE <*filename*>	.PRG or .PRS	.DBO
CREATE/MODIFY QUERY/VIEW	.QBE or .VUE	.QBO or .UPO
DEBUG	.PRG or .PRS	.DBO
DO <*filename*>	.PRG or .PRS	.DBO
LABEL FORM	.LPG	.LPO
REPORT FORM	.RPG	.RPO
SET FORMAT TO	.FMT	.FMO
SET PROCEDURE TO	.PRG or .PRS	.DBO
SET SQLPROC TO	.PRG or .PRS	.DBO

use the optional /L, a document file with the file extension .TXT will be created, showing what object files were linked.

The Debugger

The new *dBASE IV* debugger command has the format:

```
DEBUG  <filename>  /  <procedure name>
[WITH  <parameter list>]
```

The new debugger works with both .PRG and .PRS files.

SET TRAP

You can use the command SET TRAP ON/OFF to invoke the debugger when an error occurs or when you press Esc during program execution.

TYPE

The TYPE command has been modified to display line

numbers and to provide printer output to aid in debugging. The new format is:

TYPE <*filename*> [TO PRINTER/TO FILE <*filename*>] [NUMBER]

where the optional [NUMBER] clause causes line numbers to be displayed.

New Treatment of Memo Fields

Memo fields in *dBASE IV* have been extensively modified, and the way in which memo fields are stored has also been changed. Old *dBASE III PLUS* memo field files can be converted to the new format by the USE command. The new APPEND MEMO command allows data from a file to be placed in a memo field. The new COPY MEMO command copies memo fields into files having a .TXT file extension.

The new SET BLOCKSIZE TO <*expN*> command sets the BLOCKSIZE of memo files where <*expN*> can be from 1 to 32 inclusive, with a default of 1. The integer <*expN*> must be multiplied by 512 to get the actual blocksize.

The AT(<*expC*>,<*exp*>) function has been modified to take memo fields as the second argument. The LEN(<*exp*>) has been modified to take a memo field as an argument. The SUBSTR(<*exp*>,<*start*>[,<*length*>]) function can now take a memo field as the first argument.

The STUFF (<*exp1*>, <*expN1*>, –*expN2*>, <*expC2*>) function can now take a memo field as its first argument, as can the functions LEFT(<*exp1*>,<*expN*>) and RIGHT(<*exp1*>, <*expN*>).

Two new functions, MEMLINES(<*memo field*>) and MLINE(<*memo field*>,<*Nexp*>), have been added for use with memo fields. MEMLINES( ) returns the number of lines in a memo field. MLINE( ) returns the text in the Nexp line of the memo field.

User-Defined Functions

In *dBASE IV* you can define your own functions by including them in a procedure file. Your function must begin with the line:

FUNCTION <*function name*>

followed by the optional line:

PARAMETER <*parameter list*>

The RETURN command has been modified to implement user-defined functions, and now has the format:

RETURN [<*expression*>] [TO MASTER]

For example, the following code would define a function AREA(<*height*>,<*width*>):

```
FUNCTION AREA
PARAMETER height, width
Ret = height * width
RETURN Ret
```

Summary

This chapter discusses the numerous modifications to previously existing *dBASE* commands and the large number of new commands that have been added to *dBASE IV*. These commands give the *dBASE* programmer many new options for writing application programs.

The new arrays of memory variables and user defined functions are discussed. These are very useful for the application programmer.

3

The Control Center

The Control Center is the heart of *dBASE IV*. It is a graphic display from which you can access all of the other *dBASE IV* features except SQL MODE (see Chapter 10) and a few other features reached through the dot prompt.

When entering *dBASE IV*, you will end up at the dot prompt unless you have command = <*command*> in your Config.DB file. To enter the Control Center, you should use command = ASSIST. On your first entry into *dBASE IV*, *dBASE* will place all the files in your directory in a catalog called Untitled.CAT before entering the Control Center. On successive entries, *dBASE* will use the catalog in use the last time you were in *dBASE*. If you get an error message upon entry that says "File not found" and you cancel, ending up at the dot prompt, try using the ASSIST command. If the error message recurs and you can't get to the Control Center, there is probably something wrong with your catalog file. In that event, you have two choices: (1) you can delete your most recently selected catalog file, or (2) you can SET CATALOG TO some other catalog file and then try using ASSIST at the dot prompt.

After you enter *dBASE*, if your screen displays a dot and a blinking cursor, you can reach the Control Center by pressing F2, ASSIST. The Control Center gives you access to the power of *dBASE IV* through a comprehensive menu system. These menus enable you to create, modify, and organize data through simple menu options and design screens. Figure 3-1 shows a typical Control Center screen. This chapter describes the basic elements of the *dBASE IV* menu system that you can access, starting from the Control Center main screen.

In working with *dBASE IV*, you will be using *files* extensively; However, in SQL mode, these are called *tables*. A *catalog* is a file containing a list of related files.

This chapter also describes the various parts of the Control

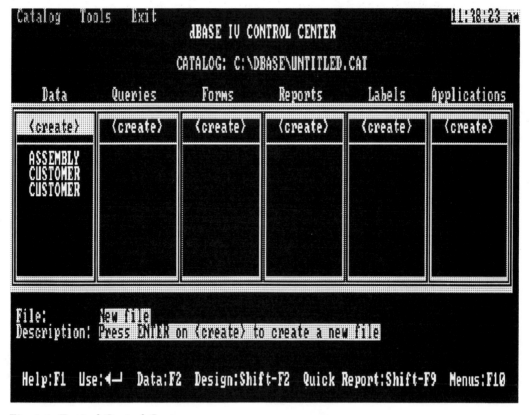

Fig. 3-1. Typical Control Center screen.

Center and the functions performed by each. In some cases, only a brief description of a submenu is included, with the full description appearing in a subsequent chapter. Since the function keys are referred to throughout this chapter, their uses are explained first.

Function Keys

Function keys let you perform common commands with less typing and without going through a menu. Some function keys have a different function when you press the shift key simultaneously. The effect of a function key may differ, depending on where your cursor is. For example, F1, the Help key, will supply help on the topic indicated by the cursor position. Also, the uses of these keys at the Control Center are different from their uses at the dot prompt. Table 3-1 gives a complete list of the function keys and their uses at the Control Center, and at the dot prompt.

Table 3-1. Function Key Values.

Key	Function	Result
At the Control Center		
F1	Help	Display on-screen help
Shift-F1	Pick	Display list of items for building expressions
F2	Data	Switch to Browse or Edit screen
Shift-F2	Design	Design database files, queries, reports, forms, or labels
F3	Previous	Move to previous field or queries design screen element
Shift-F3	Find Previous	Locate previous occurrence of search string
F4	Next	Move to next field or queries design screen element
Shift-F4	Find Next	Locate next occurrence of search string
F5	Field	Add field to layout surface or view skeleton

(Table 3-1 Continues.)

Key	Function	Result
Shift-F5	Find	Find search string
F6	Extend Select	Select contiguous data or fields
Shift-F6	Replace	Replace search string by another string
F7	Move	Move selected data
Shift-F7	Size	Change size of design elements
F8	Copy	Copy selected data
Shift-F8	Ditto	Copy data from previous record into current field
F9	Zoom	Enlarge/shrink memo fields or condition boxes
Shift-F9	Quick Report	Print a Quick Report of data
F10	Menus	Access menus for current screen
Shift-F10	Macros	Access macros

At the Dot Prompt

F1	Help
F2	Assist
F3	List
F4	Directory
F5	Display structure
F6	Display status
F7	Display memory
F8	Display
F9	Append
F10	Edit

From the dot prompt, all function keys can be reprogrammed by using the SET FUNCTION command described in your *Language Reference* manual.

(Table 3-1 Ends)

Control Center Main Menus

The three menus listed at the top of the main Control Center screen are:

□ *Catalog* provides options for managing catalogs and the files they contain.

□ *Tools* has a set of utilities for accessing DOS, for importing and exporting files, for using the PROTECT program, and for setting program parameters.

□ *Exit* allows you to leave the Control Center for either the dot prompt or DOS.

Each of these submenus is described in the following sections.

The Catalog Menu

When you enter the Control Center, if there is a valid master catalog (Catalog.CAT file), it will be opened. If you have used the master catalog previously through the Control Center, that will become the active catalog. If there is no master catalog, *dBASE IV* will check the current directory for database (.DBF) files. If none are found, your cursor will appear on the <create> marker in the Files panel of the Control Center screen, and an information box will appear on your screen, explaining what you should do to create a new database.

If *dBASE IV* doesn't find a catalog, but does find .DBF files, then all of the database, view, form, report, label, and program files will be entered into the current catalog, which will be given the default name of Untitled.CAT. These will then be displayed in the Control Center. This makes it easy for you to gain access to files without having to construct a catalog.

The files that will be automatically added to a catalog for the six Control Center panels are:

Data:	DBF, NDX
Queries:	VUE, QBE, UPD
Forms:	SCR, FMT
Reports:	FRM, FRG
Labels:	LBL, LBG
Applications:	APP.

The Catalog Menu contains six choices, which are described below.

Use a Different Catalog. If you choose this, a list of catalogs will appear with the <create> marker at the top of the list. This will enable you to create a new catalog if you wish. Once you select a catalog, the files in that catalog will be displayed in their appropriate panels.

Modify Catalog Name. This puts you in a prompt box with the current catalog name. You can edit the name here.

Edit Description of Catalog. This item will display a prompt box with the description of the current catalog. You can edit the description here.

Add File to Catalog. This option will prompt you with a file directory list of files of the type for the panel box you currently have highlighted. This list allows you to change directories and drives as described in the conventions on the list.

Remove Highlighted File From Catalog. If you choose this, the file you have highlighted in the Control Center will be removed from the active catalog. After the file is deleted from the catalog, *dBASE IV* will ask you whether or not to also delete that file from the disk.

Change Description of Highlighted File. If you choose this item, a prompt box will appear with the highlighted file's description. You can edit the description here, using up to 80 characters, but only 66 of these characters will be displayed on the Control Center screen.

The Tools Menu

The Tools Menu allows you to access the *dBASE IV* utilities, including the utilities to access DOS and manage DOS files. The utilities available through the Tools Menu are:

☐ Macros
☐ Import
☐ Export
☐ DOS utilities (Has its own full-screen modules.)
☐ PROTECT data (Has its own full-screen modules.)
☐ Settings (Has its own full-screen modules.)

When you exit utilities that have their own modules, you will be returned to the Control Center (with no menus pulled down) rather than back to the Tools Menu. This will save you from having to press an extra Esc after using any of the modules.

Macros. While the Macros submenu item resides within the Tools Menu, you can use the Shift-F10 function key at anytime when you're in *dBASE IV* to display the Macros popup menu.

There are 35 macros, 34 of which are stored in macro library files, each containing up to the full set of the 34 macros. Alt-F1 is reserved as a temporary macro, so that you can quickly record a macro for a temporary repetitive task without having to select an empty slot and name it. One macro library file can be loaded at any given time. You can play back macros by pressing Alt-F1 through Alt-F9, or by pressing Alt-F10 followed by a letter from A to Z.

The macro menu contains the following choices:

```
Begin recording
End recording
Append to macro:
Insert user-input break

Modify
Name
Delete
Copy
Play
Talk        OFF/ON

Load Library  ( )
Save Library  ( )
```

When you choose any of the menu items—Begin recording, Append to macro, Modify, Name, Delete, Copy, or Play—a macro display table will appear in which you can use your cursor to select the macro slot to operate on.

Import. The Import submenu allows you to bring in files from outside *dBASE*. The files you can import will be displayed after you select this submenu. These files and their file extensions are:

RapidFile	(.RPD)
dBASE II	(.DB2)

Framework II	(.FW2)
Lotus 1-2-3	(.WK1)
Visicalc	(.DIF)
PFS:File	
SYLK-Multiplan	
Text fixed-length fields	(.TXT)
Blank delimited	(.TXT)
Character delimited (")	(.TXT)

Note: If you are importing *dBASE II* files, you must rename the file extensions .DB2 to have them included in the list. Highlight the type of file you want to import and press Return.

Export. You can export files outside of *dBASE*. After you choose the Export submenu, a list of files to which you can export will appear on your screen. These file types and their extensions are the same ones you can import into *dBASE* (see previous section).

Select the file you want to export and press Return to export the file with its extension. The *PFS:File* and SYLK-*Multiplan* files are exported with no extensions, and ASCII text files are exported with .TXT extensions. If you want to enter a special delimiter around character fields in an exported file, highlight Character Delimited and press Return. The cursor will appear in the fill-in for this item, and you can type in the character you want to use.

DOS Utilities. The DOS Utilities subsystem provides you a full-featured set of file-manipulation and DOS-access capabilities. The work space (the area of the screen between the menu bar and the status bar) will be used as a display window. This window will normally contain a list of all the files in the current directory. It will have the headings shown in the file display window skeleton exhibited in Fig. 3-2. The heading "C:\DBASE" is the full-path directory.

The attrs column shows the status for the file attributes. For each attribute, Off is indicated by an asterisk (*), and On is indicated by

a = archive
h = hidden
r = read-only
s = system

```
                              C:\ DBASE
Name/Extension      Size      Date & Time      Attrs    Space Used
. . . . . . .
. . . . . . .
. . . . . . .
Total <marked>
Total <displayed>
_____
Files:                                       Sorted by:
```

Fig. 3-2. File Display Window skeleton.

"Total marked" and "Total displayed" indicate the number of marked files and the number of files now in the display list. Your cursor cannot be used in this area. The "Files," at the bottom of the display window, shows the selection criteria for displaying files. When two asterisks separated by a period (*.*) are shown, all files in the directory are being displayed. The "Sorted by" shows the sorting criterion for the files.

The highlight bar can be moved up or down, and files can be marked or unmarked with the Return key. Pressing the Zoom key (F9) while you are in the file list will clear the file display window contents and display a directory tree in that display window. The directory tree will show the hierarchical relationships of the directories. It will look something like the following:

```
C:\
 . - OLDDATA
 .
 .       - RECEIVBL
 .
 .       - ACCOUNTS
 .
 .       - STANDARD
 .
 .         - MEMOS
 .
 .         - PLANNING
 .
 . - NEWDATA
```

DOS Menus. You also can use the display area for the output of a DOS command or to display the contents of a file. For the latter purpose, the DOS Utilities menu bar lists the menus: DOS, Files, Sort, Mark, Operations, and Exit. Choosing the DOS Menu will allow you to issue a DOS command without leaving *dBASE IV*.

The Files Menu contains commands that affect which files are displayed in the display area. The Sort Menu contains commands that affect the order in which the files are displayed in the display area. The Mark Menu contains commands that allow you to mark, unmark, or reverse the mark of the files now marked or unmarked for deletion. The Operations Menu contains commands that allow you to perform the following operations on a file or group of files in the current directory: delete, copy, move, rename, view, and edit. Use the Exit Menu when you want to leave the DOS Utilities subsystem.

Settings. With the Settings subsystem, you can adjust the settings for certain *dBASE IV* items. These new settings will then be used in Procedural and Non-Procedural Interfaces to *dBASE IV*, but these settings will only be active in your current work session. They will not be stored in your Config.DB file.

The Settings subsystem contains the menus Options, Display, and Exit. The items in the Options Menu are shown in Table 3-2, along with their descriptions.

Table 3-2. The Options Menu.

Option	*Default*	*Description*
Bell	ON	Turns the warning bell on or off.
Carry	OFF	Copies data from the preceding record into a newly added or inserted record.
Century	OFF	Displays dates as 12/15/1986 rather than 12/15/86.
Clock	ON	Turns clock display on or off.
Confirm	OFF	Forces user to press Enter before accepting data into a new record.
Date separator	(/)	Specifies the separator to use in displaying dates.

(Table 3-2 Continues.)

Option	Default	Description
Date order	DMY/MDY/YMD	Specifies the order of the year, month, and day to be used in displaying dates.
Decimal places	(3)	Number of decimal places to be used in internal computations and the default to be used in unformatted display.
Deleted	OFF	Ignores deleted records.
Exact	OFF	Compares character strings exactly, character for character.
Exclusive	ON	Prevents shared use of files in a network.
Fixed	OFF	Uses the information from SET DECIMALS for all numeric displays.
Instruct	ON	Enables and disables display of information boxes in the NPI.
Margin	(0)	Specifies the default value for unformatted printing (same as the Offset from left option in the Print Menu.)
Memo width	(20)	Default width for displaying unformatted memo fields.
Safety	ON	Asks for confirming message before overwriting files.
Talk	ON/OFF	Controls whether output of PI commands are captured and displayed in a window.
Trap	OFF	Turns the debugger on and off.

(Table 3-2 Ends.)

The Display Menu lets you change the default display attributes of parts of the screen and objects appearing on the screen. You can set the foreground and background colors if you have a color monitor, and you can decide whether to have the object blinking. If you have a monochrome monitor, you can set the blink, the intensity, the underline, and reverse video. Submenus within the Display Menu set the colors of text, headings, boxes, status line, fields, and screen borders.

The Exit Menu

The Control Center's Exit Menu offers you two possibilities:

☐ *Exit to dot prompt,* which allows you to work on those *dBASE IV* facilities that are not available through the Control Center, and

☐ *Quit to DOS,* which is used only if you want to quit working with *dBASE IV.*

The Panel Submenus

The Control Center contains six panels, each listing a submenu from which you can lay out and design the type of file indicated by the submenu name. The submenus are:

☐ *Data:* See Chapter 4;

☐ *Queries:* See Chapter 5 (entry point for the QBE facility).

☐ *Forms:* See Chapter 6.

☐ *Reports:* See Chapter 6.

☐ *Labels:* See Chapter 6.

☐ *Applications:* See Chapter 7 (entry point of the APGEN facility).

On each of the six Control Center panels (submenus), you have two choices: *CREATE a new file* or *Work with the existing file.* Use the Left- and Right-Arrow keys to move from one panel to the next. Use the Up- and Down-Arrow keys to move within the panels from one file name to the next.

If there are more files than can be shown in a panel at one time, you can see the rest by scrolling down. Select a file to work on by moving the highlight to the file name and pressing Return.

The Data Submenu

The Data submenu will display database files containing your records and fields.

The Queries Submenu

The Queries submenu contains the QBE system for manipulating the data in your database files. With it, you can form queries that will give you specific views of the database and perform update operations.

Its querying ability is one of the primary reasons *dBASE IV* is such a powerful tool for organizing and managing data. You can specify a certain criterion and create a view to see only those records that fit the criterion. You can set up an update query to automatically update a whole file, and you can even create labels for the specific records in a view of a database file.

The Forms Submenu

The Forms submenu contains instructions for making up your own screen displays. You can design them to duplicate paper forms you already use or to enter data in a customized format.

The Reports Submenu

The Reports submenu allows you to create reports in the format you specify using data from your database files. You can also print the reports you generate from within the Control Center.

The Labels Submenu

The Labels submenu contains instructions for printing labels in the form you specify using data from your database files.

The Applications Submenu

The Applications submenu stores the programs you write to accomplish database management tasks.

Submenu Screens

All of the submenu screens contain at least the following:

☐ *Menu bar and clock*: Activate the menu bar at the top of

the screen by pressing F10, Menus, or by pressing the Alt key and the first letter of the menu you want to open. Access all menus and choose all options from the menus in the same way. The menu bar lists the available menus. To see these options, pull down the menus. After you are finished with a menu, press ESC, and it will disappear. Move from one menu to another by pressing the left- and right-arrow keys.

☐ *Status bar*: The status bar gives much information about the operation you're performing or are about to choose. It tells you the type of screen you are in, the name of the current file and its DOS path, the location of the cursor, the source database file or view, and the keyboard mode (such as Caps for CAPS LOCK).

☐ *Navigation line*: The navigation line at the bottom of your screen shows the keys you can use to move the cursor on your screen;

☐ *Message line*: When the cursor is in a menu, the message line gives a brief explanation of the highlighted menu option. When the cursor is not in a menu, the message line shows information such as prompts.

Getting Help

To get help, press the F1 Help key. It will show information about the item on which you have placed your cursor. For example, if you put your cursor on the <create> marker in the Data panel and press F1, *dBASE IV* will display the help box on creating a database file. The help box will be superimposed on your screen. All help boxes contain four parts:

☐ *Title line*: This tells you the topic covered by the help text.

☐ *Text area*: This contains the explanation of the topic. There may be more than one page; if so, you can see the next page by pressing F4, Next. (If you hear a beep, *dBASE IV* is signalling that a new topic begins on that page.)

☐ *Buttons*: At the bottom of the help box, you will see four "buttons." These provide options for the help display. Activate any button by highlighting it and pressing Return, or by typing its first letter and pressing Return. The available buttons are:

- *Contents*: Displays the help table of contents. (For more details on the topic you want help on, press the PgDn key. For more general information on that topic, press PgUp.)
- *Related Topics*: Quick way to reach other relevant topics. When you pick one, help on that topic is displayed.
- *Backup*: Retraces your steps through the HELP system in reverse order.
- *Print*: Prints the current help page;

☐ *Navigation line*: While help is on your screen, the navigation line at the bottom of the screen shows:

- *F3 PREVIOUS*: Pressing this will show the previous page of text. Help boxes are in logical order by topic. You'll hear a beep when you reach a different topic.
- *F4 NEXT*: Shows the next page of help text.
- *ESC:EXIT*: Removes the help box from your screen, leaving the display on which you were working.

When you are finished with the help message, press either Return or Esc to close the help box.

Quitting dBASE IV

You can leave *dBASE IV* by choosing QUIT TO DOS from the Exit Menu in the Control Center. To get back into *dBASE IV*, type dbase at the DOS prompt.

Summary

You have now learned how to access all of the *dBASE IV* features except SQL mode by making use of the graphic display called the Control Center. The main menus of the Control Center are:

- ☐ Catalog, containing options for managing catalogs and the files they contain.
- ☐ Tools, containing a set of utilities for accessing DOS, importing and exporting files, the PROTECT program, and program parameter settings.
- ☐ Exit, which allows you to leave the Control Center for either the dot prompt or DOS.

Each panel in the Control Center contains its own submenus. These panels are:

Data (See also Chapter 4)

Queries (See also Chapter 5)

Forms (See also Chapter 6)

Reports (See also Chapter 6)

Labels (See also Chapter 6)

Applications (See also Chapter 7)

Each of the above panels and their submenus are explained briefly in this chapter, and in more detail in the other chapters indicated.

You have also learned how to get HELP while you're working at the Control Center.

4

Database Files

This chapter describes what can be done in the Data panel of the Control Center. When the Control Center screen appears on the monitor, look for the catalog name above the Control Center panels in the middle of the screen. This will be the catalog you will be working with. The files in that catalog will be listed in the Data panel at the leftmost panel of your screen. If no files are listed, you will probably want to add some files to your catalog. You can press either Return with the highlight on < create > in the left panel or F10 to go to the Catalog pull-down menu.

Pressing Return with the highlight on < create > will cause the Database File Design screen to appear. The Catalog pull-down menu will give you the option of adding a file to the catalog. These two choices are discussed in the following sections.

After you have created and added files to the catalog, the files in the catalog will appear on the Control Center screen in the Data panel separated by a horizontal line. The files above the line are opened for use and have their own work area. The files below the line are not open and do not occupy a work area. You cannot remove an open file from the catalog. Procedures for opening or closing files are described later in this chapter. If there is a file in the current catalog, you can BROWSE or EDIT records in that file.

Creating a New File

If you press Return with the highlight on <create> in the Data panel of the Control Center, the Database File Design screen (Fig. 4-1) will be displayed. By using the Database File Design screen, you will be able to *name the fields*, determine the *field types*, decide the *width* of each field, decide how many *decimal*

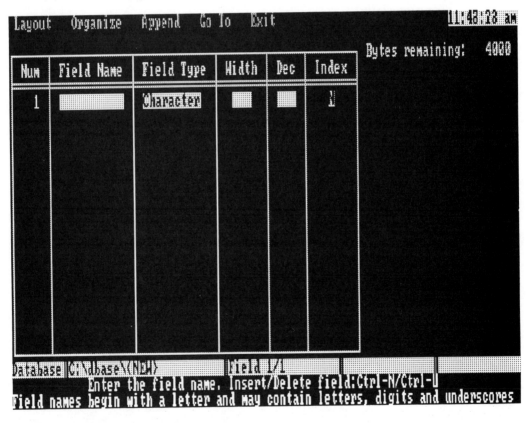

Fig. 4-1. The Database File Design Screen.

places numeric fields have, and decide whether the file will be *indexed* on a designated field.

While designing the database file structure, you can insert a blank field above the current field by pressing Ctrl-N. When you edit the blank field, you are actually placing a new field above the one on which you have been working. You can delete the current field by pressing Ctrl-U.

When you finish designing the fields, press Return twice or Ctrl-End (or you can press F10 and select *Save this database structure* from the Layout Menu described later in this chapter), and you will be prompted for the file name. After you provide a name and hit Return, the structure will be saved under that file name with a .DBF file extension. A prompt will then ask whether you want to enter data records. If you answer yes, you will be presented with an EDIT screen where you can begin to enter new records.

From the Database File Design screen, you can go to the menu bar by pressing F10. The five menus to choose from on the menu bar are:

- ☐ *Layout*
- ☐ *Organize*
- ☐ *Append*
- ☐ *Go To*
- ☐ *Exit*

The Layout Menu

The Layout Menu has three options:

- ☐ *Print database structure:* The Print popup menu will appear on the screen with eight options, which will allow you to set up your printout and then print. The eight options are:

  [1] *Begin printing,* which allows you to start the printout.

  [2] *Eject page now,* which allows you to eject a page before starting the printout.

  [3] *Use print form,* which allows you to choose a form file to use during the printout.

[4] *Save settings to print form,* which allows you to save any settings for your printer that you may have changed (using the following three options) to the print form file.

[5] *Destination,* which allows you to choose the screen, a file, or the printer for your output.

[6] *Control of printer,* which allows you to set print control options.

[7] *Output options,* which allows you to decide on any special options you might want for your output.

[8] *Page dimensions,* which allows you to set up the page dimensions for your output.

☐ *Edit database description*: The Edit Database Description Dialog will appear on your screen with the current description. You can either accept the description, by pressing Return, or edit it, and then press Return to accept it.

☐ *Save this database file structure*: You will be able to save the file structure you have created after being prompted to name it.

The Organize Menu

The *Organize* menu has eight options divided into two groups: The first group allows you deal with indexes, and the second group allows you to sort or deal with marked records by deleting them or unmarking them. The options on the Organize menu are *Create new index, Modify existing index, Order records by index, Activate NDX index file, Remove unwanted index tag, Sort database on field list, Unmark all records,* and *Erase marked records.*

The Append Menu

The *Append* menu gives you three options for appending records: *Enter records from the keyboard, Append records from a dBASE file,* or *Copy records from a non-dBASE file.*

The Go To Menu

The *Go To* menu allows you to choose a field description to edit. The options are *Top field, Last field,* and *Field number.* If you choose *Field number,* you will be prompted for a field number.

The Exit Menu

The *Exit* menu has two options: *Save changes and exit* and *Abandon changes and exit.*

Adding Existing Files to the Catalog

If you want to add already-created files to the catalog, you press F10 to obtain a pull-down menu under Catalog at the menu bar. Using the Down-Arrow key, position the highlight on the *Add file to catalog* option, and press Return. A list of directories and files in the current directory will appear at the right of your screen. The directories will be distinguished from the files by angle brackets (< and >). Using the Up- and Down-Arrow keys, you can choose from the list by pressing Return. If you select a directory, a new list of files and subdirectories in that directory will appear. If you select a file, that file will be added to the current catalog and will appear in the leftmost panel on your Control Center screen.

Opening and Closing Files

If you highlight a file name in the Data panel of the Control Center and press Return, a prompt box will appear on your screen. If the file appears below the line in the Data panel, the file is currently closed, and the leftmost option, *Use file* on the prompt box, will be highlighted. By pressing Return, the file will be opened, placed in a work area, and its name moved above the line in the Data panel of the Control Center.

If you want to BROWSE the file, move the highlight to the *Display data* option of the prompt box and press Return. The file will be opened, placed in a work area, and the BROWSE screen will be displayed. Upon returning to the Control Center, you will see that the file has been moved above the line in the Data panel of the Control Center, which means it is open and occupies a work area. If you press Return, the prompt box will be displayed with the highlight on the leftmost option, which is *Close file*. If you press Return, the file will be closed and removed from the work area it currently occupies, and its name will be moved below the line in the Data panel of the Control Center.

BROWSE

If a file appears in the Data panel of the Control Center, you can BROWSE the file by placing the highlight on the file name and pressing Return. This will cause the prompt box to appear on your screen. If you want the BROWSE screen displayed with records from the file highlighted in the Data panel of the Control Center, move the highlight to the *Display data* option and press Return. If you then press F2, the BROWSE screen will be replaced with the EDIT screen. The F2 key is a toggle between BROWSE and EDIT. You can also get into BROWSE by pressing the F2 key while you are in the Control Center. The BROWSE command is much the same in *dBASE IV* as it was in *dBASE III PLUS*. See Chapter 2 for changes in the BROWSE command in *dBASE IV*.

In BROWSE, you can do such tasks as edit fields and mark records for deletion. First select a record by using the Up-Arrow and Down-Arrow keys, which will move the highlight to whatever record you want to modify. Then press F10 to have the Records Menu appear under Records on the bar at the top of the screen. The Records Menu has six choices:

☐ *Undo change to record*: If you have changed the record, you can select this option to undo the change.

☐ *Add new records*: With this option, the BROWSE screen will be positioned just after the last record with a blank record ready for you to fill in.

☐ *Mark record for deletion:* The currently highlighted record will be marked for deletion. If the currently highlighted record is already marked for deletion, this option will be replaced by the option *Clear deletion mark.*

☐ *Blank record:* The currently highlighted record will be blanked out, and you can replace it with a different record.

☐ *Lock record:* You cannot use this option unless you have a multiuser system. If you do, this option can be used to lock the record while you change it. If you press F10 again, you will see that this option has been replaced by *Unlock record,* which you can choose to unlock the record. (See Chapter 9 for further details on the locking system.)

☐ *Follow record to new position:* You will be able to reset a SET switch that allows you to follow a record to its new position when fields in an index key are modified. The default for this switch is Yes.

If, after you press F10, you use the Right-Arrow key, the Fields Menu will appear at the top of your screen under the word Fields on the menu bar. The Fields Menu has four options:

☐ *Lock leftmost fields:* With this option, a prompt box will appear, allowing you to choose the number of fields that are to remain stationary. If, for example, you fill in the prompt box with the number two, the two will be placed in the curly braces following the *Lock leftmost fields* option. The effect will be that, if you scroll the fields using the Ctrl-Right-Arrow and Ctrl-Left-Arrow keys, the two leftmost fields will remain stationary.

☐ *Blank field:* The current value in the field where the highlight is will be blanked, ready for you to enter a new value.

☐ *Freeze field:* A prompt box will appear, asking you to enter the field name of the field to be frozen, which will confine the editing to the field chosen.

☐ *Size field:* You will be able to change the size of the currently highlighted field by using the Right- and Left-

Arrow keys. When you are finished resizing the field, press Return to end the sizing operation.

If you bypass the Fields Menu at the menu bar on the BROWSE screen, the Go To menu will appear on your screen. The Go To menu has eight options:

☐ *Top record:* In this option, the highlight will be moved to the top record in the file.

☐ *Last record:* In this option, the highlight will be moved to the last record in the file.

☐ *Record number:* You will be prompted for the record number you want to move to. After you enter it, the highlight will move to that record.

☐ *Skip:* you will be prompted for the number of records you want to skip, and the highlight will be moved forward that number of records.

☐ *Index key search:* You can only select this option if there is an index in use with your file. If there is, a search will be made for an exact match (see the *Match capitalization* option) of the key with the search string. If the search is successful, the highlight will be moved to the matching record.

☐ *Forward search:* You will be prompted for a search string. After you enter the search string and press Return, a forward search will be made for an exact match (if the *Match capitalization* toggle is set to Yes. If an exact match is found, the highlight will be moved to the matching record. If the *Match capitalization* toggle is set to No, a search will be made for an exact match independent of the case of the letters; and if a match is found, the highlight will be moved to the matching record. If a match is not found, a box will appear on your screen telling you the record has not been found and to press any key to continue.

☐ *Backward search:* This option is the same as the *Forward search* option, except that the search will be made for records prior to the highlighted record.

☐ *Match capitalization:* This option is a toggle between Yes and No. If the toggle is set to Yes, the search string must not only match the field value exactly, but the capital letters must match the capital letters and the small letters must match the small letters.

If you choose the Exit menu on the menu bar, you will have two options:

☐ *Exit*: This option returns you to the Control Center screen.

☐ *Transfer to query design*: This option will transfer you to QBE. (See Chapter 5, which is devoted entirely to QBE.

EDIT

To EDIT records in a file in the catalog, you must first bring up the BROWSE screen. Then you can toggle between BROWSE and EDIT by pressing the F2 key.

In EDIT, only a single record appears on the screen at any given time. The fields of the record are placed in sequential lines down, rather than across the screen. In EDIT, you can move between fields by using the Up- and Down-Arrow keys. In EDIT, there are three menus on the menu bar: *Records, Go To*, and *Exit*. The *Fields* Menu in BROWSE would not make sense in EDIT. The three menus, *Records, Go To*, and *Exit*, have exactly the same options they have in BROWSE. The treatment of these menus in BROWSE applies to the menus in EDIT.

Summary

This chapter discusses the data panel of the Control Center. The BROWSE and EDIT commands can be reached from the data panel, and new data files can be created from this panel. The procedures and the menus for manipulating data files are discussed in detail.

5

Query By Example (QBE)

Query By Example (QBE) is, like SQL, an interactive query language (designed by IBM) for relational database management systems. Each includes slightly different facilities: SQL is more extensive than QBE, but you may find QBE somewhat easier to learn. Now, *dBASE IV* offers both QBE and SQL so that you may use whichever query language you like. With QBE (as with SQL), you tell the system what you want, not how to get it. QBE and interactive SQL are both part of the Non-Procedural Interface to *dBASE IV*.

In *dBASE IV*, QBE has two major capabilities. The first is forming queries to define virtual files (called views) for use in reports, labels, and *ad hoc* inquiries. The view is called a virtual file because the data it contains are not actually stored in the database. Only the view definition is stored. This allows the data to be retrieved whenever needed. The data in the view vary as the data in the base file(s) vary. For the *dBASE III PLUS* user, views in *dBASE IV* are a superset of views in *dBASE III PLUS* where views are defined with ASSIST or in the *dBASE* language with the USE command, the SET RELATION command, the SET FIELDS command, and the SET FILTER command.

The second capability is forming queries to specify global updates to a database file. You can use queries to:

☐ Link two or more database files to form a new virtual file (join).

☐ Form a subset of the records in a file (selection or filter).

☐ Form a subset of the fields in a file (projection).

☐ Organize the records in a file (sort).

☐ Summarize a group of records (aggregate operator).

These capabilities and the requirements for using them are explained in the sections that follow:

How to Form Queries

A query is defined by using the query design subsystem, which includes:

☐ File skeletons
☐ View skeletons
☐ Condition boxes
☐ Calculated fields

The work area in QBE where you use the query design subsystem is called a "blackboard," which is shown in Fig. 5-1.

Before QBE performs or saves a query, it will check to see that all the files in the current query are linked together and that all the example variables have a match. This process is called *semantic checking*. If QBE finds any problems, it will produce an error message.

File Skeletons

The file skeleton(s) is at the top of the blackboard. A file skeleton is a graphic representation of a file in tabular form. The fields of the file are represented as column headings. The file

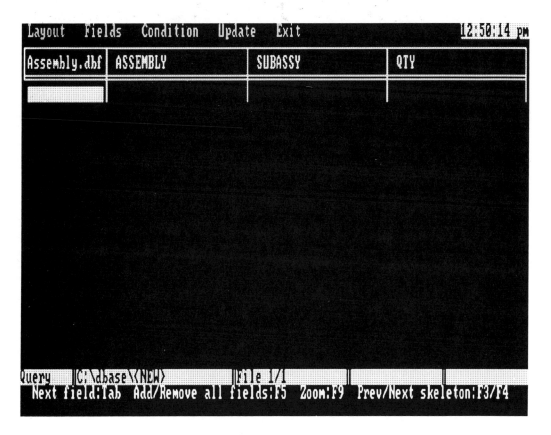

Fig. 5-1. The Query Design Subsystem Blackboard.

skeleton can represent either a database file or a view. It will look
like Fig. 5-2. The name of the file, "Customer.DBF," is shown
in the leftmost box of the file skeleton, with an initial capital, and
contains the file extension .DBF to make it clear that this is a file,
not a field. The other columns show the names of the fields in
this database file. If you have more fields than can fit on the screen
at one time, scroll horizontally to see them. The file name will
be locked during horizontal scrolling, and the column names will
be locked during vertical scrolling.

If you have more than one file skeleton with the same name
for a specific field, the default example is:

<file name> <field name>

Customer.dbf	CUST_NO	CUST_NAME	CUST_ADDR	PURCHASE

Fig. 5-2. A File skeleton.

Each line in the file skeleton represents an example of a row in the result. If you enter a query with multiple expressions on one line, the resulting records must satisfy each expression on that line. If you enter a two-line query, then two groups of records will be in the result, with each group satisfying the expressions on one of the two lines.

To form queries, you must use "example" variables (this is the meaning of the name, Query By Example). You will use example variables for filtering and for linking. You can enter four types of information in the columns under the field names of the file skeleton:

☐ Filtering criteria
☐ File linking
☐ Updating
☐ Aggregating operators

These types of information are discussed later in this chapter.

The View Skeletons

Queries that define a view have a view skeleton (Fig. 5-3); other queries do not. The skeleton appears—and stays—at the bottom of your screen. It is a picture of the fields that you want to appear in the view. The name of the view is in the leftmost box and is separated from the first field name by vertical double lines. If all the fields do not fit on the screen at one time, scroll horizontally to see the rest.

Each column in a skeleton is 21 characters wide. If your entry is wider than 21 characters, scroll horizontally within the column.

View Orders	DATE	CUST_NAME	INV_NO	ITEM	PRICE

Fig. 5-3. A View skeleton.

By using the F9 (Zoom) key, you can see up to 78 characters of the entry.

The Condition Box

When you select "Add condition box" from the Condition Menu, a box will appear just above the view skeleton. It will allow you to enter expressions that are more complex than those you can put within a field. Its use is optional, and you can have only one condition box for each query. The condition box can have many lines, but only three will be displayed in the unzoomed mode. By using the F9 (Zoom) key, you can display all the contents of the condition box, up to 78 characters wide and 13 lines deep.

You can create a logical expression by entering the expression directly into the box. It can be any valid *dBASE* logical expression involving any of the fields in any of the files in the query, and it can contain *dBASE* function references. The expression you put in the condition box (Fig. 5-4) acts like a filter for the entire query. It is applied to each potential row in the query. If the expression is evaluated as true, the row is included in the result. If the expression is evaluated as false, the row is not included.

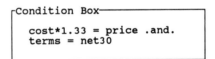

Fig. 5-4. A Condition Box.

```
┌Condition Box─────────────
 cost*1.33 = price .and.
 terms = net30
```

Calculated Fields

Just above the Condition Box, you will find the calculated Field Skeleton (Fig. 5-5). It has the same shape as a file skeleton. You can enter into a column heading any valid *dBASE* expression that involves the fields in the query. The calculated value can be included in the view skeleton. You cannot use calculated fields as links or as sort fields; otherwise, they are just like any other field in the query.

Calc'd Flds	cost*1.4	net30

Fig. 5-5. A calculated field skeleton.

Example Variables

Example variables are normal *dBASE* variables that you use to give QBE an example of what you are looking for. They can be no more than 10 characters long, must begin with a letter, and can contain no embedded blanks. Letters, numbers, and underscores can be used for the name of an example variable. The example variable must occur at least twice. The default example variable for each column is its field name. Example variables are used for filtering and for linking.

Filtering

Filtering in QBE is the same as SELECTing in SQL. In other words, you filter out the record(s) you want by entering an expression describing it in the column for a specific field. When you enter a single value, you are asking for only the subset of records where this field matches the specified value. For example, if you wanted to retrieve only the records for Customer No. 223, you would enter 223 under the field name for Customer No. as shown in Fig. 5-6.

Customer.dbf	CUST_NO	CUST_NAME	CUST_ADDR	PURCHASE
	223			

Fig. 5-6. *Filtering for a single value.*

In *dBASE IV* QBE, all character-string values must be enclosed in quotation marks. For example, if you want only those customers living in Boston, you would enter "Boston" (including the quotes) under the field Customer Address, as in Fig. 5-7.

Customer.dbf	CUST_NO	CUST_NAME	CUST_ADDR	PURCHASE
			"Boston"	

Fig. 5-7. *Filtering for a string value.*

When you specify an example value, any one of the relational operators in Table 5-1 can be used, which includes values that are equal to the field value, as well as values that are unequal.

Table 5-1. Relational Operators in QBE.

Operator	*Meaning*
>	Greater than
<	Less than
=	Equals
< >	Not equal
#	Not equal
> =	Greater than or equal to
< =	Less than or equal to
$	Contained in
Like	Pattern match
Sounds like	SOUNDEX match

Any of the operators in Table 5-1 can be used with your example variable. If, instead of including only Boston customers, you want to exclude Boston customers and include all others, you would precede "Boston" with one of the two unequal operators, either # or < >, as shown in Fig. 5-8.

If you don't enter any operator in front of the example variable, QBE assumes you mean equal (=). Therefore, it is not necessary to use the equal sign if you do mean equal.

When you use the operator "like," you must follow it by a quoted pattern. For example, to specify that you want names like

Customer.dbf	CUST_NO	CUST_NAME	CUST_ADD	PURCHASE
			#"Boston"	

Fig. 5-8. Filtering for all except the string value.

Customer.dbf	CUST_NO	CUST_NAME	CUST_ADD	PURCHASE
		like "Johns*n"		

Fig. 5-9. Filtering for a string like "pattern."

Johnson, Johnsen, or Johnston, use like with the asterisk (*) wildcard indicator, since there may be either one or two unknown letters (Fig. 5-9).

You may know the sound of what you are looking for, but not the exact spelling. The facility *dBASE IV* has for handling this problem is called SOUNDEX. You can use the operator "sounds like" for this function; you must follow it by a quoted character string. For example if you are searching for something that sounds like "write," but could be "right" or "rite," you can do it as shown in Fig. 5-10. In general, operators in QBE must be placed *before* the quoted string. This contrasts with the *dBASE IV* Procedural Interface, where operators are placed *after* the string.

Customer.dbf	CUST_NO	CUST_NAME	CUST_ADD	PURCHASE
		sounds like "rite"		

Fig. 5-10. Filtering for a similar sound.

You can also use the following aggregate (or built-in) functions for filtering:

plus	(+)
minus	(−)
multiplication	(*)
division	(/)
exponent	(**) and (^)

Multiple expressions on the same line are added together to form the search condition. For example, you can enter < 2000 under Customer No., and "Boston" under customer address, as in Fig. 5-11. The search condition expressed is "All customers whose invoice number is less than 2,000 and whose address is Boston."

Customer.dbf	CUST_NO	CUST_NAME	CUST_ADDR	PURCHASE
	<2000		"Boston"	

Fig. 5-11. Filtering with more than one search condition.

Two conditions on separate lines are interpreted as "the first condition or the second condition." For example, you can put <2000 on one line, and "Boston" on the next line as in Fig. 5-12. The search condition "All customers whose invoice number is less than 2,000 or whose address is Boston." This query will yield all customers whose invoice number is less than 2000 regardless of where they live, and all customers who live in Boston, regardless of their invoice numbers. Those customers who have invoice numbers less than 2000 and who also live in Boston will appear only once in the result.

Customer.dbf	CUST_NO	CUST_NAME	CUST_ADDR	PURCHASE
	<2000			
			"Boston"	

Fig. 5-12. Filtering for either of two search conditions.

Multiple expressions can be placed in one column if you want to indicate a range of values. For example, if you want to specify customer numbers between 1500 and 2000, you would enter both numbers under the customer number field, as in Fig. 5-13. This query will yield records with the range of invoice numbers from 1500 to 2000, but it will not include the endpoints 1500 or 2000.

In general, each line in the file skeleton represents an example row in the result. Queries with more than one expression on one

Customer.dbf	CUST_NO	CUST_NAME	CUST_ADDR	PURCHASE
	>1500, <2000			

Fig. 5-13. Filtering for an expression.

line yield results where each record satisfies each of the expressions in that line. Queries with two lines yield results consisting of two groups of records where each group satisfies the expression on one of the two lines.

Filters can be applied to memo fields in the same way they are applied to character fields. While entering a filter, you can press Shift-F1 to get lists of field or example variable names, operators, and functions to help you construct the filter.

Linking Files

Linking is actually another form of filtering. If you want to link two files together (this operation is called a "join"), place an example variable in the linking column of each of the two files. (Example variables used in linking obey regular *dBASE* syntax.) This will convey to QBE that records in these two files, which have the same value in this column, will be joined. The common field will then be displayed just once in the result. This is called the *inner* or *natural join*.

For example, to join a file of Invoices with a file of Customers, on Customer No., place the same example variable in the CUST__NO field in each of those files. After you do this, a virtual file (or view) will be created consisting of all the fields in the Customers file and all the fields in the Invoices file with the common field, Customer No., appearing only once (Fig. 5-14).

Customer.dbf	CUST_NO	CUST_NAME	CUST_ADDR	PURCHASE
	208			

Invoices.dbf	DATE	CUST_NO	TERMS	ITEM
		208		

Fig. 5-14. Filtering by using a join.

The search condition for Fig. 5-14 is "Join together all records in the Customers.DBF file with any record in the Invoices.DBF file that has the same Customer No." The number 208 has no special significance. We could have entered 503 or any other number or character string. The point is that you must give the same example in the CUST_NO column of both file skeletons to convey to QBE that the two files must be joined on the CUST_NO field.

You might want to see all customer records, regardless of whether there is a corresponding invoice record. The join of customers and invoices might not include such items as customers for whom, through error, no customer number was assigned. To do so, you would use an "outer join."

Instead of entering the same value under the field name for invoice number as you would for the natural join, enter Every C under CUST_NO in the Customers file and C under CUST_NO in the Invoices file. This procedure is shown in Fig. 5-15, which will create a new virtual file where every customer's name will be listed, along with all the other fields from both files. If no record with the same customer number as that in the Invoices files exists in the Customers file, then blanks will be used for customer name. In this way, you will pick up any record in the Customers file where customer number has been omitted.

You can also perform self-joins with QBE. A *self-join* occurs when you make a query that involves two different records from the same file. For example, you might need to know who is the supervisor of a certain employee. If all employee records are in

Customer.dbf	CUST_NO	CUST_NAME	CUST_ADD	PURCHASE
	Every C			

Invoices.dbf	DATE	CUST_NO	TERMS	ITEM
		C		

Fig. 5-15. Filtering by using an outer join.

the same file, then you need to link information within that file to find the answer.

In *dBASE IV* QBE, you must set up two file skeletons to form a self-join. The final section in this chapter tells how to get two file skeletons on your screen. Assume that you have the following employee and manager list in your employee file, which is called Emp.DBF

EMPNO	NAME	MRG_NO
45	Jim	48
46	Chuck	65
47	Stan	30
48	Juli	87

If you are looking for the name of Jim's supervisor, you must set up the two file skeletons shown in Fig. 5-16. The result will be the view shown in Fig. 5-17, which identifies Jim's supervisor.

Emp.dbf	EMPNO	NAME	MGR_NO
	45		M

Emp.dbf	EMPNO	NAME	MGR_NO
	M		

Fig. 5-16. *Filtering with a self join.*

Emp.dbf	EMPNO	NAME	MGR_NO
	48	Juli	87

Fig. 5-17. *View resulting from a self join.*

Updating

In QBE, "update" is a general term meaning delete, replace, append, or unmark. The Update Menu contains two items. The first is the *Specify Update Operation*, which will give you the following submenu of update operations applied to a specific file:

☐ Mark records for deletion

☐ Replace values in *<file name>*
☐ Append records to *<file name>*
☐ Unmark records from *<file name>*

The second item is *Perform the Update*, which is only available for an update query. When you select this option, QBE first does a semantic check, then it asks you for confirmation. It will then perform the specified change. After the change has been made, you will get a message box telling you how many records were changed and giving you the opportunity to look at the newly updated file.

Each update applies one of these two terms to a specific file. You can only perform one update operation for each query. The operations are explained in the following sections.

Updating Views

When using BROWSE or EDIT with a .DBF file, you can change as well as peruse data. This is not true of views because only certain views can be updated. If you try to update a nonupdatable view, a message will appear telling you that this is not possible.

The following rules apply to updating views:

☐ If the view contains a calculated field, you cannot update that field.

☐ If a field in the view is defined by an aggregate operator, the view cannot be updated.

☐ If a view definition is derived from more than one file skeleton, the view cannot be updated.

You can BROWSE views that cannot be updated.

Deleting

Deleting is similar to linking and filtering in that values that appear in a column are used to filter. Then all records that satisfy the filter are marked for deletion. A delete operation with no filter conditions is the same as a DELETE ALL command in the Procedural Interface.

If you want to update by deleting, when the word MARK appears in the leftmost column of the Target file skeleton, put a value(s) in a column just as you would filter a view or a query. Any record satisfying that value will be marked for deletion. The absence of specified filter conditions is equivalent to DELETE ALL, and all rows having that filter value will be marked for deletion. Figure 5-18 shows how to delete Employee No. 21, and Fig. 5-19 shows how to delete everyone in Group No. 3.

Target Emp. dbf	EMPNO	NAME	GROUP_NO	SALARY
Mark	21			

Fig. 5-18. Marking an employee for deletion.

Target Emp. db	EMPNO	NAME	GROUP_NO	SALARY
Mark			3	

Fig. 5-19. Marking a group for deletion.

Replacing

When using the Replace operation, values that you put in the column will be used for filtering, unless you precede the value by the word "with," in which case they become the new value. (This is the same as the REPLACE command in the Procedural Interface.) For example, Replace can be used either to change an individual salary or to issue a change in all salaries within a specified category. Figure 5-20 gives a 5 percent raise to all employees in Group No. 5.

Target Emp. dbf	EMPNO	NAME	GROUP_NO	SALARY
Replace			5	with salary*1.05

Fig. 5-20. Replacing specified fields with a new value.

Appending

The append operation can be used to add one record, to copy records from other files, or to construct new records by consolidating fields. Figure 5-21 illustrates adding a new employee to the Emp.DBF file.

Target—— Emp. dbf	EMPNO	NAME	GROUP_NO	SALARY
Append	92	"Doe"	13	50000

Fig. 5-21. Appending a new record.

Unmark

Unmark is used to recall records that are currently marked for deletion. The records specified by unmark will no longer be marked for deletion. (This is the same as the RECALL command in the Procedural Interface.) To give the employee marked for deletion in Fig. 5-18 a second chance, you would unmark his record, as shown in Fig. 5-22.

Target—— Emp. dbf	EMPNO	NAME	GROUP_NO	SALARY
Unmark	21			

Fig. 5-22. Unmarking a record previously marked for deletion.

Aggregating Operators

The following aggregate operators are used to summarize a group of records:

SUM
AVG
MIN
MAX
CNT

The operators SUM, AVG, and CNT can be followed by the word "unique." which will ensure that duplicate records are not included. Aggregate operators can only be used on file skeletons; they cannot be used in the condition box.

More than one aggregate operator can be used in a given file skeleton. For example, you might want to count employees and get the sum of their salaries in a specified group. You can do this in one operation by entering COUNT under the name field, the group number under the field with that name, and SUM under the salary field, as shown in Fig. 5-23.

Emp. dbf	EMPNO	NAME	GROUP_NO	SALARY
		COUNT	4	SUM

Fig. 5-23. Using aggregate operators.

The GROUP BY Operator

When using one of the aggregation operators, you can also have specified groups of records aggregated by placing the term GROUP BY in the column containing the grouping field. For example, if you want the total salary figure for each group within each department, instead of having QBE compute them one at a time, enter SUM under salary and place the term GROUP BY under the field for department number, as well as the field for group number.

Since you want more than one grouping, you must specify the order of the groupings. The sorting will be in ascending order (lower numbers before high numbers, A before Z) unless you specify otherwise. The setup for a SUM of salaries grouped first by Department, then by Group, both in descending order, is shown in Fig. 5-24.

Emp. dbf	NAME	DEPT_NO	GROUP_NO	SALARY
		GROUP BY, DESC1	GROUP BY, DESC2	SUM

Fig. 5-24. Salaries summed over sorted departments and groups.

Query Operations

The seven query operations that you can enter in the leftmost box of a file skeleton are:

(Blank)
Unique
Find
Append
Delete
Replace
Unmark

A *Blank* operation field is the same as defining the view and is the default operation. You can also use blank (or define view) for *ad hoc* retrievals. To do this, set up the query and then browse the resulting view.

A *Unique* query operation prevents any duplicate records from appearing in the view. The file itself may contain any number of duplicates, but when the unique operation is specified, each record in the view will be different from every other record in the view.

The *Find* query operation lets you browse a database file and be positioned at the first record of that file defined by a filter condition. You will see the record in context with the other records in the file. If you press F2 for a Find query, it will switch you to either Browse or Edit. The cursor will be positioned on the first record satisfying the filter condition. (This is like executing the FIND command from the dot prompt and then the BROWSE command.)

The *append, delete, replace,* and *unmark* query operations are referred to as "updates." In QBE, an update is a global change to a database file.

Designing Your Queries

To move among the objects on the query screen (file skeletons, calculated fields skeleton, condition box, view skeleton), use the Prev/Next (F3/F4) function keys. To move among columns in a skeleton (file, calculated field, or view), press Tab and Shift-Tab.

To move within a column, press the right- and left-arrow keys to move the cursor one character at a time and the up- and down-arrow keys to move the cursor one row at a time. Home, End, and similar keys work the same as they do in Browse. Table 5-2 shows the available key strokes in QBE. When you press the F1 (Data) key, the QBE processor first does a semantic check. For a view definition, pressing F2 will switch you to either Browse or Edit. You can toggle between Browse and Edit by pressing F2. The equivalent to this menu item from the dot prompt is to SET VIEW TO <*filename*> and then BROWSE or EDIT.

Table 5-2. Summary of Keystrokes Available in QBE.

Keystroke	Action
F1	Help
Shift-F1	Display list of field names, example variable names, functions and operators.
F2	For view queries, perform query and browse data.
	For update queries, browse data of target file.
	F2 on an update query does not perform the query.
F3	Go into edit mode in previous object. If at first object, go to last object.
F4	Go into edit mode in next object. If at last object, go to first object.
F5	When inside calc field or file skeleton, add/remove field from view.
F6	When inside a view skeleton, extend select one field at a time.
F7	When inside a view skeleton, move field.
F8	Display (at dot prompt).
F9	Zoom/Unzoom.
F10	Open the pull-down menu that was used last.
Ctrl-End	Save and exit.
Ctrl-PgDn	Go to last row in current column.

(*Table 5-2 continues.*)

Keystroke	Action
Ctrl-PgUp	Go to first row in current column.
Ctrl-Return	Save and continue.
Del	Delete one character.
Uparrow	Go to previous line.
Dnarrow	Go to next line.
Leftarrow	Move one character left.
Rightarrow	Move one character right.
Ctrl-Leftarrow	Move left one word.
Ctrl-Rightarrow	Move right one word.
PgDn	Go to next page of file skeleton.
PgUp	Go to previous page of file skeleton.
Home	Move cursor to leftmost box.
End	Move to last column.
Shift-Tab	Move left one column.
Tab	Move right one column.

(Table 5-2 ends.)

Put fields in the view skeleton by pressing the toggle F5 (Field) key while you are positioned on one of the fields in a file skeleton or the calculated fields skeleton. If that field is already in the view skeleton, QBE will remove it. You can do this same thing by choosing the menu item "Add field to view" from the Fields Menu while you are positioned on a field.

If you choose "Remove field from View" while you are positioned in a field column of a file skeleton, QBE will delete the currently selected field from the view skeleton.

If you press F5 while positioned on the data cell (the leftmost cell), QBE will put all the fields for that file into the view skeleton. If all the fields for that file are already in the view skeleton, pressing F5 will remove all of them from the view skeleton. If some, but not all of the fields for that file are already in the view skeleton, pressing F5 will add the rest.

Menus

On the Queries Design screen, you will use a graphic interface to create queries and to update. The series of menus you will encounter starts with the Topline Menu, the menu bar for which contains the choices:

Layout   Fields   Condition   Update   Exit

Each of these Topline choices is a menu itself. These menus and the choices they offer are explained in the following sections.

The Layout Menu

The Layout Menu (Fig. 5-25) contains commands that add, delete, and link files, which are described in the following paragraphs.

Fig. 5-25. The Layout Menu.

```
Add file to query
Remove file from query

Create link by pointing

Write view as database file
Edit description of query
Save this query
```

Add File to Query. This option presents a list of database files. If a catalog is active, the list will contain files from the catalog. Otherwise, the list will contain files from the disk. After you choose a file, the new file skeleton will be displayed below the last file skeleton, and the cursor will be inside the new file skeleton.

Remove File from Query. The file skeleton containing the current selection will be removed after you confirm that action.

Create Link by Pointing. The cursor should be in a column of a file skeleton. The QBE processor will ask you to move the cursor to a column in another file skeleton and press Return. After you do this, QBE will link the two files on the two selected fields by placing the next available LINKn example variable in the two columns.

Save This Query. The QBE processor will first do a semantic check and then present a prompt box with the current name filled in. You can press Return to accept the current name, or you can change the name and then hit Return. If you choose a new name, that name will become the current name. The extension for every query file you save is .QBE. The extension for every update query file that you save is .UPD.

Write View as Database File. You can only choose this item if the query is a view definition. It will allow you to create a database file (.DBF file) from the data in the current view. This will be a snapshot of the virtual file and make it a physical file. The QBE processor does a semantic check and then presents a prompt box that will allow you to choose the name for the .DBF file. The name of the current view will be filled in. You can accept that or type in a different name. At this point, the .DBF file is created.

Edit Description of Query. You can modify the catalog description of the current query.

The Fields Menu

The Fields Menu is shown in Fig. 5-26. The commands in the Fields Menu affect individual fields in a skeleton. Their meanings are defined in the following paragraphs.

Add Field to View. This item will cause the currently selected field to zoom down to the view skeleton (if it is not already there). This gives the same result as pressing the F5 key. You can only

Fig. 5-26. The Fields Menu.

```
Add field to view

Remove field from view

Edit field name

Create calculated field

Sort on this field

Include indexes          NO/YES
```

use this command for view definition and unique queries. Fields will appear in the view skeleton from left to right in the order in which you add them to the view. You can change this order by first selecting the field in the view skeleton, then using the F7 (Move) key.

Remove Field from View. If your current selection is a field in the view skeleton, it will disappear from the view skeleton when you choose this menu item. If your current selection is a file or calculated field skeleton that appears in the view skeleton, the same thing will happen. If your selection is somewhere else, the QBE processor will display an error message. You can only use this command for view definition and unique queries.

Edit Field Name. Choose this command when you want to rename a selected column in either the view skeleton or the calculated fields skeleton. For calculated fields, the new name followed by an equal sign (=) will appear above the calculated field expression in the column heading. For table fields, the new name will be placed above the old name on the border of the view skeleton.

Create Calculated Field. The calculated field skeleton will appear (if it is not already there). QBE will then add an empty column to the skeleton.

Sort on This Field. A prompt box will appear with the following choices:

☐ Ascending ASCII (A..Za..z,0..9)
☐ Descending ASCII (z..aZ..A,9..0)
☐ Ascending Dictionary (Aa..Zz,0..9)
☐ Descending Dictionary (zZ..aA,9..0)

Include Indexes No/Yes. Toggling to Yes on this item gives you the opportunity to include any indexes associated with the database file as pseudofields, excluding single fields. You can then sort, link, or filter on this pseudofield, which will be faster than on nonindexed fields. Toggling to No will delete the pseudofield. The default is No.

The Condition Menu

The Condition Menu is shown in Fig. 5-27. Choose items in

```
┌─────────────────────────────┐
│ Add condition box           │
│ Delete condition box        │
│ Show condition box   YES/NO │
└─────────────────────────────┘
```

Fig. 5-27. The Condition Menu.

this menu to affect the presence or absence of the condition box. The commands are described in the following paragraphs.

Add Condition Box. An empty condition box will appear (if one isn't already there).

Delete Condition Box. Choosing this command (after you answer Yes to a prompt) will delete the condition box and its contents. (You could also accomplish this by selecting the condition box and pressing the DEL key.)

Show Condition Box Yes/No. When you toggle this to Yes, the condition box will be displayed; when you toggle to No, QBE will replace the condition box with

$$>>CB<<$$

At times, you might want to do this to save space.

The Update Menu

The Update Menu is shown in Fig. 5-28. It contains commands that you will use in connection with update queries. Their meanings are described in the following paragraphs.

```
┌─────────────────────────────┐
│ Perform the update          │
│ Specify update operation    │
└─────────────────────────────┘
```

Fig. 5-28. The Update Menu.

Specify Update Operation. The submenu of operations will appear. The commands in the submenu are:

Replace
Append
Delete
Unmark

The update operation you chose will appear in the leftmost cell of the file skeleton, and this file will become the target file for the query. The word *"target"* will appear at the left corner of the file skeleton.

If there already was an operation for the query, the newly chosen operation will replace the old one. If you change a view definition query to an update operation, the view skeleton will be deleted. You can also put your cursor on the operation cell, delete the operation, and change the operation to define the view. You can also specify the operation by moving the cursor to the cell and typing in the operation manually instead of using this menu.

Perform the Update. You can only select this option for an update query. QBE will first do a semantic check and then ask you to confirm. It will subsequently perform the specified change to the target file. After the changes are made a message box will tell how many records were changed (Fig. 5-29). If you press F2, QBE will switch you to BROWSE so that you can look at the newly updated file.

```
90 records deleted from BUYERS.DBF

Press F2 to browse BUYERS.DBF

Press any other key to continue in query
```

Fig. 5-29. Message Box after selecting "Perform the update."

The Exit Menu

The commands in the Exit Menu are shown in Fig. 5-30. This menu is consistent with other menus in the *dBASE IV* Non-Procedural Interface. The meanings of the menu items are as follow.

Fig. 5-30. The Exit Menu.

```
Save changes and exit

Abandon changes and exit

Return to <module>
```

Return to *<Previous Module>*. QBE will switch you back to the subsystem from which the query subsystem was called. If the current query was modified since it was last saved, you will see a prompt box that will give you the option of saving the current query definition or discarding it.

Save Changes and Exit. This command will switch you back to the Control Center after saving the current query.

Abandon Changes and Exit. This command will switch you back to the Control Center and will discard the current query.

Return to *<Module>*. This command will switch you back to the subsystem from which the query subsystem was called.

Summary

In this chapter you learned how to use the Query panel of the Control Center. The Query Panel contains Query By Example, (QBE), which is an interactive query language that lets you tell the system what you want, not how to get it.

To form queries, you use the query design subsystem in a work area called a *blackboard*. The design system consists of

File skeletons
View skeletons
Condition boxes
Calculated fields

How to use Example Variables to construct your queries also is explained.

In QBE, you "filter" to select the records that will satisfy your query. This chapter gave the rules for the different ways of filtering, including linking files and using a join.

The term "updating" in QBE includes the following operations:

Updating
Deleting
Replacing
Appending
Unmarking

Aggregate operators in QBE are used with groups of data. They are:

Summation
Averaging
Maximizing
Minimizing
Counting

The term GROUP BY is used with the aggregate operators to gather data into the groups you specify.

QBE has seven query operations:

(Blank)	To define a view
Unique	To prevent the duplicating of records
Find	To browse a database file
Append	
Delete	To make global changes to a database file.
Replace	
Unmark	

This chapter shows you how to design your queries using the graphic interface of the queries design screen.

6

Forms, Reports, and Labels

Extensive facilities are provided in *dBASE IV* for designing customized forms, reports, and labels to suit your own needs. Forms are screen objects designed to be displayed on a monitor; reports and labels are print objects designed to be printed. (Memo fields and programs are also considered to be print objects.) Following this approach, print objects use the *Style* option, while screen objects use the *Display* option. For example, on the Forms Design screen, the *Style* option is dimmed, meaning that it is unavailable for form design.

Print objects must be shown on the screen before they are actually printed. If your printer does not have italic, bold, superscript, or subscript, they appear as underlines.

Forms

A form can be designed by one of two methods: you can display the data in a database file or view on the Browse screen, or you can display it on an Edit screen. The display on the Browse screen is always a standard table format, with each row representing a record. The display on the Edit screen is more flexible in that you can add boxes or lines, omit certain fields, or add calculated fields.

Constructing forms from a view enables you to create many forms that are derived from the same base, but which will look very different because they make use of different sets of data. The names of all the forms currently in your catalog will appear in the Forms panel of the Control Center.

The following section describes the *dBASE IV* form-constructing facilities. For help in discovering different ways of designing effective forms, see your Ashton-Tate documentation called *Using the Menu System*.

Form Files

When you design a form using the Edit screen, this design is stored in a "form." As you use the form, you might want to improve on your original design. To do so, return to the Forms Design screen and modify it. The files used by the Forms Design screen have an .SCR file extension, and are listed in the Forms panel on the Control Center main screen. At the same time, *dBASE IV* creates a file with a .FMT extension that is used to display the form on the screen. You can modify the .FMT file, but any changes you make will be overwritten the next time you use the .SCR file because *dBASE IV* automatically creates a new .FMT file whenever you use the Forms Design screen to modify an .SCR file.

Quick Layout

If you do not want to design a form yourself, use the Quick Layout provided by *dBASE IV* on the Edit screen. It consists of each field of a database file or view on a separate line running down the left side of your screen. The field data appear to the right of the field name. If you want to design a customized form, use the Forms Design screen.

The Forms Design Screen

The Forms Design screen (Fig. 6-1) contains menus and a work

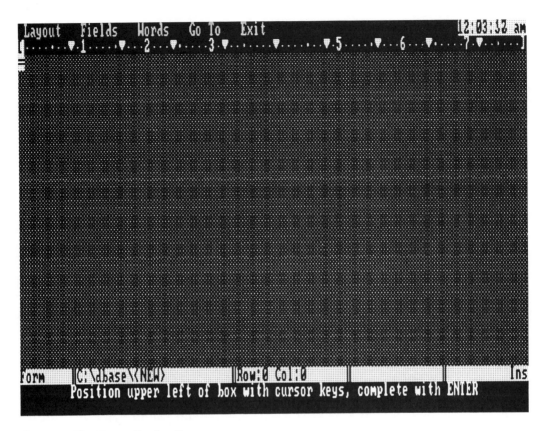

Fig. 6-1. The Forms Design Screen.

surface. The work surface uses the layout editing mode described in Chapter 3. Five design elements can be put on a form, including:

☐ Fields from an underlying database file or view
☐ New calculated fields not already in the view
☐ Text
☐ Boxes
☐ Lines

You cannot make your form wider than the screen, but you can make it longer. You must scroll up and down to see all of the form.

Forms have the same advantages as views. You can restrict the form to certain columns of the file, omitting other, perhaps sensitive or unnecessary, columns; you can use calculated fields in a form; and you can assign "picture" functions to fields on a form that will make it easier to enter or display data.

Forms Design Menus

The menu bar on the Forms Design screen contains five menus, which are:

☐ *Layout*
☐ *Forms Fields*
☐ *Words*
☐ *GO TO*
☐ *Exit*

Each of these menus is described below.

Layout. The Layout Menu displays the Quick Layout design discussed previously. It allows you to place all fields of the underlying database file or view on the form with a "field template" for each. The template shows the width and type of the data entry area for each field. After the Quick Layout design appears, you can modify or delete any of the fields that have been placed in the work surface. The Layout Menu has five options:

☐ *Box*
☐ *Line*
☐ *Use different database file or view*
☐ *Edit description of form*
☐ *Save this form*

The *Box* option on the Layout Menu lets you draw a box on the form to enclose related material. This option also allows you to make the border of the box with a single line, with a double line, or with some special character. To use a special character, type in the character you will use and press Return. For a list of special, IBM extended ASCII characters, press Shift-F1 (Pick), choose the one you want, and press Return.

To show where you want the box, place the cursor in the upper left corner of your intended box, then move the cursor toward the lower right corner. You will see the temporary box being drawn. When you reach the lower right corner, the box will be complete. Press Return and the box will become permanent. (Use the Color option in the Words Menu on the Forms Design screen to change the appearance of the box.)

The *Line* option in the Layout Menu, like the *Box* option, lets you decide where and how you want to draw lines. You have the choice of a single line, a double line, or a line made up of special characters designated by the Using Special Character option. Here again, you can call up the list of IBM extended ASCII characters by pressing Shift-F1 (Pick), select a character, and press Return.

After selecting your line type, put the cursor where you want to start the line. Press Return and move the cursor in the direction that you want the line to be. When you are finished drawing, press Return. If you make a mistake while drawing, use the Backspace key to delete.

If your printer does not contain the special character you decided to use, *dBASE IV* will instruct the printer to use the closest possible character. In the absence of other characters, this substitution will be: dashes (-) or equal (=) signs for horizontal lines, plus (+) signs for corners, and colons (:) for vertical lines.

Every form is associated with a database file or view. The *Use different database file or view* option lets you choose another source of data to use with the current form. But this is only a temporary change unless you save the form. If you don't save it, the next time you use the form, it will point to the original data. When using another file, be sure that the fields match those already on the forms design work surface. If not, you will get an error message.

The *Edit description of form* option lets you change the catalog description of the form by simply changing the existing description displayed on the screen. The *Save this form* option lets you save the current form under its current name or under a new name.

Forms Fields Menu. The Forms Fields Menu is for adding, deleting, and modifying fields on the forms design work surface. the three basic types of fields available are fields from the underlying database file or view, calculated fields, and special memory variable fields. You can apply color to forms with, for example, the border one color and the field another. Also, you can use different print styles, such as italics; these will be seen only when the forms are printed, however.

The *Add field* option increases the number of fields on a form. Do so by first putting the cursor where you want the new field to be, then selecting this option. A two-column list will appear on your screen containing the current fields on the form. The first column will contain the original columns of the underlying file or view, the second column will contain any calculated fields that have been added.

You must name the new field. After you do, a Validation submenu will appear on your screen. Use this submenu to add information about the field. The information at the top of the box (Field name, Type, Length, Decimals) comes from the database file or view definition and cannot be modified from the Forms Design screen. However, the information below these items can be modified from this screen. You can accept this information as it stands by pressing Ctrl-End, you can modify it as explained in the following section, or you can abandon this process by pressing Esc. When you finish modifying the information, place your cursor where you want the field to be and press Ctrl-End.

To add a new calculated field, choose the <create> option. If you want to modify a calculated field already in the current form, select the name of the calculated field. In either case, a Validation submenu, as shown in Fig. 6-2, will appear. You can change any attribute in the submenu for a calculated field since it is defined only for the Forms Design screen and has no predefined attributes. It is best to assign a name to the calculated field (although it is not mandatory). If you don't, it will not appear on the field list for the *Modify field* and *Remove field* options. Once in the calculated field, you can enter up to 90 characters of explanation in the *Description* option. Press Shift-F1 (Pick) for assistance if needed to complete the options.

The options on a Validation submenu are slightly different, depending on the type of field you are adding or modifying. You can specify the width of a field and the type of characters expected in each column by selecting the *Template* option. A prompt box will appear on your screen that contains the possible template characters. There are more template characters available for forms than for reports or labels. The attributes you want to assign to each field can be specified by choosing the Picture Functions Menu. The picture functions for character fields are:

Fig. 6-2. The Validation Submenu.

- ☐ Alphabetic characters only (not available for reports or labels)
- ☐ Upper-case conversion
- ☐ Literals not part of data (not available for reports or labels)
- ☐ Scroll within display width (not available for reports or labels)
- ☐ Multiple choice (not available for reports or labels)
- ☐ Trim
- ☐ Right align
- ☐ Center align
- ☐ Horizontal stretch

☐ Vertical stretch

☐ Wrap semicolons

The picture functions available for numeric fields are:

☐ Positive follow with CR
☐ Negative follow with CR
☐ Use ( ) around negative numbers
☐ Show leading zeros
☐ Blanks for zero values
☐ Financial format
☐ Exponential format
☐ Trim
☐ Left align
☐ Center align
☐ Horizontal stretch
☐ Vertical stretch

You will find more information about specific picture functions under the @SAY command in your Ashton-Tate documentation called *Language Reference*.

To limit what values can be accepted and to specify Read Only and other restrictions, choose the Edit Options Menu. The possible *Edit* options and their descriptions are:

☐ *Editing allowed* controls whether the contents of the currently selected field can be edited.

☐ *Permit edit if* controls whether a user will be allowed to enter into a field, depending on whether a criterion is met.

☐ *Message* lets you enter a message that will be displayed whenever a user places the cursor on the current field.

☐ *Carry forward* will copy data from the corresponding field field in the previous record.

☐ *Default value* allows you to set up an initial data string for the current field, which can be modify later if necessary.

☐ *Smallest allowed value* and *Largest allowed value* let you you define the allowed range for any new values. If a user enters values outside this range, an error message will appear showing the allowed values.

☐ *Accept value when* lets you state any condition(s) that must be met before new data will be accepted. The condition(s) can be any valid *dBASE IV* expression.

☐ *Unaccepted message* is the error message that will appear when a user's entry does not meet the *Accept value when* requirement.

Operations with Memo Windows and Markers. The memo fields on your form can be expanded into memo windows, which are usually smaller than the full-screen zoom displays of memo fields. These allow you to edit the data inside the memo field while it is still in the context of the form. When a memo field is set to be displayed as an open window, it is called a *static window*. Memo fields can appear initially on a form as memo markers or memo windows. Memo markers can be expanded to their memo windows and to full-screen display. Static memo windows can be expanded to full-screen display, but they can never be reduced to memo markers.

dBASE IV uses case to indicate whether a memo field marker is empty, with lowercase characters (e.g., memo) indicating empty and uppercase (e.g., MEMO) indicating not empty. Static memo windows can be deleted, copied, moved, or resized. Memo markers can be deleted, copied, or moved, but they cannot be resized since they always have the same dimensions.

You can remove a field from the work surface by choosing the name of the field from a list of all the fields currently on the work surface. But the *Remove field* option will remove all occurrences of that field, not just the one you may have picked. The template of the current field can be edited directly on the work surface by pressing Ctrl-Home, and the *Modify field* option can be used to change the options for a field in the Validation submenu. Furthermore, the *Insert memory variable* option lets you place a memory variable on the form which is useful for SQL.

Words, Go To, and Exit

The Words, Go To, and Exit Menus are the same for Forms and Reports and are described in the section entitled "Reports."

Reports

Reports make use of the information stored in your database. They can be used to fill in your customized forms, to prepare form letters, to group sales figures, to print annual information, etc. In general, with reports you can:

- ☐ Group related data
- ☐ Present fields where and as you want them
- ☐ Paginate
- ☐ Display statistical operations on data
- ☐ Insert data into text

Many report options are available in *dBASE IV*, some of which are only briefly described here. Our main purpose is to explain what facilities are available to you in designing reports by working with fields and bands.

The Reports Design Work Surface

By working in the reports design work surface (Fig. 6-3), you can include in your report fields from the current database file or view, special fields you create for the report, text you type into the report, and boxes and lines. You can work in either of two modes—word wrap or layout editing—on the reports design work surface.

The *word wrap* mode is used as you would a word processor (with text as one long character string) to create introductory explanations for the data or to create form letters. The *layout editing* mode works more like a bulletin board, where you lay out fields on the surface, then move them around, as you add fields, boxes, and lines to the report.

The reports design work surface uses *report bands* to divide the report into different parts so that you can see more of the screen at one time. Five basic bands, which appear automatically and can be used in either layout or editing mode, are:

- ☐ Page header
- ☐ Report intro

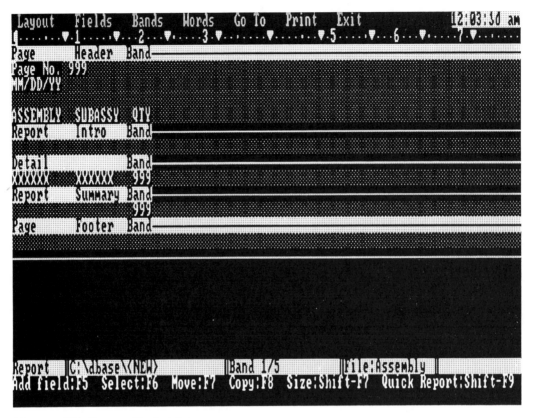

Fig. 6-3. The Reports Design Screen.

☐ Detail
☐ Report summary
☐ Page footer

Also included are "group bands" that organize records in the report by collecting them into groups. Each group band is actually two bands, a group intro band and a group summary band. You might want to start a new group every 100 records, or you might want to group records according to sections of the alphabet or every time a value, such as "city," in a specified column changes. You can also use *dBASE IV* expressions to form groups. However, group bands will only work properly if your records are indexed (or sorted) according to the grouping you want; if not and if you are sorting on "city" for example, the result could be a different group each time the city changes even though the same city may occur many times. You can sort and group records with a query, then use the view created by that query as the basis for the report.

One of the main purposes for using group bands is to apply statistics, such as an average, to different groups. Such information is shown in the group summary band. The possible summary functions are:

- ☐ Average
- ☐ Count
- ☐ Maximum
- ☐ Minimum
- ☐ Sum
- ☐ Standard deviation
- ☐ Variance

You can add group bands and nest them within already existing ones, and you can remove group bands.

When working on group bands, you may want to close some and open others; although only the open ones will print. This system allows you to use the form for different purposes, depending on which bands you leave open at a given time.

Report Menus

There are seven menus are available to you on the reports screen:

- ☐ *Layout*
- ☐ *Fields*
- ☐ *Bands*
- ☐ *Words*
- ☐ *Go To*
- ☐ *Print*
- ☐ *Exit*

The functions of these menus are described in the following sections.

Layout Menu. The Layout Menu contains a "quick layout" that gives you three types of automatic report designs: column, form, and MailMerge. You can remove any fields you don't want and move other fields into the positions you desire on this layout. MailMerge is principally to aid you in writing form letters.

Fields Menu. With the Fields Menu, you can add or remove fields on the reports design work surface. The types of fields that can be added are: fields from the underlying database or view, new calculated fields created for this report, special predefined fields, and summary fields.

Bands Menu. The Bands Menu lets you add or remove group bands from the Reports Design screen and allows you to add special characteristics to individual bands. These include text pitch, print quality, line spacing, and page headings. However, if you specify different text pitches, your screen display will not be the same as the printed report since all characters in the screen display take up the same amount of room, whereas they may not in the printed report.

Words Menu. The Words Menu is the same for forms, reports, and labels, It also appears when you write memo fields or programs and provides options for the editor. From the Words Menu and its submenus, you can:

- ☐ Select different type faces (fonts) of print, such as Times, Roman, and Helvetica. You can also select special user-specified fonts with settings in your Config.DB file. For details, see your the "Customizing *dBASE IV*" chapter in your Ashton-Tate documentation called *Language Reference*.
- ☐ Select different emphasis styles for text, such as normal, bold, underline, italic, superscript, and subscript.
- ☐ Combine different emphasis styles with different fonts in selected fields within the same report.
- ☐ Assign any one of 16 colors to the foreground of the report and any one of eight colors to its background.
- ☐ Restore deleted text.
- ☐ Move text within the current margins.
- ☐ Modify left and right margins.
- ☐ Set paragraph indentations and enable automatic indent.

☐ Add to and remove lines from the report.

☐ Set tabs.

☐ Insert page breaks.

☐ Read and write text files, which enables you to exchange text between a design surface and other files.

Go To Menu. The Go To menu (Fig. 6-4) lets you quickly access specific records in a database file. The eight options on the Go To Menu, along with their functions, are as follows:

☐ *Top Record* displays the first record in the current database

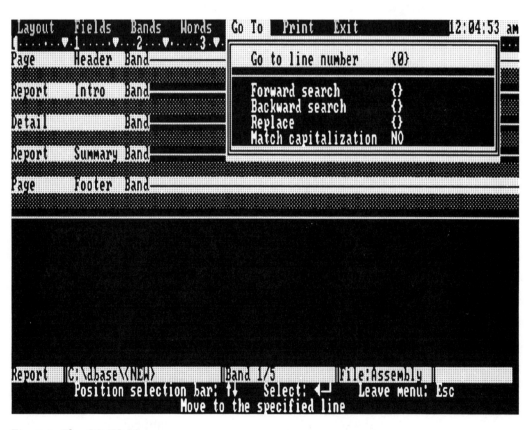

Fig. 6-4. The GO TO Menu.

file in the order determined by the current master index.

☐ *Last Record* displays the last record in the current database file in the order determined by the current master index.

☐ *Record Number* displays the record with the number you specified with the cursor appearing inside the record. You can use this option only if the current view is derived from one underlying table, not when it is from two or more tables.

☐ *Skip* lets you skip a given number of records forward or backward. The default, which is 10 records, can be changed after you choose this option. Specify a number followed by a plus sign to skip forward or a number followed by a minus sign to skip backward.

☐ *Forward Search* offers a fast way to find specific records. When you tell *dBASE IV* what field to look in and what to look for, it will find the next record matching the search condition. You can use the wild cards * and ? in stating the search condition.

☐ *Backward Search* works just like *Forward Search* except that it searches toward the beginning of the file instead of toward the end.

☐ *Match Capitalization* tells *dBASE IV* that a record must be capitalized in the same way as the search criterion. For example, if this option is set to Yes, then a search criterion of *SAME* will not accept *Same* or *same* as a valid match. If this option is set to No, then the search criterion of *SAME* will find *Same*, *same*, *SAme* and *SAMe*, as well as *SAME*.

☐ *Index Key Search* allows you to search for matches in the master index. A prompt box will display the current index expression; you then enter a search string to use on it. (A variety of searching techniques is explained in your Ashton-Tate *Language Reference Manual*.)

Print Menu. The specifics of the Print Menu are described in the final section of this chapter.

Exit Menu. The Exit Menu gives you the choice of "Save changes and exit" or "Abandon changes and exit." If you have modified a view, form, report, or label, *dBASE IV* will ask if you want to save the modifications. If not, they will be abandoned at this point. Changes saved earlier with a SAVE command, will not be undone. The only ones abandoned will be from the current session.

Printing Reports

Reports are printed through the Print Menu, shown in Fig. 6-5. Place the cursor on the name of the report in the Reports panel

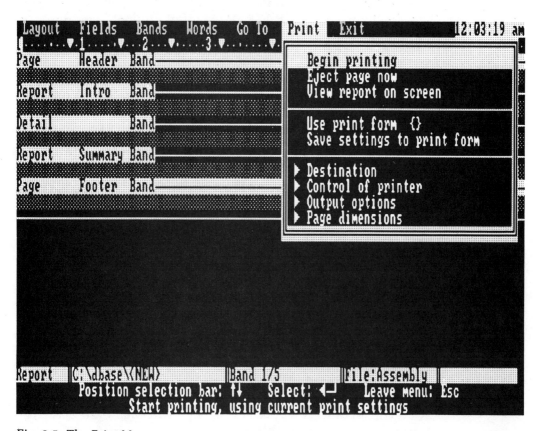

Fig. 6-5. The Print Menu.

of the Control Center. The open bands feature is used to print different versions of a report.

The Quick Report, like the Quick Layout, is always available. It will print every field in the database file or view and use the field names for column headings. It will also sum every numeric field. To print a Quick Report, press Shift-F9 (Quick Report). If you are designing a report when you press Shift-F9, the report printed will be the one you are designing instead of the usual Quick Report.

The Print Menu does not contain any styling options; instead, these appear in the Words Menu. Several items in *dBASE IV* have similar print menus with only minor differences among them. Since the differences will appear in prompts on each menu, only the general characteristics of all print menus are described.

The Print Menu, shown in Fig. 6-5, contains the following options:

☐ *Begin Printing* tells *dBASE IV* to start printing. If the settings on the menu are satisfactory, this is the only option you need. Press S to stop printing temporarily, and Esc to stop printing entirely.

☐ *Eject Page Now* makes the printer eject a page so that you can start and end pages at their perforations.

☐ *View Report on Screen/View Labels on Screen* shows the report or label on the screen as it will be printed except that reports are shown one screenful at a time with lines wrapped that are wider than the screen.

☐ *Generate Sample Label* enables you to check the alignment of labels, printer, and label design. (It is found only on the Print Menu for labels.)

☐ *Use Print Form* lets you use previously specified print settings. If you have a report form with its own control codes that you use repeatedly, save these settings to a print form and then load this print form. You can select the name of the print form from a screen list of all .PRF files.

☐ *Save Settings to Print Form* lets you create or modify a print form.

☐ *Destination* lets you indicate where you want to send the print file (i.e., to different printers, to a file, or to the screen).

☐ *Control of Printer* allows you to give instructions to the printer about the size and quality of the printing, the way new pages are to be handled, and the special codes needed to initiate the printer.

☐ *Output Options* lets you specify which pages and how many copies are to be printed.

☐ *Page Dimension* allows you to specify how and where the text is placed on the page (i.e., height, width, offset, and line spacing of the pages).

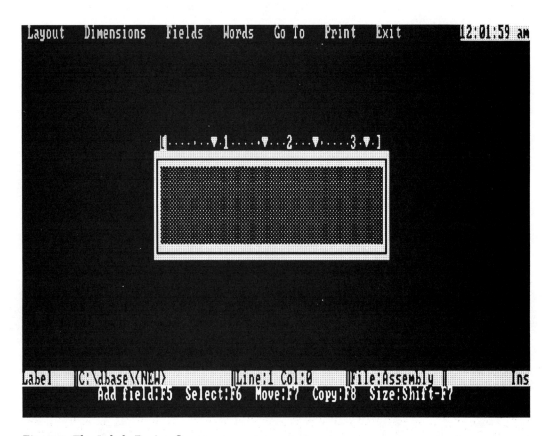

Fig. 6-6. *The Labels Design Screen.*

Labels

With *dBASE IV*, you can design many kinds of labels, such as mailing labels, name badges, stickers, shipping tags, and medical information labels. Figure 6-6 shows the Labels Design screen.

Seven menus are available from the Labels Menu bar: Layout, Dimensions, Fields, Words, Go To, Print, and Exit.

The Layout Menu helps you design new labels or modify existing ones. The Dimensions Menu lets you specify the shape, spacing, and contents of the label.

The Fields Menu allows you to place fields from the database file or view onto the work surface, as well as calculated fields created for the label, and predefined fields such as Date and Time.

The Words, Go To, and Print Menus are the same as those described previously under the section entitled "Reports." The Exit Menu options are *Save changes and exit* or *Abandon changes and exit.*

Summary

Chapter 6 explains how you go through the Control Center to create your own forms, reports and labels with *dBASE IV*. If you don't want to design your own form, report or label, you can use the Quick Layout provided by *dBASE IV* on the Edit Screen.

If you want to create a custom form, report or label, *dBASE IV* provides a design screen for each, with a wide variety of available type sizes, borders, and colors.

You can use information stored in your *dBASE IV* database in constructing your forms, reports and labels.

7

APGEN

In *dBASE IV*, an application generator (APGEN) is used to design applications. With APGEN, you can set up a sequence of menus and programs, called an application, which will make it easy to perform everyday tasks needed to keep your database files up to date or to generate reports and labels. Also, APGEN gives you a method for documenting your applications so they can be modified in the future. If you have a lot of experience using *dBASE*, you can use APGEN to generate turnkey applications for sale to the public. In addition to generating an application, APGEN can be used to test, document, and run a generated application.

A complete description of all the things you can do in APGEN is beyond the scope of this book. Here we will describe some of the possibilities to get you started and then leave you to your own devices using the documentation supplied by Ashton-Tate. The process of becoming expert with APGEN is comparable to learning a programming language and, in fact, includes, among other things, learning the *dBASE* template language, which is included in the *dBASE IV* developer's package.

Three template files—Document.MAC, Menu.MAC, and Quickapp.MAC—come with *dBASE IV*. These files make it possible to use APGEN to generate documentation, code, and quick applications. However, you cannot modify these templates unless you have the *dBASE IV* developer's package.

APGEN is designed to encourage a top-down approach to designing your applications. First, you must enter the name, description, and other attributes into the "Application Definition Dialog." Next, you must create the "application object," which can be used as an introductory screen for your application. Third, you must select the attributes, options, and main menu of the application. These steps are described in the following sections.

Once you have set up the main menu, you will know something about the menu bar at the top of the blackboard, which is really a list of menus of things you can do in APGEN. The menus, called pull-down windows, are Design, Application, Generate, Preset, and Exit. If you have been working on a menu as an object and you return to the menu bar, the Application Menu will be replaced with two menu options called *Menu* and *Item*. If you have been working on a list, the Application Menu will be replaced with two menu options called *List* and *Item*. You can select a menu by using the Left- and Right-Arrow keys to display the menu you want. Once the selected menu is displayed, you can use the Up- and Down-Arrow keys to highlight the option you want and press Return to select it.

In most cases, selecting a menu option will result in the display of another menu or list from which you can select an option, and so on. The resulting hidden structure of menus, sub-menus, sub-submenus, and so on, is called a *menu tree*. For APGEN, the menu tree is very extensive and becoming familiar with it requires practice. To help you, we have provided a section for each pull-down window menu previously listed and preset its capabilities.

The Application Definition Dialog

To create an application, you must either select <create> from the Applications panel in the Control Center or perform a CREATE APPLICATION command at the dot prompt. In either case, the Application Definition Dialog (Fig. 7-1) will be displayed on your screen.

```
                          Application Definition
     Application name:  _____
     Description:       _____
     Main menu type:    Bar
     Main menu name:    _____
     Database/view      _____
     Set INDEX to:      _____
            ORDER:      _____
```

Fig. 7-1. *The Application Definition Dialog.*

The items in The Application Definition Dialog have the following meanings and requirements:

☐ *Application name* must be filled in with a valid *dBASE* or DOS variable name. The application will be stored in a file with this name with the .APP file extension.

☐ *Description* is a brief statement about the application, which will be converted into the generated code.

☐ *Main menu type* is either Bar, Pop-up, or Batch; the default is Bar. The three types of menus can be toggled by hitting the space bar.

☐ *Main menu name* is a name that you must give the main menu before the application can be generated. You can either enter a name or use Shift-F1 to bring up a list at the right of your screen from which you can select a name.

☐ *Database/view* is the default database or view to be used at the level of the main menu. You must either type in a name or use Shift-F1 to bring up a list from which to select.

☐ *Set INDEX to* is a line on which to enter indexes to be used with your database. Shift-F1 will provide you with a list.

☐ *ORDER* is the order in which to use the index files and is used as the argument to the SET ORDER command, and must have the same syntax as arguments to the SET OR-DER command. Again, Shift-F1 will provide you with a list.

Once the Application Definition Dialog is completed, press

Ctrl-End to save it and display the APGEN menu bar or press Esc to cancel the application and return to the Control Center. If you choose to continue by pressing Ctrl-End, you will find yourself in the application object box superimposed on the blackboard with the APGEN menu bar at the top and help instructions at the bottom.

The Application Object

If you have completed the Application Definition Dialog and pressed Ctrl-End to record it, you will have arrived at the application object. The application object is a box superimposed on the blackboard that you can edit to produce an (optional) initial information box for the end user. The keystrokes to edit the application object are in Table 7-1. They can be used to edit any object in the application or on the blackboard. When you have finished editing the application object, press F10 to move the cursor to the menu bar.

Table 7-1. Editing Keystrokes.

Keystroke	*Result*
LEFTARROW	Move one position left.
RIGHTARROW	Move one position right.
Ctrl-LEFTARROW	Move to start of word.
Ctrl-RIGHTARROW	Move to end of word.
Ctrl-T	Delete current word.
Ctrl-Y	Delete line.
Ctrl-N	Insert line.
Ctrl-W	Save and return to originating menu.
Ctrl-H	Delete previous character.
Ctrl-BKSP	Delete previous character.
UPARROW	Move one position up.
DOWNARROW	Move one position down.
PGUP	Move to previous item in menu.

(Table 7-1 Continues.)

Keystroke	*Result*
PGDN	Move to next item in menu.
HOME	Move to first item.
END	Move to next item.
TAB	In edit insert tab. In dialog move to next field.
ENTER	In menu execute highlighted item. In dialog move to next field.
Ctrl-END	Save and return cursor to originating entity.
ESC	Return to originating entity.
SPACEBAR	In a toggle field, move to next toggle item. In an edit, move one space.

(Table 7-1 Ends.)

Laying Out the Main Menu

Assuming you have finished editing the application object and have pressed F10 to move the cursor to the menu bar, you will find that a design pull-down window has appeared in the upper lefthand corner of the blackboard with five choices: Design, Application, Generate, Preset, and Exit. At this point, your screen will look like Fig. 7-2.

You should select either horizontal bar menu or popup menu by using the arrow keys and pressing Return. After you press Return, a box will appear on the right side of your screen with <create> on the top line. After selecting this option by pressing Return, a wide box will appear on your screen with six lines in it and three titles:

Name:
Description:
Message line prompt:

These are for the name of your menu (which must also be a valid file name), a description of your menu, and a prompt that you want on the bottom line of your screen when the menu occurs in your application. After filling out the items in this box, press

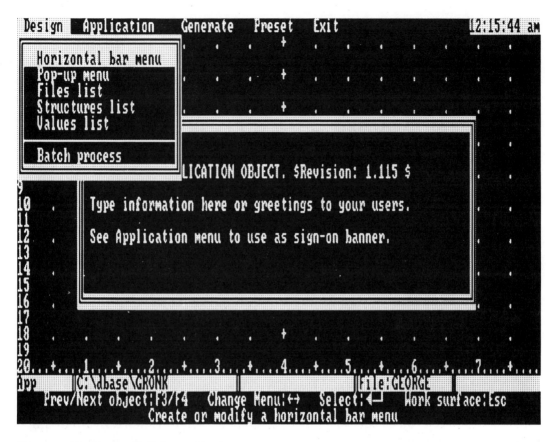

Fig. 7-2. The Design Pull-down Window.

Ctrl-End, which creates the menu and positions the cursor inside the menu on the blackboard.

At this point, you can start putting in the options for the bar or popup menu. For each option, you must press F5 to start typing and F5 again when you are finished with the option. If you want to move or copy the bar menu, use the F7 and F8 function keys, respectively, and then the arrow keys. To change the size of the bar or popup menu, use the Shift-F7 key and then the arrow keys to resize the menu. At this point and in the further design of your application, you should read the help instructions at the bottom of your screen to see what choices you have.

Selecting Additional Attributes and Options

When designing your menu, you can choose to press the F10 key to return to the menu line. At the top of your screen you will see six words: Design, Menu, Item, Generate, Preset, and Exit. (Notice that this is different from the way the screen appeared before you selected horizontal bar or popup menu from the Design screen because Menu has been interpolated between Design and Item, and Item has replaced Application. If you had selected one of the list items, such as Files list, from the Design Menu, there would still be six words, but List instead of Menu would have been interpolated between Design and Item.) For each of these, APGEN provides a menu (a design pull-down window) of things you can do. You can move from one of these menus to another by means of the Right- and Left-Arrow keys.

To modify your display options, choose the Right-Arrow key to display the menu pull-down window. Then, by using the Down-Arrow key, move the highlight to the modify display options line and press Return. The result will be a menu from which you can select frame style, standard colors, and enhanced colors. When choosing one of these, you will obtain a list of colors from which you can select the foreground and background colors. By following the help at the bottom of the screen, you will be able to navigate your way back to the menu pull-down window.

The Design Menu

The Design Menu has the following six options:

- ☐ *Horizontal bar* is a horizontal list of options usually across the top of the screen.
- ☐ *Popup menu* is a list of options in a box that can be associated with a bar menu.
- ☐ *Files list* contains a list of files to be selected, usually all with the same file extension.

□ *Structure list* contains a list of fields in the current database file or view.

□ *Values list* contains values for a specific column of the current database file or view.

□ *Batch process* is a list of actions on the Actions Menu that are to be performed sequentially. A batch process will not be visible to the end user.

If you select any option on the Design Menu, a list of all entities of that kind in the current catalog is displayed with a <create> option at the top. If you select <create>, a blank form appears with the name, description, and message line prompt for you to complete. (In the case of batch processes, no message line prompt appears.) When the form has been filled out, the blackboard appears with the menu, list, or batch process as the current object.

If you don't select <create>, but select one of the items on the list instead, that item appears on the blackboard to be modified as the current object. You can either modify the current object or press F10 to return to the menu bar at the top of the screen. If you decide to return to the menu bar, you will find the second word there to be Menu, List, or Batch, depending on which option you selected from the Design Menu.

The Application Menu

The Application Menu has eight options relevant to the application as a whole. They are treated in the following sections.

Name and Describe

If you select the *Name and describe* option, the current name and description of your application will be displayed. If you change the name, a new application will be created. You may edit the description as you wish, but the name must be a valid file name.

Assign Main Menu

If you select the *Assign main menu* option, a two-line form will appear on the screen. The first line is "Main menu type:," and you can toggle bar, pop, and batch to select the type. The second line is "Main menu name:." You can type in the name or use Shift-F1 to have a list of menus of the given type displayed on the screen from which you can select the main menu name.

Display Sign-On Banner

Selecting the *Display sign-on banner* option means that you want to use the current object as the sign-on banner at run time. A box will appear on the screen requesting confirmation. If you select No, the runtime application will begin with the main menu.

Edit Program Header Comments

The information entered using the *Edit program header comments* option will appear as the beginning comment in the generated code for the option. All you can enter is the application author, the copyright notice for the application, and the *dBASE* version for the application.

Modify Application Environment

If you select the *Modify application environment* option, the Runtime Environment Menu will be displayed. It has four options that are treated in the following subsections.

Display Options. If you select the *Display options* option, the Display Options submenu (Fig. 7-3) will be displayed on your screen. You can toggle the Frame style line in the Display Options submenu. The toggle values are Double, Single, and Panel, with the default being Double. The selected value will be the border for all menus and lists in your application. Selecting any other line will cause the color palette to be displayed. The selections include:

```
┌─────────────────────────┐
│ Frame style:            │
├─────────────────────────┤
│ Standard colors         │
│    Text                 │
│    Headings             │
│ Enhanced colors         │
│    Boxes                │
│    Status line          │
│    Input fields         │
└─────────────────────────┘
```

Fig. 7-3. The Display Options submenu.

☐ *Standard colors* sets one color for all text and headings.

☐ *Text* selects the color for all text.

☐ *Headings* selects the color for all headings.

☐ *Enhanced colors* sets one color for boxes, the status line, and fields.

☐ *Boxes* sets the color for box frames.

☐ *Status line* sets one color for the clock and error box borders.

☐ *Input fields* sets the color for fields in Browse, for options in menus and lists, and for fields that can be edited.

Environment Settings. The *Environment settings* option displays the Environment Setup Dialog on your screen. The Environment Setup Dialog lets you set BELL, CARRY, CENTURY, CONFIRM, ESCAPE, SAFETY, and DELIMITERS.

Search Path. The *Search path* option allows you to set the disk drive and search path for storing output at run time.

View/Database and Index. The *View/database and index* option displays the Database or View Dialog on your screen. The Database or View Dialog lets you select the database file, indexes, and index order for the level with which you are currently working.

Generate Quick Application

The *Generate quick application* option lets you create and generate a single menu (popup) application. When you select it, the Quick Application Setup Dialog is displayed on your screen, which has eight fields:

☐ Database file
☐ Screen format file
☐ Report format file
☐ Label format file
☐ Set INDEX to
☐ ORDER
☐ Application author
☐ Application menu heading

The first five can be chosen from lists by pressing Shift-F1. The ORDER field must be filled out with the same syntax as the SET ORDER TO command. You may, if you wish, leave the last two fields blank. The default for the application author is what has been entered on the sign-on defaults under the Preset Menu. The default for the Application Menu heading is the application name.

When you are through filling out the Quick Application Setup Dialog, press Ctrl-End, which will display a confirmation box that says:

Select YES to generate the quick application; select NO to cancel

If you select YES, the quick application will be generated, based on the information in the Quick Application Setup Dialog. If you select NO, the quick application will be canceled and you will return to the Application Menu.

Save Current Application Definition

The *Save current application* option saves the current application to disk, and you can continue editing.

Clear Work Surface

By selecting the *Clear work surface* option, you will be able to save the current object to disk or return the current object to the state it was in when it was saved the last time. A prompt will appear on the screen allowing you to make this choice.

The Menu Menu

The Menu pull-down menu allows you to modify or define various attributes of either a horizontal bar menu or a popup menu. The same options are available for both types, except that there is one additional option for a horizontal bar menu. The additional option lets you attach pull-down menus to horizontal bar options. The options are discussed in the following sections.

Name and Describe

The *Name and describe* option displays a Name, Description, and Prompt Dialog on your screen with the current name, description, and prompt filled in. You can change the name if you want to create a new object with the same attributes as the current one. You can also modify description and prompt.

Override Assigned Database or View

The *Override assigned database or view* option displays the Database or View Dialog on your screen. However, when this option is chosen here, the Database or View Dialog will show the current values and allow you to enter other values on the lower half of the dialog. The values can either be left as they are or modified for use at the current level.

Write Help Text

The *Write help text* option displays a full-screen editing window. You can use this window to write 16 lines of HELP text. Then you can press either Ctrl-End to save the text or Esc to abandon the text and return to the menu bar.

Modify Display Options

Selecting the *Modify display options* option will cause the

Display Options submenu to be displayed on your screen.

Embed Code

The *Embed code* option allows you to enter before and after codes to be embedded. You are given a choice of before or after and then a full-screen editing window is displayed on your screen. You can use this window to enter 16 lines of *dBASE* code. After that, you can press Ctrl-End to save, or Esc to abandon.

Attach Pull-Down Menus

The *Attach pull-down menus* option is available only if the object is a horizontal bar menu. Choosing this option will cause a confirmation box to appear on your screen. The confirmation box will ask you if you want associated menus pulled down automatically. If you choose YES, the result for your application will be like the current situation in APGEN where you move across the bar menu at the top, and the pull-down menus occur with their various options. If you choose NO, the end user will have to select the item on the bar menu by pressing Return in order for the associated menus or lists to appear on the screen.

Save and Put Away Current Menu

Choosing the *Save current menu* option saves the current menu to disk. After it is saved, it will still remain on the blackboard so that you can continue to edit it.

You can use the *Putaway current menu* option to close and remove the current menu from the blackboard. You will be given the choice of saving any changes you may have made or abandoning them.

Clear Work Surface

The *Clear work surface* option enables you to save the current object to disk or return the current object to the state it was in when it was saved the last time. A prompt will appear on the screen, allowing you to make this choice.

The List Menu

The List pull-down menu is almost identical to the Menu pull-down menu. The difference is that the *Attach pull-down menus* option is replaced by an *identify* option. The *Identify* option will be *Identify files in list* if the current object is a list of files. If the current object is a list of fields, the *Identify* option will be Identify fields in list; and if the current object is a Values list, the *Identify* option will be Identify values in list.

The *Identify* option will display a one-line identification dialog on your screen, preceded by "File specifications:," "Fields:," or "Field to list values for:." If it is "File specifications:," you can use the asterisk wild card and separate entries by commas. If it is "Fields:," you can enter the fields separated by commas or press Shift-F1 to obtain a list of choices. If it is "Field to list values for:," you can either type in a field name or press Shift-F1 to obtain a list of choices.

The Batch Menu

The Batch Menu has six options:

☐ *Name and describe*
☐ *Override assigned database or view*
☐ *Embed code*
☐ *Save current batch process*
☐ *Put away current batch process*
☐ *Clear work surface*

These choices also occur on the Menu and List pull-down Menus, and are described in those sections.

The Item Menu

The Item Menu is used to make changes to the various aspects of a menu, list, or batch object. The 10 options on the Item Menu are described in the following subsections.

Show Item Information

The *Show item information* option (Fig. 7-4) displays the Item Information dialog on your screen. All of the entries in the Item Information Dialog are display only; you cannot change anything. The OK in the lower left corner will be highlighted, and you can return to the Item Menu by pressing Return.

The "This item will:" field alone requires a comment; namely, this field contains the action defined for this item by means of the *Change action* option.

```
 Object:  _____
 Item:          _____

 Current database/view: _____  using index _____
 This Item will: _____

 OK
```

Fig. 7-4. *The Item Information Dialog.*

Change Action

The *Change action* option displays the Item Actions Menu on your screen, as shown in Fig. 7-5. In the Item Actions Menu, you can use the *Text (no action)* option to define a menu that contains information displayed but not selectable. You can also select the *Open a menu* option to open a menu when the end user selects the current item. Choosing this option causes the self-explanatory Open a Menu Dialog to be displayed on your screen.

```
 Text (no action)
 Open a menu                       ACTIVATE MENU
 Browse (add, delete, edit)              BROWSE
 Edit form (add, delete, edit)             EDIT
 Display or print
 Perform file operation
 Run program
 Quit
```

Fig. 7-5. *The Item Actions Menu.*

If you select the *Browse* option, the Browse a Database or View Dialog will be displayed on your screen (Fig. 7-6). The end user will be in BROWSE. You must set up the conditions for a BROWSE session using the *Browse a Database or View* Dialog.

```
                      Browse a Database or View

     FIELDS:  _____
     FILTER:  _____

     Fields to LOCK onscreen:    0   FREEZE edit for field:  _____
     Maximum column WIDTH:       0   FORMAT file:            _____

     Allow record ADD?          YES  Allow record EDIT?          YES
     Allow record DELETE?       YES  KEEP image on exit?         NO
     Display Browse MENU?       YES  Use PREVIOUS Browse table?  NO
     FOLLOW record after update? YES COMPRESS display?           NO
```

Fig. 7-6. *The Browse a Database or View Dialog.*

The FIELDS entry must use the same syntax as the FIELDS option of the BROWSE command. The FILTER entry must use the same syntax as the SET FILTER TO command. The number of fields to LOCK during the BROWSE session will be used as the argument to the LOCK option of the BROWSE command. The FREEZE and WIDTH entries will be used as the argument for the FREEZE and WIDTH options of the BROWSE command.

The FORMAT file entry is the name of a .FMT file to be used as the argument to the SET FORMAT command. The Allow record ADD, EDIT, DELETE, KEEP image on exit, Use PREVIOUS Browse Table, Display Browse MENU, and FOLLOW record after update entries if answered NO will cause BROWSE to be entered with the NOAPPEND, NOEDIT, NODELETE, NOCLEAR, NOINIT, NOMENU, and NOFOLLOW choices, respectively. If the COMPRESS display entry is answered by YES, BROWSE will be entered with a *Compress* option.

The *Edit form* option will enable the end user to edit the current database file. When you select this option the Append/Edit Via Form File Dialog will appear on your screen (Fig. 7-7). The Append/Edit Via Form File Dialog is to be filled out in much the same way that the Browse a Database or View Dialog was filled out, keeping in mind the EDIT command. The Mode entry is a toggle for which the possible values are Append and Edit.

```
┌─────────────────────────────────────────────────────────────────┐
│                  Append/Edit Via Form File                        │
│   FORMAT file: _____      Mode: Append                 │
│                                                                   │
│   FIELDS:     _____        │
│   FILTER:     _____        │
│   SCOPE:      _____                                    │
│   FOR:        _____        │
│   WHILE:      _____        │
│                                                                   │
│   Allow record ADD?            YES    Allow record EDIT?      YES  │
│   Allow record DELETE?         YES    KEEP image on exit?     NO   │
│   Display Edit MENU?           YES    Use PREVIOUS Browse Table? NO│
│   FOLLOW record after update?  YES                                 │
└─────────────────────────────────────────────────────────────────┘
```

Fig. 7-7. The Append/Edit Via Form File Dialog.

If you select the *Display or print* option from the Item Actions Menu, you can set up an action whereby the end user will be able to print or display information. The Print or Display Menu will appear on your screen (Fig. 7-8).

```
┌─────────────────────────────────────────┐
│   Report              REPORT FORM         │
│   Labels              LABEL FORM          │
│   Display/list        DISPLAY/LIST        │
└─────────────────────────────────────────┘
```

Fig. 7-8. The Print or Display Menu.

If you select the *Report* option from the Print or Display Menu, the Print a Report Dialog will be displayed on your screen (Fig. 7-9). The Print a Report Dialog will set up a report to be printed by the end user.

```
┌─────────────────────────────────────────────────────────────────┐
│                      Print a Report                               │
│   FORM name:_____                                      │
│   HEADING:  _____          │
│                                                                   │
│   Report format:      Full detail                                 │
│   Heading format:     Plain                                       │
│   Before printing:    Skip to new page                            │
│   Send output to:     Printer                                     │
│                                                                   │
│   FILTER:     _____        │
│   SCOPE:      _____                                    │
│   FOR:        _____        │
│   WHILE:      _____        │
└─────────────────────────────────────────────────────────────────┘
```

Fig. 7-9. The Print a Report Dialog.

The FORM name on the Print a Report Dialog is the report form you want used. Press Shift-F1 for a list of report forms. The HEADING is a heading that will appear on each page of the report. Report format, Heading format, Before printing, and Send output to are toggles. FILTER will be used as the argument to the SET FILTER COMMAND. SCOPE, FOR, and WHILE are used as the <*scope*>, FOR option, and WHILE option arguments to the REPORT FORM command, and must have the same syntax.

If you select the *Labels* option from the Print or Display Menu, the Print Labels Dialog will be displayed on your screen. (Fig. 7-10).

```
                          Print Labels

     FORM name:   _____

     Send output to:    Printer

     Print SAMPLE?      YES

     FILTER:   _____
     SCOPE:    _____
     FOR:      _____
     WHILE:    _____
```

Fig. 7-10. The Print Labels Dialog.

The Print Labels Dialog is used in much the same way as the Print a Report Dialog, with the following exception: You must use the LABEL FORM command. If you choose the YES option for Print SAMPLE?, the *Sample* option will be used with the LABEL FORM command.

The *Display/list* option from the Print or Display Menu will enable the end user to DISPLAY or LIST records from a database file or view. The Display/List Database Records Dialog will appear on your screen (Fig. 7-11). The Display/List Database Records Dialog should be filled out similarly to the Print Labels Dialog, keeping in mind the *dBASE* DISPLAY and LIST commands.

The *Perform file operation* option from the Item Actions Menu will display the File Operations Menu on your screen. This menu will allow you to define an action that will allow the end user to perform a file action such as UPDATE, SORT, REINDEX, CREATE INDEX, IMPORT, or EXPORT.

```
┌─────────────────────────────────────────────────────────────┐
│               Display/List Database Records                   │
│  PAUSE at full page/screen? YES                               │
│  Send output to:           Printer                            │
│                                                               │
│  Include RECORD NUMBERS?    YES                               │
│                                                               │
│                                                               │
│  FIELDS: _____     │
│  FILTER: _____     │
│  SCOPE:  _____                               │
│  FOR:    _____     │
│  WHILE:  _____     │
│                                                               │
└─────────────────────────────────────────────────────────────┘
```

Fig. 7-11. *The Display/List Database Records Dialog.*

The *Run program* option from the Item Actions Menu, will allow you to select a program that will be run by the end user. The *Quit* option from the Item Actions Menu will enable you to set up your exit for the end user.

Override Assigned Database or View

The *Override assigned database or view* option for the Item Menu is the same as for the Application Menu and the Menu Menu and is described in those sections.

Embed Code

The *Embed code* option is described in the section entitled Menu Menu.

Bypass Item on Condition

The *Bypass item on condition* option will display the Bypass Item on Condition Dialog on your screen. Your entry in the By-

```
┌─────────────────────────────────────────────────────────────┐
│                                                               │
│  Skip this item if:                                           │
│  _____            │
│                                                               │
└─────────────────────────────────────────────────────────────┘
```

Fig. 7-12. *The Bypass Item on Condition Dialog.*

pass Item on Condition Dialog should be a condition for the SKIP FOR clause in the *dBASE* DEFINE BAR command.

Position Record Pointer

The *Position record pointer* option will display the Set Position in File Dialog on your screen. See Fig. 7-13. If you choose Display POSITIONING MENU at RUNTIME by toggling this field to YES, a menu of positioning choices will be displayed at run time. If you choose SEEK first occurrence of key, you must enter an argument for the SEEK command. If you choose GOTO, you must enter either TOP or BOTTOM or a record number.

The remaining three choices call for a <scope> argument, a FOR condition, or a WHILE condition for the LOCATE command.

```
Choose ONE of the following positioning methods:

Display POSITIONING MENU at RUN TIME? NO
SEEK first occurrence of key:_____
GOTO: _____
LOCATE SCOPE:   _____
       FOR:     _____
       WHILE:   _____
```

Fig. 7-13. The Set Position in File Dialog.

Reassign Index Order

Use the *Reassign index order* option to specify the index or tag for the action being defined. If you select this option, the Reassign Index Order Dialog will appear on your screen (Fig. 7-14). You must enter a correct argument for the SET ORDER TO command on the Reassign Index Order Dialog.

```
Set ORDER to:  _____
```

Fig. 7-14. The Reassign Index Order Dialog.

131

Define Logical Window

To use the *Define logical window* option, enter the appropriate DEFINE WINDOW options for the action being defined. If you select this option, the Define Logical Window Dialog will be displayed on your screen (Fig. 7-15). The entry in window NAME field on the Define Logical Window Dialog must be usable as the *<window name>* argument in the DEFINE WINDOW command. *Display border as-is* a toggle field. The entries you make in the *Border characters* field will be used as the argument to the SET BORDER TO command. The entry you make in the *Color* field will be used as the argument to the *Color* option of the DEFINE WINDOW command. The upper-left and lower-right corner fields will determine where the window will appear on the screen.

```
Window NAME: _____

Display border as: Single
Border characters (For CUSTOM borders):_____
Colors: _____

UPPER LEFT  corner at row   2, column   0
LOWER RIGHT corner at row  20, column  79
```

Fig. 7-15. The Define Logical Window Dialog.

Write Help Text

When you select the *Write help text* option, a full-screen editing window will appear for you to enter up to 16 lines of help text. When you are finished, press Ctrl-End to save your help text or Esc to abandon it.

Assign Message Line Prompt

The *Assign message line prompt* option will display the Assign Message Line Prompt Dialog on your screen. (Fig. 7-16). If you don't like the prompt displayed under the first line of the Assign Message Line Prompt Dialog, you can enter a different

```
This message line prompt is currently assigned to the <objecttype>:

It will be used for this item unless you enter a different prompt below:
```

Fig. 7-16. The Assign Message Line Prompt Dialog.

prompt under the second line of the dialog, then press Ctrl-End to save it.

The Generate Menu

The Generate Menu has three options, *Begin generating*, *Select template*, and *Display during generation*.

Begin Generating

If you select the *Begin generating* option, you must have already selected the template. The template will determine whether application design documentation or *dBASE* code will be generated. To generate documentation, you must have selected the document.mac template. To generate *dBASE* code, you must have selected the Menu.MAC template. Finally, to generate a quick application, you must have selected the Quickapp.MAC template.

If you select the *Begin generating* option, and the main menu has not been assigned, the Main Menu Dialog will be displayed on your screen (Fig. 7-17). The main menu type is a toggle of bar, pop, and batch. You can either enter the main menu name or press Shift-F1 to have a list of menus of the type you chose displayed so you can select one. You must press Ctrl-End to begin generation.

```
The following information must be
provided before generating can proceed:

Main menu type: Bar
Main menu name:
```

Fig. 7-17. The Main Menu Dialog.

Select Template

The *Select Template* option will be displayed on your screen (Fig. 7-18). On the Template Dialog, you can either type in the name of the template or press Shift-F1 to have a list of available templates displayed on your screen.

Three templates—Document.MAC, Menu.MAC, and Quickapp.MAC—come with *dBASE IV*. When this book was being written, the names of these template files had not been determined. Therefore, check your *dBASE IV* documentation to be sure of the template file names.

Fig. 7-18. The Template Dialog.

```
┌──────────────────────────────────────┐
│  Template: _____     │
└──────────────────────────────────────┘
```

Display During Generation

The *Display during generation* option will display a confirmation box on your screen. You can then choose to display the code or the documentation that is generated.

The Preset Menu

The Preset Menu is used to set defaults and system information. It has four options: *Sign-on defaults, Display options, Environment settings,* and *Application drive/path.*

Sign-on Defaults

The *Sign-on defaults* option will display the Sign-on Defaults Dialog on your screen (Fig. 7-19). After you finish filling out the Sign-on Defaults Dialog, press Ctrl-End to save the information and return to the Preset Menu.

```
┌─────────────────────────────────────────────────────────┐
│  Application author: _____ │
│  Copyright notice:   _____ │
│  dBASE version:      _____ │
└─────────────────────────────────────────────────────────┘
```

Fig. 7-19. The Sign-on Defaults Dialog.

Display Options

The *Display options* option will display the Display Options submenu on your screen. See the section entitled Application Menu for an explanation.

Environment Settings

The *Environment settings* option will display the Environment Setup Dialog on your screen. See the section entitled Application Menu for an explanation.

Application Drive/Path

The *Application drive/path* option will display the Drive and Search Path Dialog on your screen (Fig. 7-20). On the Drive and Search Path Dialog, fill in the drive or press Shift-F1 for a list of drives from which you can select. Fill in the search path with the default search path at runtime.

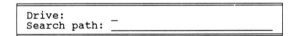

Fig. 7-20. The Drive and Search Path Dialog.

The Exit Menu

The Exit Menu allows two options: *Save all changes and exit* and *Abandon all changes and exit*. Choose one of these to exit.

Alphabetic List of APGEN Menu Nodes

Table 7-2 is a table of entities you might want to find in the menu tree and how to find them.

Table 7-2. Nodes in the APGEN Menu Tree.

Object	*How to Get There*
APPEND/EDIT via Form file dialog	Select EDIT form from the Item Actions Menu.
Assign Main Menu	Application Menu.
Assign Message Line Prmpt dialog	Select Assign Message Line Prompt from the Item Menu.
Batch process	Design Menu.
Batch menu	Select Batch process from Design Menu and return from object by pressing F10.
Bypass Item on Condition dialog	Select the Bypass Item on Condition option from the Item Menu.
Browse a Database or View dialog	Select Browse from the Item Actions Menu.
Clear work surface	Application Menu, Menu Menu.
Color palette	From the Display options submenu by selecting any nontoggle option.
Database or View dialog	Select View/database and Index from Runtime Environment Menu or select Override Assigned Database or View option from the menu pull-down.
Define Logical Window dialog	Select Define Logical Window from the Item Menu.
Display/List Database Records dialog	Select Display/List from the Print or Display Menu.
Display options submenu	Select Display options from Runtime Environment Menu, select Modify Display options from the menu pull-

(Table 7-2 Continues.)

Object	How to Get There
	down, or select Display options from the Preset Menu.
Drive and Search Path dialog	Select Application Drive/Path option from the Preset Menu.
Display sign-on banner	Application Menu.
Edit program header comments	Application Menu.
Environment setup dialog	Select Environment settings from Runtime Environment Menu or select Environment settings from the Preset Menu.
Files list	Design Menu.
File Operations Menu	Select Perform file operation from the Item Actions Menu.
Generate quick application	Application Menu.
Horizontal bar menu	Design Menu.
Item Actions Menu	Select Change action from the Item Menu.
Item information dialog	Select Show Item information from the Item Menu.
List menu	Select list from Design Menu and return from object by pressing F10.
Main Menu dialog	Select Begin generating from the Generate Menu. Main Menu Dialog will only be displayed if the Main Menu has not been assigned.
Menu Menu	Select bar menu or popup menu from Design Menu and return from object by pressing F10.
Modify application environment	Application Menu.
Name and describe (application)	Application Menu.
Name and describe (batch process)	Select batch process from Design Menu. Then select <create>.
Name and describe (list)	Select list from Design Menu. Then select <create>.

(Table 7-2 Continues.)

Object	How to Get There
Name and describe (menu)	Select menu from Design Menu. Then select <create>.
Open a menu dialog	Select Open a menu from the Item Actions Menu.
Popup menu	Design Menu.
Print or display menu	Select Display or Print from the Item Actions Menu.
Print Labels dialog	Select Labels from the Print or Display Menu.
Print a Report dialog	Select Report from the Print or Display Menu.
Quick Application Setup dialog	Select the Generate quick application option from the Application Menu.
Reassign Index Order dialog	Select the Reassign index order option from the Item Menu.
Runtime environment menu	Select the Modify application environment option from the Application Menu.
Save current application definition	Application Menu.
Set Position in File dialog	Select Position Record Pointer from the Item Menu.
Structure list	Design Menu.
The Template Dialog	Select the Select Template option from the Generate Menu.
Values list	Design Menu.

(Table 7-2 Ends.)

Summary

In this chapter the new application generator is discussed. It can be reached from the Application panel of the control center. It is designed to make it easy to generate application programs for use with *dBASE IV*. The complete menu tree for the application generator is discussed in detail; and Fig. 7-2 lists the menus and how to get to them.

8

The dBASE IV Procedural Interface

The *dBASE IV* Procedural Interface is very much like the Procedural interface in *dBASE III PLUS*. It is the interface that allows you to run program files that you have written yourself, using *dBASE* commands. It can be contrasted with the *dBASE IV* Non-Procedural Interface where, for example, you execute one command at a time, at the dot prompt, or select choices from a menu in the Control Center. The term *procedural* implies execution of a program or procedure.

If you have a set of operations on your database that you perform repeatedly, you will find it useful to write a program that encompasses those operations so that you will not have to type them in repeatedly. At the dot prompt you can just type:

DO < *program filename* >

where < *program filename* > is the name of the file containing your *dBASE* program. The file name must be a legal DOS file name with a .PRG file extension. In this chapter, we give some examples of programs that you might want to modify for your own use.

One way in which the procedural interface in *dBASE IV*

differs from that in *dBASE III PLUS* is that SQL commands can now be embedded in programs to make it even easier to program in *dBASE*. (Embedded SQL is the subject of Chapter 13.) Another way in which the procedural interface differs from *dBASE III PLUS* is that *dBASE IV* has a complete set of commands and functions for transaction processing. Transaction processing is useful for making certain that your database is kept in a consistent state.

In this chapter, we confine ourselves to examples using *dBASE* commands only. The same examples are given in Chapter 13 using embedded SQL so that you can compare the two methods of programming.

Transaction Processing

The term *Transaction* refers to a set of modifications to the database, all of which have to be completed in order for the database to be kept in a consistent state. For example, if you are posting sales from a file that has a logical column, "posted," which is either true (.T.) or false (.F.) to indicate whether or not the sale has been posted, and you enter a sale in the Sales Table, the database is temporarily inconsistent because the posted column still has a false entry indicating the sale has not been posted. Thus, a transaction would include both entering the sale in the Sales Table and changing the entry in the posted column to .T.

To provide for this situation, *dBASE* has a set of commands and functions. The commands are BEGIN TRANSACTION, END TRANSACTION, and ROLLBACK. Use the BEGIN TRANSACTION command just before the beginning of a transaction, and when the transaction is completed, use the END TRANSACTION command. If something goes wrong during the transaction, use the ROLLBACK command to set everything back where it was before the transaction was begun.

The format for BEGIN TRANSACTION is:

```
BEGIN TRANSACTION [<path>]
```

where <path> is optional and is the path to a directory where a transaction log file will be kept, which file contains all of the changes to database files that must be rolled back in the event of a ROLLBACK.

Transactions cannot be nested. It would not make sense to have a BEGIN TRANSACTION start before a previous transaction has ended.

BEGIN TRANSACTION can result in error messages when the transaction log file cannot be created. If a transaction log file already exists, for example, the error message ''Unterminated transaction file exists, cannot start new transaction'' will occur. If the directory path in < *path* > does not exist, the error message will be ''Path does not exist.'' If the transaction log file cannot be created for some other reason, the error message ''Cannot create transaction register file'' will occur. If you attempt to nest transactions, the error message ''Cannot nest transactions'' will be displayed.

All commands that cause changes to database files or the environment, but not to memory variables, will be recorded in the transaction register file. These commands are:

APPEND	COPY
BROWSE	CREATE
CHANGE	EXPORT
DELETE	IMPORT
EDIT	INDEX
RECALL	JOIN
REPLACE	SET CATALOG TO
UPDATE	SORT
TOTAL	

Once the BEGIN TRANSACTION command has been issued, the above commands will cause changes to database files. The environment to be recorded in the transaction register file and the database files affected will be marked to show that they are in an inconsistent state. Commands causing the overwriting of existing files during transactions are not allowed and would result in an error message. As a result, the following commands are never allowed while a transaction is in progress:

CLEAR ALL

CLOSE ALL/DATABASE/INDEX
DELETE FILE
ERASE
MODIFY STRUCTURE
INSERT
PACK
RENAME
ZAP

The following commands are not allowed during a transaction if they would cause a file to be closed:

CREATE
INDEX ON
SET CATALOG TO
SET INDEX TO
USE

The END TRANSACTION command will cause the transaction register file to be deleted, all locks to be released, and all marked files to be unmarked.

The ROLLBACK command has the following format:

ROLLBACK [<*database filename*>]

where <*database filename*> is the name of any database file involved in the current transaction. If this optional parameter occurs, an attempt will be made to restore this file to its state prior to the beginning of the transaction. Otherwise, an attempt will be made to restore all files involved in the transaction to their state prior to the transaction.

A failure of the ROLLBACK command will leave the database in an inconsistent state and the user will have to try to restore it manually. Therefore it is a good idea to limit the size of transactions as much as possible so that restoration will not be a big task.

A rollback does not terminate a transaction. That can only be done by an END TRANSACTION or CANCEL command. If a CANCEL command is issued during a transaction, the transaction will automatically be rolled back and terminated. If a SUSPEND command is issued during a transaction, the transaction will remain active. And if a ROLLBACK is issued in the SUSPEND mode, the user will not be allowed to RESUME. A RESUME will be the same as issuing a CANCEL. Thus, RESUME is the same as issuing a ROLLBACK and an END TRANSACTION.

If a file that is marked as being inconsistent is put in use by the USE command, a warning will be displayed to that effect, and the user will not be allowed to make any changes to that file without a successful ROLLBACK. If a successful ROLLBACK cannot be performed, a RESET IN < *alias* > command may be performed to remove the inconsistency tag on the file. That may result in an inconsistent database, however.

The functions for use with transaction processing are ROLLBACK( ) and COMPLETED( ). By default, the ROLLBACK( ) function returns a logical .T. After a ROLLBACK command is issued and before the ROLLBACK is successfully completed, the ROLLBACK( ) function returns .F. After the ROLLBACK is successfully completed, ROLLBACK( ) returns .T. again. Similarly, the COMPLETED( ) function ordinarily returns .T. When a transaction is begun and until the end of a transaction, COMPLETED( ) will return false (.F.). After the end of the transaction, COMPLETED( ) will return true (.T.) again.

Program Examples

Posting Sales

Suppose you have created the following files shown in Fig. 8-1. (To CREATE files see Chapter 4.)

Now suppose that with these files, you want to post the transactions that you have in the Trnsacts file. You will need to move the rows of the file, one row at a time, into memory variables, look up the salesperson's ID and the price, and enter the result in the Sales file. Then, you will reduce inventory accordingly; and finally, you will want to update the Trnsacts file to show that the row has been posted. If an error occurs while processing a row, before the Trnsacts file has been updated, you will want to ROLLBACK the changes that have been made until such a time

```
Trnsacts
(type       CHAR(10),      * "SOLD", "RETURNED", "LOST", etc.
item        CHAR(15),      * "DESK", "CHAIR", "TELEVISION", etc.
model       CHAR(16),      * like "ZENITH1108YY3".
invoice     CHAR(8),       * invoice identifier.
no_units    SMALLINT,      * how many were sold, or returned, etc.
s_first     CHAR(15),      * salesperson's first name.
s_iast      CHAR(15),      * salesperson's last name.
posted      LOGICAL);      * .T. if it's been posted, .F. otherwise.

Salesper
(s_id       CHAR(4),       * salesperson's id number as CHAR.
s_first     CHAR(15),      * salesperson's first name.
s_last      CHAR(15),      * salesperson's last name.
address     CHAR(15),      * salesperson's street address.
city        CHAR(15),      * city salesperson lives in.
phone       CHAR(12));     * salesperson's phone number.

Sales
(s_id       CHAR(4),       * salesperson's id number as CHAR.
item        CHAR(15),      * "DESK", "CHAIR", "TELEVISION", etc.
model       CHAR(16),      * like "ZENITH1108YY3".
invoice     CHAR(8),       * invoice identifier.
no_units    SMALLINT,      * how many were sold, or returned, etc.
tot_amt     NUMERIC(10,2)) * total amount of the sale.

Inventry
(item       CHAR(15),      * "DESK", "CHAIR", "TELEVISION", etc.
model       CHAR(16),      * like "ZENITH1108YY3".
price_pu    NUMERIC(10,2), * like 438.99. price per unit.
no_on_hnd   SMALLINT);     * number on hand.
```

Fig. 8-1. Database files for the "Posting Sales" example.

that the cause of the error has been determined and you have dealt with it. The code for this is shown in Fig. 8-2.

Getting a Salesperson's Total Sales

Periodically you may wish to find the total sales of all the salespeople and print them in descending order. The code in Fig. 8-3 shows how to do this.

Having done so, you can run a report using Tot__sale (see Chapter 6).

```
SET TALK OFF

* Set up the work areas.
* The USE command has been modified in dBASE IV so that the
* work area can be named in the command by means of the IN clause.
* For the modifications to the USE command see Chapter 2.
USE SALESPER IN 2
USE SALES IN 3
USE INVENTRY IN 4
USE TRNSACTS IN 1

* Now set up an ARRAY to hold the transaction.
ARRAY TRNSACT[8]

* Start a loop on the Trnsacts file.
GO TOP
DO WHILE .NOT. EOF()
    IF .NOT. posted

        * Now move the transaction into the ARRAY TRNSACT using
        * the new COPY TO ARRAY command. Since the ARRAY
        * TRNSACT is one-dimensional, so we have to use the scope
        * NEXT 1.
        * See Chapter 2 for the format of the COPY TO ARRAY
        COPY TO ARRAY TRNSACT NEXT 1
        * Now the values for this record are in the ARRAY.
        * TRNSACT[1] contains type.
        * TRNSACT[2] contains item.
        * TRNSACT[3] contains model.
        * TRNSACT[4] contains invoice.
        * TRNSACT[5] contains no_units.
        * TRNSACT[6] contains s_first.
        * TRNSACT[7] contains s_last.
        * TRNSACT[8] contains posted.

        * Now BEGIN a TRANSACTION.
        * If for some reason an error should occur while
        * entering this transaction record, you want to be able
        * to ROLLBACK the changes you have made so the database
        * will not be in an inconsistent state.

        ON ERROR DO Error_hd
        * You need to set up a program or procedure to do
        * something about errors during a transaction. For
        * example,you may want to attempt a ROLLBACK.

        BEGIN TRANSACTION
        DO CASE
```

Fig. 8-2. The posting program in .PRG form.

```
                    * Here we do only one case, namely sales.
                    CASE RTRIM(TRNSACT[1]) = 'SOLD'

                         * Now look up the salesperson's id.
                         SELECT SALESPER
                         GO TOP
                         LOCATE FOR S_FIRST = TRNSACT[6] .AND. ;
                              S_LAST = TRNSACT[7]
                         STORE S_ID TO m_s_id

                         * Now, look up the item in Inventry and
                         * subtract the number of units sold from the
                         * number on hand.
                         SELECT INVENTRY
                         GO TOP
                         LOCATE FOR item = TRNSACT[2] .and. ;
                              model = TRNSACT[3]
                         REPLACE no_on_hnd WITH no_on_hnd - TRNSACT[5]

                         * Put the price into a memory variable.
                         STORE price_pu to m_price

                         * Now post the transaction to the Sales file.
                         SELECT Sales
                         APPEND BLANK
                         REPLACE s_id WITH m_s_id
                         REPLACE item WITH TRNSACT[2]

                         REPLACE model WITH TRNSACT[3]
                         REPLACE invoice WITH TRNSACT[4]
                         REPLACE no_units WITH TRNSACT[5]
                         REPLACE tot_amt WITH TRNSACT[5] * m_price

                         * Place other cases here.
                    CASE RTRIM(TRNSACT[1]) = 'RETURNED'
                         * Lines of code.
                    CASE RTRIM(TRNSACT[1]) = 'LOST'
                         * Lines of code.
               ENDCASE

               * Now mark this transaction posted.
               SELECT TRNSACTS
               REPLACE posted WITH .T.
               END TRANSACTION
               ON ERROR
               * This terminates the ON ERROR DO above, because the
               * transaction has been completed.
          ENDIF
          SKIP
     ENDDO
     RETURN
```

(Fig. 8-2 ends.)

```
     * First, you need to have CREATEd a temporary file to hold the
     * names of the salespeople and their total sales.
     Tot_sale
     (s_first  CHAR(15),          * salesperson's first name.
     s_last    CHAR(15),          * salesperson's last name.
     Sum       NUMERIC(10,2));    * salesperson's sales total.

     SET TALK OFF
     USE SALESPER IN 2
     USE SALES IN 3
     USE TOT_SALE IN 5

     * Zap the tot_sale file in case it still has records from a
     * previous run.
     SET SAFETY OFF
     ZAP
     SET SAFETY ON
     SELECT Salesper
     GO TOP

     * Now do the following for each salesperson.
     DO WHILE .NOT. EOF()
         STORE S_ID TO MS_ID
         STORE S_FIRST TO MS_FIRST
         STORE S_LAST TO MS_LAST
         SELECT SALES
         GO TOP
         LOCATE FOR S_ID = MS_ID
         STORE 0.00 TO M_SUM

         * Now do the following for each sale by this person.
         DO WHILE .NOT. EOF()
             STORE TOT_AMT + M_SUM TO M_SUM
             CONTINUE
         ENDDO

         * If you are only interested in a report on those salespeople
         * who actually had some sales, use the following IF and
         * ENDIF.  Otherwise you can leave out the IF and ENDIF.
         IF M_SUM > 0.00
             SELECT TOT_SALE
             APPEND BLANK
             REPLACE S_FIRST WITH MS_FIRST,S_LAST WITH MS_LAST
             REPLACE SUM WITH M_SUM
         ENDIF
         SELECT SALESPER
         SKIP
     ENDDO
```

Fig. 8-3. *Program to determine salesperson's total sales.*

Replacing Inventory

Suppose you have a file on suppliers with the following columns: "item" CHAR(15), "model" CHAR(16), "supplier" CHAR(30), "address" CHAR(15), "city" CHAR(15), "zip" CHAR(15). Further suppose that you want to reorder those items which you have sold more of in the last two months than you currently have on hand. You want to keep a two-month supply on hand. You can create a structure, Orders, to hold your orders. Orders will have the following fields: "item" CHAR(15), "model" CHAR(16), "number" SMALLINT, "cost" NUMERIC(10,2), "supplier" CHAR(30), "address" CHAR(15), "city" CHAR(15), "zip" CHAR(15).

You may also want to collect information on those items that have not sold in the last two months. For that you will need a file No__sales with columns "item" CHAR(15) and "model" CHAR(16). Start by setting up two memory variables, say "mf__date" for the date two months ago and "ml__date" for today's date.

You need a file of suppliers for this example. Assume it has been created as follows:

```
Supplier
(item         CHAR(15),
model         CHAR(16),
supplier      CHAR(30),
address       CHAR(15),
city          CHAR(15),
zip           CHAR(15));
```

The .PRG file shown in Fig. 8-4 will get the results you want into the Orders file and the No__sales file.

After you have run this program, you will probably want to run a report using the Orders and No__sales files. See Chapter 6 on reports.

```
* First declare an ARRAY, INVENTOR, to hold records from the
* Inventry file.
ARRAY INVENTOR[4]
CLOSE ALL
SET TALK OFF
USE INVENTRY IN 1
USE SALES IN 2
USE ORDERS IN 3
ZAP
* ZAP Orders to make sure it is empty before you start.
USE NO_SALES IN 4
ZAP
* ZAP No_sales to make sure it is empty before you start.
USE SUPPLIER IN 5
SELECT INVENTRY
GO TOP
DO WHILE .NOT. EOF()

     * This DO WHILE loop works its way through each inventory
     * item and model, checking the number of sales.
     * Now move the inventory item into the ARRAY INVENTOR using
     * the new COPY TO ARRAY command. Since the ARRAY
     * INVENTOR is one-dimensional, so you have to use the scope
     * NEXT 1.
     * See Chap. 2 for the format of the COPY TO ARRAY command.
     COPY TO ARRAY INVENTOR NEXT 1
     * Now INVENTOR[1] contains item.
     * Now INVENTOR[2] contains model.
     * Now INVENTOR[3] contains price_pu.
     * Now INVENTOR[4] contains no_on_hnd.

     * Now check sales for this item.
     SELECT SALES
     LOCATE FOR ITEM = INVENTOR[1] .AND. MODEL = INVENTOR[2]
     STORE 0 TO M_COMP
     * Use M_COMP to store the number of units sold.
     DO WHILE .NOT. EOF()
          * Now check if the sale was within the last two months.
          IF DATE > MF_DATE .AND. DATE < ML_DATE
               * If you get here, the sale was in the right time
               * period.
               STORE M_COMP + NO_UNITS TO M_COMP
          ENDIF
          CONTINUE
          * This CONTINUE takes you to the next sale of the
          * current inventory item and model.
     ENDDO

     * Here you have finished all sales of this item and model.
     * M_COMP has the number of units sold.
```

Fig. 8-4. *Inventory replacement and "no-sales" program.*

```
      * Now test M_COMP against the number
      * of units on hand.
      IF M_COMP > INVENTOR[4]

            * If you get here, you sold more than you have on hand,
            * so you need to make an entry in the Orders file.
            SELECT ORDERS
            STORE M_COMP - INVENTOR[4] TO M_DIFF
            * M_DIFF has the number of units to order.

            * Now you need to get the supplier's name and address to
            * make the order.
            SELECT SUPPLIER
            LOCATE FOR ITEM = INVENTOR[1] .AND. MODEL = INVENTOR[2]
            STORE SUPPLIER TO M_SPLR
            STORE ADDRESS TO M_ADD
            STORE CITY TO M_CITY
            STORE ZIP TO M_ZIP
            SELECT ORDERS

            * Now insert all the necessary information for the
            * order in the Orders file.
            APPEND BLANK
            REPLACE ITEM WITH INVENTOR[1]
            REPLACE MODEL WITH INVENTOR[2]
            REPLACE NUMBER WITH M_DIFF
            REPLACE COST WITH M_DIFF * INVENTOR[3]
            REPLACE SUPPLIER WITH M_SPLR
            REPLACE ADDRESS WITH M_ADD
            REPLACE CITY WITH M_CITY
            REPLACE ZIP WITH M_ZIP
      ELSE
            IF M_COMP = 0

                  * If you get here, there haven't been any sales of
                  * this item and model, so you need to enter it in
                  * the No_sales file.
                  SELECT NO_SALES
                  APPEND BLANK
                  REPLACE ITEM WITH INVENTOR[1], MODEL WITH INVENTOR[2]
            ENDIF
      ENDIF
      SELECT INVENTRY

      * Now SKIP to the next inventory item and model.
      SKIP
ENDDO
```

(Fig. 8-4 ends.)

Summary

This chapter discusses the procedural interface of *dBASE IV*, in which programs can be written in the *dBASE* programming language. Several program excerpt examples can be compared with the examples in Chapter 13, where the same things are accomplished using embedded SQL.

9

Security and Integrity

Two main concerns are connected with information kept in database management systems. The first is the ease with which data can be accessed by unauthorized persons. The second is the integrity or continuing accuracy of the data when many persons are engaged in working with it. Both of these matters need to be considered when the database is installed and kept track of as it is put to use.

In *dBASE IV*, a number of security features are incorporated that will allow you to guard against the unauthorized use of your database. These consist of a system of GRANTing access, called PROTECT, a provision for data encryption, and the use of views as security devices.

Additional security features in SQL mode allow you to limit access to SQL tables, as well as to a set of SQL catalogs, used by the system to route queries efficiently. Also, the RUNSTATS, DBCHECK, and DBDEFINE commands bring into the SQL tables any changes made in the data when you were not in SQL mode. All of the SQL security measures are under the control of the *dBASE* PROTECT system.

The features provided by *dBASE IV* for maintaining security

Table 9-1. Levels of dBASE Security.

Level	User Definition	Result
Log-in	User name and password	Controls access to dBASE IV
Access	File and Field	Controls access to data files, fields in data files, and application code
Data Encryption	User and File Group	Automatic encryption and decryption of data

and integrity of the information in your database are described in the sections that follow.

dBASE Security

The core of the *dBASE* security system, the PROTECT command, is optional; you don't have to use it. It can be used with either a single microcomputer or in a local area network (LAN) environment. The database administrator (DBA) can make use of the PROTECT command to ensure security. PROTECT is a menu-driven command invoked within *dBASE IV*. It contains three types of database protection:

☐ Log-in security
☐ Access level security
☐ Data encryption

The functions of these security measures are shown in Table 9-1 and are explained in the following subsections.

The Dbsystem.DB File

When a DBA creates a protected database system, *dBASE IV*

builds and maintains a password system file, called Dbsystem.DB, containing a record for each user who accesses a protected system. Each of these records, called a *user profile*, contains the user's log-in name, account name, password, group name, and access level.

Dbsystem.DB is an encrypted file that cannot be decrypted. Only the DBA can print it out (See the section entitled "Printing Security Information".)

If Dbsystem.DB is not available, the log-in system will not work, but the database file security will remain in force so that encrypted files cannot be used. To be certain that Dbsystem.DB is always available, make sure that it is in the directory from which you start *dBASE IV*.

Log-In Security

With PROTECT you can create a password-protected system whereby no user can gain access unless that user supplies (1) a group name, (2) a log-in name, and (3) a password. When password-protection is in force, PROTECT will display the user Log-in screen any time *dBASE IV* is accessed, even if you invoke *dBASE IV* at the operating system level with a call for an applications program.

Access-Level Security

You can control access to database files and the fields within those files by setting up a *privilege scheme*. To do this, you assign *user access levels* that determine the user's file and field access privileges. You can assign user access levels from Nos. 1 through 8, with a low number giving greater access privileges. You then establish an access level for each user in the *user's profile*, and you establish additional access levels for file and field privileges in the *file privilege scheme*.

When this access-level security system is in place, *dBASE IV* will determine what the user can do with a file by matching the user access level with the file's privilege scheme as soon as the user logs in. If you do not use PROTECT to create a privilege scheme for a database file, all users can read and write to all fields in the file. If you do use PROTECT to create a file privilege scheme, the following privileges are the default and are granted initially until you change them:

- ☐ View records in a database file (read privilege)
- ☐ Change database file record contents (update privilege)
- ☐ Append new records to a database file (extend privilege)
- ☐ Delete records from a database file (delete privilege)

At the field level, you can grant the following access privileges to each field in a database file for each access level:

- ☐ *Full*: Read and write the field in the database file (the default);
- ☐ *Read-Only*: Read but not write the field; and
- ☐ *None*: Neither read nor write the field.

With these constraints, a user can be prevented from even seeing fields that you do not want displayed.

Data Encryption

If PROTECT is in use on your database system, then your database files and their associated index and memo files are encrypted in a file with a .CRP extension. This means that data cannot be read until it is decrypted. When files are encrypted, they are translated from source data to another form that makes them impossible to read without a decryption key.

After a file is encrypted, you should delete the unencrypted (.DBF) file from the directory, and then rename the encrypted file so that it has a .DBF extension. Index files are only encrypted when you REINDEX or when you create them with an encrypted database file.

The size of your file will determine the time required for encryption. The encryption occurs when you select Save on the PROTECT Exit Menu or when you exit PROTECT. To control when copied files are encrypted, use the SET ENCRYPTION command. After a database is protected, the DBA and the application programmer maintain control over encryption of copied files. SET ENCRYPTION is ON by default in a protected database system.

How to Install a Protected Database System

To install a PROTECTed database system, you must take the following steps:

[1] Initiate the PROTECT command. This is done from within *dBASE IV* at the dot prompt by entering PROTECT and pressing Return.

[2] Define the DBA's password, which can have a maximum of 16 alphanumeric characters in either upper- or lowercase form. It will not be displayed on the screen. The first time you use PROTECT, the system will prompt you to confirm the password, and you must enter it again. After that, you only enter it once. You will have three chances to type it correctly; after that, PROTECT will terminate the session. The security system can only be changed if the DBA's password is entered. Once this is done, the system will display the User's Menu that allows you to define user profiles.

[3] Define user profiles. Use the Users Menu to create or modify a user profile in the Dbsystem.DB file. Follow the steps below to add or change a user profile.

a] Access the Users Menu. The cursor is at the first field.

b] Enter a user log-in name (1–8 alphanumeric characters). Press Return.

c] Enter a user password (1–16 alphanumeric characters). Press Return.

d] Enter a group name (1–8 alphanumeric characters). Press Return.

At this point, PROTECT will check to see if the user profile has been defined. If so, the rest of the menu items will be completed with their current values. You can then change any of them except the group name. If you edit the group name, there will be no way to access files associated with the original group name. If you delete the group name before all files associated with that group are copied from decrypted form, there will be no way for anyone to access those files.

e] Enter the full name (1–24 alphanumeric Characters) if desired. Press Return.

f] Select a user access level (a number from 1 through 8). You must assign an access level to each user within each group. This level will be matched with file access levels in the Files Menu to determine whether the user can access database files. It will also determine the type of access the user can have to each file and to each field within each file.

g] Store the user profile. The user profile information is not saved until you do this. The full name is the only optional item in the user profile; you must specify group, log-in name, and password or the profile will not be created. The user group name will be matched with the file group name to enable file access. To delete a user profile, simply enter the log-in name, the password, and the group name, then move the highlight on the Users Menu to Delete user from group and press Return.

[4] Define file privilege levels and field privileges. See section on file privilege schemes and field access.

[5] Save the security information. After setting all file and field access privileges, select *Store file privileges* to save them. (After you have defined or changed 8 file privilege schemes, you must store them before you can continue using the Files Menu.)

File Privilege Schemes and Field Access

Use the Files Menu to create and change access levels for file privileges and assign field access privileges for each file access level. To define file and field privileges for a database file:

[1] Access the Files Menu

[2] Select a file

[3] Assign the file to a specific group

[4] Establish the most restrictive access level for each file privilege.

[5] Select an access level for field privilege assignment.

[6] Select field privileges for each field at each access level, as required.

[7] Store the file and field privilege scheme.

A file is encrypted using *Select NewFile*, stored using *Store File Privileges*, and saved using *Exit*. With these choices, you can change the file privilege scheme or accept the default values, which are:

☐ Access levels for all file privileges are set to 8.
☐ Field privileges are set to FULL.

Table 9-2 shows the values you can enter and the default values for items on the Files Menu.

You can only create database file privilege schemes for up to 8 database files at a time. You will get an error message if you try to set up an 9th file. To avoid this, after you have completed the 8th scheme, move to the Exit Menu and select Save or Exit to save the 8 schemes you have created. You can then move back to the Files Menu and make up to 8 more schemes.

You can only assign a file to one group. The group name will be matched with a user group name to enable data decryption. For greatest efficiency, try to organize users and files into groups that reflect application use (e.g., by department or area).

To establish file privilege levels, select *File access privileges* from the Files Menu, and the *File Access Levels* Menu will appear. Access level 1 has the greatest privilege, and access level 8 has the least. To limit access, the higher the privilege level (i.e., the closer to access level 1), the fewer users you should assign to it. These access rights that you assign on the File Access Levels Menu

Table 9-2. Item Values on the Files Menu.

Menu Item	Value Type	Value	Default
Select new file	Menu list item	File selected from file list	First file in list
Group Name	User-defined CHAR string	1-8 alphanumeric CHARs	None
Read privilege	Integer	1 through 8	8
Update privilege	Integer	1 through 8	8
Extend privilege	Integer	1 through 8	8
Delete privilege	Integer	1 through 8	8
Access Level	Integer	1 through 8	1
Field Access privilege (set for each field at each access level)	Enumerated data type	Fields selected from field list	First field in list
		FULL, R/O, NONE	FULL*

* Once field privileges are set for an access level, the field privileges
  for more restricted levels that are not set default to FULL.

cannot override a read-only restriction established on the file at
the operating-system level.

File privileges determine permissions for DELETE, EXTEND,
READ, and UPDATE. For each type of file privilege, you can
specify the most restricted access level to have the privilege. Then
all levels less restricted than that will be granted the privilege,
and levels more restricted than that will not. For example, if you
specify 5 as the UPDATE privilege level for the file Clients.DBF,
then all users with access levels of 1 through 5 will be able to
UPDATE that file, and users with access levels of 6 through 8 will
not. To assign and change file privileges, highlight the item, press
Return, and enter the value, or use the Up- and Down-Arrow keys
to change the value.

To establish a field access level, move the highlight to

access level and enter the access level for which you wish to define field access. The possible field privileges are:

☐ FULL, which grants the right to read and update (write) the field. (default).

☐ R/O, which grants the right to read the field only (no update capability).

☐ NONE, which prevents access. The user cannot read or update the field, and the field appears as though it has been removed from the database file.

File privileges take precedence over field privileges. In other words, if a file privilege limits a user to read-only access, the only possible field privileges that user can have are R/O and NONE.

Field privileges are established by moving to *Establish field privileges* and pressing Return. A fields list will appear next to the Files Menu. This fields list will contain all fields defined in the database file and the current field access privilege assigned to them. These are all set to FULL initially. To change the field privilege:

[1] Move the highlight to the field for which you want to change the privilege.

[2] Use Return to toggle the preset values FULL, R/O, and NONE.

[3] When the field privilege you want is displayed, move to the next field you want to change.

Continue this procedure until you have set all fields for the access level that you want, then return to the Files Menu by pressing Return.

Set the next access level and move the highlight back to *Establish field privileges* (by pressing Return) to assign field privileges at that level. This process continues until you have assigned all the field privileges you want to change. When you specify a level and then change field privileges, the changes you make affect that field only at that access level; all other fields and access levels remain as they were.

To cancel a file privilege scheme at any time while you are defining or modifying it, move to the last option on the menu, *Cancel current entry* and press Return. This will delete the definition in progress.

Printing Security Information

There is no way for you or any other user to examine the contents of Dbsystem.DB because it is maintained as an encrypted file. Therefore, you may want to keep a hard copy of some of the information kept in it.

The Reports Menu will allow you to either display or print the following security information about users and files:

☐ The User Information Report lists the names of all system users, their passwords, group names, account names, and levels.

☐ The File Information Report lists the name of each *dBASE* file, the group to which the file is assigned, file privileges, name of each field in the file, and the field privileges.

Exiting from PROTECT

The Exit Menu contains three options:

☐ *Save* will post all new and updated user profiles and file privilege schemes that have been stored during the current PROTECT session. The user profiles will be saved in the current Dbsystem.DB file. File privilege schemes will be saved in the database file structure. User profiles can be saved at any point during a PROTECT session. You must save file privilege schemes after you define or change 8 of them. Database files are encrypted when the file privilege scheme is saved.

☐ *Abandon* will cancel all new and updated user profiles and file privilege schemes not already saved in the current PROTECT session.

☐ *Exit* will terminate the current PROTECT session. Any new and updated user profiles and updated file privilege schemes that have not been encrypted and saved will be encrypted and saved when you choose Exit.

Locking

In a multiuser (or networking) system, locking procedures are necessary to avoid deadlock. *dBASE IV* contains an extensive locking system for this purpose. You can set it for either automatic locking or you can explicitly request it when you need it. The locking system is explained in detail in Chapter 14.

SQL Security and Integrity

When you work in SQL mode, there is an additional security system provided by the SQL commands GRANT and REVOKE, which are discussed in the next subsection. There are also commands for ensuring that relevant work outside of SQL mode is brought into the SQL complex of tables and indices. This is accomplished by the RUNSTATS, DBCHECK, and DBDEFINE commands, to be discussed. Also, SQL mode maintains a set of catalog tables, to be described, with file extensions .DBF (*dBASE IV* non-SQL catalogs have file extension .CAT).

Other security features available within SQL mode are (1) the locking system, previously described, and (2) the use of views, to be described.

GRANT and REVOKE

With the same identification provided by the PROTECT command, you can assign or restrict privileges to work with the tables in SQL mode. These privileges do not override any restrictions set using PROTECT in *dBASE* mode; they can only be used to further restrict privileges assigned by the PROTECT command.

The GRANT command allows you to specify the following

privileges in relation to existing database tables and views:

ALTER
CREATE INDEX
DELETE
INSERT
SELECT
UPDATE

Any of these privileges can be granted at any time, thereby adding to privileges the user may already have. The syntax is:

```
GRANT [ALL] [PRIVILEGES]/<privilege list>
ON <table name>
TO (PUBLIC/<user list>)
[WITH GRANT OPTION];
```

where:

☐ [PRIVILEGES] includes the items listed in Table 9-1. The entire list can be granted by using the optional word ALL, or any selection of items on the list can be specified.

☐ <privileges list> is the list of items selected from the list in Table 9-1 in lieu of GRANTing ALL privileges.

☐ <table name> is the name of the table on which you are granting privileges in the event you wish to restrict privileges to designated tables, instead of granting privileges on the entire database. If no table is specified, the privileges granted apply to all tables and views in the database.

☐ PUBLIC is the term used to GRANT privileges to all users at once without having to specify the IDs of each person.

☐ <user list> is the list of users to whom privileges are being granted when you GRANT to specific users only and not to all users.

☐ [WITH GRANT OPTION] is an optional privilege that you can grant, allowing the grantee to, in turn, grant those same privileges to any other user(s).

For example, you can GRANT ALL privileges, including the right to GRANT ALL privileges to others, to a user with the ID of CHUCK by entering:

```
GRANT ALL
TO   Chuck
WITH GRANT OPTION;
```

These privileges will cascade downward (i.e., Chuck can now grant any or all of his privileges to other users, with or without giving them the WITH GRANT OPTION privileges).

You can also restrict such privileges to a specific table or view by entering:

```
GRANT ALL

ON    Sales

TO    Chuck
WITH GRANT OPTION;
```

To give the privilege of performing a restricted number of operations on that table, without the privilege of passing it on to other users, enter:

```
GRANT UPDATE, INSERT, DELETE
ON    Sales
TO    Chuck;
```

To give those same privileges to all users, enter:

```
GRANT UPDATE, INSERT, DELETE
ON    Sales
TO    PUBLIC;
```

You cannot grant the privilege WITH GRANT OPTION to PUBLIC (nor is it necessary, since all users would already have the privilege when it is granted to PUBLIC.)

Use the REVOKE command to remove privileges in the same way as you use the GRANT command. The syntax is:

```
REVOKE [ALL] [PRIVILEGES]/<privilege list>
ON <table name>
FROM (PUBLIC/<user list>);
```

where the meanings of the terms are the same as listed under the explanation of the GRANT syntax.

If, for example, you have previously granted access to PUBLIC on the Sales Table and now wish to restrict it to a few users, enter the following two commands:

```
REVOKE      ALL
ON          Sales
FROM        Public;
```

and

```
GRANT  ALL
ON     Sales
TO     Chuck, Stan, George, Cindy;
```

If you previously awarded privileges accompanied by the WITH GRANT OPTION statement, the REVOKE will cascade just as the GRANT statement did. In other words, if you gave Chuck the right to grant, and he gave it to Stan, who gave it to George, then your revocation of Chuck's privilege will revoke the privileges he gave to Stan, and the one Stan gave to George. However, privileges and revocations do not cascade upward: If Stan revokes George's privileges, this does not affect Stan's own privileges, nor Chuck's.

On the other hand, if someone else also gave George the same privileges, these will still stand until actively revoked by the grantor, even though Stan has revoked those same privileges for George. In other words, unless the privileges were acquired through the cascading feature, each grantor must revoke privileges he gave in order to prohibit a user from exercising the privileges he was given.

Data Encryption in SQL Mode

Encryption was discussed in detail in the first section. In SQL mode, the tables get encrypted when they are created. Encrypted data can only be decrypted in SQL mode, not in dBASE.

Views as Security Devices

If certain tables contain sensitive information, yet must be accessed by personnel needing to work on nonsensitive columns, you can CREATE a view containing only the nonsensitive parts of the table and GRANT access only to the view, not to the whole table. (Views are discussed in detail in Chapter 12).

Transaction Processing

In multiuser systems, it is important to be able to complete a unit of work before changes are made by another user. One complete unit of work is called a "transaction." For example, entering the payment of a salary also entails deducting that same amount from Cash on Hand, entering the amount paid for such items as FICA and withholding tax in other accounts. Until all these are completed, the database may be out of balance. Therefore (depending on how your database is set up), it may be advisable to ensure that a complete set of these entries is entered before the relevant tables or files are accessed by another user. There is also the possibility of a system breakdown, which might leave only part of the set of entries recorded in the database.

To avoid the different types of interruptions that may occur and thus destroy the integrity of the database, you should use the BEGIN TRANSACTION command. This will ensure that any changes made before you issue the END TRANSACTION command will be rolled back if they are not completed. The ROLLBACK feature will remove any partially completed transactions and leave the database as it was before you issued the BEGIN TRANSACTION command.

The syntax for starting a series of related entries is:

BEGIN TRANSACTION;

To end the series, the command is:

END TRANSACTION;

Transaction processing in *dBASE IV* when you are not in SQL mode is discussed in Chapter 4.

SQL System Catalogs

To keep track of all database objects (i.e., tables, views, synonyms, indices), *dBASE IV* SQL maintains a set of System Catalog tables. Every time you create a new database with the CREATE DATABASE command, a new set of Catalog tables is set up for that database. *dBASE IV* uses these System tables when it executes your queries and updates.

You can look at the information in a System Catalog table at any time by using SELECT, just as you would any other table; but you cannot perform any other SQL operations directly on these tables (unless you are the SQL DBA). The names and descriptions of the System tables are shown in Table 9-3. At the same time, you must keep the information in these tables up to date since they are used by the system. For this purpose, use the RUNSTATS, DBCHECK, and DBDEFINE commands described in the following sections.

Table 9-3. dBASE IV SQL System Catalog Tables.

Table Name	Description
SYSAUTH	Describes the privileges held by users on tables and views, with one row for every user (including PUBLIC) holding privileges in the current database.
SYSCOLAU	Describes the privileges held by users to UPDATE columns in a table or view, with one row for each user holding privileges to an individual column in the current database.
SYSCOLS	Describes each column in every table and view including the Catalog tables.
SYSIDXS	Describes every index in the database and the table for which it is defined.
SYSKEYS	Describes every column (index key) used in each index.

(Table 9-3 Continues.)

Table Name	Description
SYSSYNS	Contains all synonym definitions for each table and view.
SYSTABLS	Contains information describing every table and view in the current database.
SYSVDEPS	Describes the relation between views and tables in the current database (so that if tables are dropped, views based on those tables will also be dropped).
SYSVIEWS	Contains the view definitions and the limitations on use of each view.
SYSDBS	Contains information about all SQL databases.
SYSTIMES	Used in the multiuser environment to ensure that users' internal copies of the catalog tables reflect the most recent catalog updates.

(Table 9-3 Ends.)

RUNSTATS

dBASE IV uses statistical information to optimize its performance. Therefore, it is important to the efficiency of the system that the columns in the system catalogs be kept up-to-date. Whenever you create or add objects to a database, or add or change access privileges, the system catalogs are automatically updated. But, when you drop objects; add columns to tables; change definitions of tables, views, and indices; or use INSERT, DELETE, or ADD operations, the columns in the catalogs are not automatically updated.

To accomplish this statistical updating, use the RUNSTATS command. The syntax is:

```
RUNSTATS [<table name>];
```

where [<table name>] is the name of the table (and its associated indices) that you want *dBASE IV* to update in the catalogs. Use the table name if you have made extensive changes to a single table. Omit use of the table name if you want several tables or the entire active database updated in the catalogs.

RUNSTATS will only update columns that have SMALLINT, INTEGER, DECIMAL, NUMERIC, or FLOAT datatypes. The columns updated by RUNSTATS are shown in Table 9-4.

Table 9-4. Catalog Columns Updated by RUNSTATS.

Column	Table	Description
Colcard	Syscols	Number of distinct values in the column
High2key	Syscols	Statistical entry
Low2key	Syscols	Statistical entry
Firstkcard	Sysidxs	Number of distinct values in first column of index key
Fullkcard	Sysidxs	Number of distinct values in the full index key
Nleaf	Sysidxs	Number of B-tree leaves in index
Nlevels	Sysidxs	Depth of index B-tree
Updated	Systabls	Last date that ALTER TABLE or RUNSTATS command was run; date of creation for views
Card	Systabls	Cardinality (the number of rows) in table; 0 for views
Npages	Systabls	Number of disk pages a table occupies

DBCHECK and DBDEFINE

SQL commands issued after the structure of a database table has been modified in *dBASE* mode may give incorrect results or may not operate at all. To avoid this, you should always make certain that system catalogs are up to date before accessing data with SQL commands by using DBCHECK. The syntax is:

```
DBCHECK [<.DBF file>];
```

where [<.DBF file>] gives you the option of specifying a table (and its associated indices). If you do not specify the .DBF file, then DBCHECK will check all files in the active database. This command can only be used in interactive SQL.

The DBCHECK command will check the SQL System Catalog

table and index files in the active database to determine whether the tables are consistent with current structures. If the table entries are not consistent, you will receive an error message for every database file that does not match the definitions in the database's System Catalog tables.

If you receive one or more error messages after issuing the DBCHECK command, you should run the DBDEFINE utility to bring the catalog descriptions up to date. The syntax is:

DBDEFINE [<.DBF file>];

where[<.DBF file>] gives you the option of specifying a file to be brought up to date in the catalogs (i.e., where you have received only one error message after issuing the DBCHECK command). If you received several error messages, indicating that several updates need to be performed, then omit the file name and DBDEFINE will update all table catalogs in the active database.

Summary

The levels of *dBASE IV* security include:

☐ Log-in security, where only authorized personnel are allowed to log in to the database.

☐ Access level security, restricting the extent of access given to individuals.

☐ Data encryption, whereby information entered into the database is encrypted so that it is readable only to those individuals who have been given the decryption key.

The *dBASE IV* PROTECT system allows for the installation of all levels of security.

An automatic locking system insures against disruption of the system by simultaneous use. Locking is discussed further in Chapter 14 on networking.

A separate security system within SQL mode allows you to GRANT and REVOKE privileges to specific individuals for access to columns, tables and views.

The commands RUNSTATS, DBCHECK and DBDEFINE enable you to keep the SQL System catalogs up to date, and to bring into SQL Mode the files created in *dBASE*.

10

SQL: Creating Database Objects

The Structured Query Language (SQL), as it is used in *dBASE IV*, is described in this chapter, as well as in Chapters 11, 12, and 13. If you are not a programmer, you can skip Chapter 13 because it discusses embedding SQL in a *dBASE* program.

SQL is an efficient, easy-to-learn query language originated by IBM for use with relational databases. It has been standardized by the American National Standards Institute (ANSI) as "Database Language SQL" and is fast becoming the most widely used query language. Its history and development, as well as currently available variations in its syntax, have been well documented in computer literature over recent years and, therefore, will not be repeated here. For an in-depth look at these developments, see *SQL, The Structured Query Language* (TAB BOOKS Inc., 1988), and the references contained in that text.

The SQL language consists of three types of statements:

☐ *Data Definition Statements*, which are for setting up database objects, consist of the commands CREATE DATABASE, SHOW DATABASE, DROP DATABASE, CREATE TABLE, ALTER TABLE, DROP TABLE, CREATE

INDEX, and DROP INDEX. They are discussed in this chapter.

☐ *Data Manipulation Statements* are for transferring data into tables, querying the database to obtain answers about the contents of the database, inserting new data, updating the information in the tables, and creating views. Data Manipulation Statements are SELECT, INSERT, UPDATE, DELETE, and CREATE VIEW. They are discussed in Chapters 11 and 12.

☐ *Data Control Statements* are for instituting security measures and for ensuring the integrity of the information in the database. The Data Control Statements are GRANT, REVOKE, RUNSTATS, DBCHECK, and DBDEFINE. They were discussed in Chapter 9, along with other *dBASE IV* security features.

In addition, the SQL language contains connecting words and clauses used in conjunction with the Data Definition, Manipulation, and Control statements that make it possible to perform arithmetic, logical, and comparison operations on the data, as well as on group and order data. SQL also includes "expressions" consisting of constants combined with operators. The clauses, operators, and expressions are discussed in Chapter 11.

All of the SQL commands, clauses, operators, and connecting words are called "reserved words"; these cannot be used to name database objects. These reserved words are listed in Table 10-1. Chapter 13 discusses embedded SQL and shows how to write programs that can be embedded in the *dBASE* programming language. Appendix A contains a list of SQL error messages, along with a brief explanation of the meaning of each.

Starting SQL

dBASE IV offers two SQL facilities. Interactive SQL allows you to enter SQL commands for creating and maintaining

Table 10-1. SQL Reserved Words.

ADD	DISTINCT	PRIVILEGES
ALL	DROP	PUBLIC
ALTER	EXISTS	REAL
AND	FETCH	REVOKE
ANY	FLOAT	ROLLBACK
AS	FOR	RUNSTATS
ASC	FROM	SAVE
AVG	GRANT	SDF
BETWEEN	GROUP	SET
BLANK	HAVING	SMALLINT
BY	IN	START
CHAR	INDEX	STOP
CHECK	INSERT	SUM
CLOSE	INTEGER	SYLK
CLUSTER	INTO	SYNONYM
COUNT	KEEP	TABLE
CREATE	LIKE	TEMP
CURRENT	LIST	TO
CURSOR	LOAD	UNION
DATA	LOGICAL	UNIQUE
DATABASE	MAX	UNLOAD
DATE	MIN	UPDATE
DBCHECK	NOT	USER
DBDEFINE	NUMERIC	USING
DECIMAL	OF	VALUES
DECLARE	ON	VIEW
DELETE	OPEN	WHERE
DELIMITED	OPTION	WITH
DESC	OR	WKS
DIF	ORDER	WORK

databases. Embedded SQL lets you build application programs using the SQL language. Since SQL commands operate the same interactively as they do in an application program, you can use everything you do in interactive mode when you build your application programs.

dBASE IV has retained the standard SQL terminology while incorporating SQL into the *dBASE* structure. Therefore, the database objects called "files" in *dBASE* are called "tables" in SQL mode. This maintains the spirit of the relational database which, as far as the user is concerned, consists entirely of tables.

You cannot get to *dBASE IV's* interactive SQL mode through the Control Center. Instead, you must go to SQL mode from the dot prompt. If you are operating in *dBASE IV's* menu system, you must first exit from the menus and display the dot prompt. Then enter:

```
SET SQL ON
```

and press Return.

If you want to be able to start up in the interactive SQL mode automatically, enter the following into your Config.DB file:

```
SQL = ON
```

You can enter SQL statements on the SQL prompt command line, or you can press F9 (Zoom) to activate an editing window on which you can enter SQL statements. A maximum of 1024 characters can be put in a SQL statement.

If you are working at the SQL prompt, you must enter the SQL statement on a single line. If you are working in the editing window, you can enter a SQL statement on one or more lines. You must enter a semicolon (;) and press Return at the end of every SQL statement to have *dBASE* execute the statement.

The *dBASE* commands and functions that can be used in SQL mode are shown in the tables in Appendices B and C, respectively. If you use one of these *dBASE* commands, do not end the statement with a semicolon (;). Just press Return at the end of the statement. Use the semicolon as a terminator only to end statements that include a SQL command. (For *dBASE* commands, use the semicolon at the end of a line of code whenever the command is continued on the next line.)

The CREATE DATABASE Command

Before you create the relational tables in SQL, you must create a database to hold them. You should create a database for each of your applications. You can use the CREATE DATABASE command only in interactive SQL mode. The syntax is:

CREATE DATABASE [<*path*>] <*database*>;

where:

☐ [<*path*>] is the optional path to the subdirectory that will hold your database. The new database will be created in the directory specified by the path. If you do not specify a path, the database directory will be created as a subdirectory of your current directory named <*database*>.

☐ <*database*> is the name you want this database to have.

For example, you may want to create a database to hold your Accounts Receivable tables. To do so, enter:

CREATE DATABASE AcctRec;

When you use the CREATE DATABASE command, it creates a DOS file directory with the same name as the new database. It will also define a set of SQL catalog tables for this new database. The name and DOS path to the database directory are stored in a row entry of the master catalog table SYSDBS. (The catalog tables are described in Chapter 9.)

The START and STOP DATABASE Commands

After you create a directory, you must enter the START DATABASE command in order to use it. The syntax is:

START DATABASE <*database name*>;

where < *database name* > is the name of the database you want to start. After this command is executed, all subsequent activity on tables and views will be in the database named here.

You should enter the START DATABASE command immediately after entering interactive SQL mode. (It is also the first command you should enter after you start executing statements in a SQL program file.) Only one database can be active at a time. To change to another database, you must execute the STOP DATABASE command, then activate another one with START DATABASE. This will replace your current database with the new database.

For example, to activate the Accounts Receivable database:

```
START DATABASE AcctRec;
```

After you finish working with Accounts Receivable and want to go to the Accounts Payable database, enter:

```
STOP DATABASE;
```

You do not need to name the database to be stopped, since there can be only one open at a time; the only one that can be stopped is the current one. To work in the Accounts Payable, database, enter:

```
START DATABASE AcctPay;
```

The SHOW DATABASE Command

Enter the SHOW DATABASE command if you need to know what databases are available. It will list the name of each database, the DOS path to each database directory, the user ID of the person who created each database, and the date each database was created. All of this information is stored in the master catalog table, SYSDBS, which is maintained in the *dBASE IV* SQLHOME program directory. The syntax for the SHOW DATABASE command is:

```
SHOW DATABASE;
```

Creating Tables

To define a new table, use the CREATE TABLE command. The syntax is:

```
CREATE TABLE <table name>
(<column name>  <data type>  <width>
[,column name>  <data type>  <width>, . . . ]);
```

where:

- [ ] *<table name>* is the name you are giving to the new table. Follow DOS file-naming conventions in choosing the table name: it can be no more than eight characters long; cannot contain any embedded blank spaces; may consist of letters, numbers, and underscore characters; and must begin with a letter. It cannot be a reserved word. A table can have a maximum of 255 columns of no more than 4000 bytes. (These are the same rules for naming tables as those with the *dBASE* CREATE/MODIFY STRUCTURE command.)

- [ ] *<column name>* is the name you are giving to a new column. It can be no more than 10 characters long; cannot contain any embedded blank spaces; may consist of letters, numbers, and underscore characters; and must begin with a letter. It cannot be a reserved word. (These are the same rules for naming columns as those with the *dBASE* CREATE/MODIFY STRUCTURE command.) The list of columns, their data types, and (where necessary) widths must be enclosed in parentheses, and each column listing must be separated from the other column listings by a comma.

- [ ] *<data type>* is the type of data of the values to be entered in the designated column. *dBASE IV* SQL supports the data types shown in Table 10-2. The data type entered in this space must be one of those in the table.

Table 10-2. dBASE IV SQL Data types.

Datatype	Description
SMALLINT	Holds an integer with up to six digits (including sign). Values entered may range from – 99,999 to + 999,999.
INTEGER	Holds an integer containing up to 11 digits (including sign). Values entered may range from – 999,999,999 to + 99,999,999,999.
DECIMAL(x,y)	Specifies a numeric-type number of x digits (including sign) with y decimal places (digits to the right of a decimal point).
NUMERIC(x,y)	Holds a signed fixed decimal point number with x total digits (including sign and decimal point) and y decimal places (significant digits to the right of the decimal point). The value of x may range from 1 to 20 and y may range from 0 to 18; y cannot be greater than $x - 2$.
FLOAT(x,y)	Holds an x-digit floating point number (including sign and decimal point) with y decimal places. You may specify up to 20 total digits with up to 18 decimal places. Values can be entered as constants, memory variables, or columns. Constants may include numbers with an exponent (for example, $- 1.45E127$). The range of numbers is from 10^{-308} to 10^{+308}.
CHAR(n)	Holds a character string of up to n characters. You must specify a length (a maximum of 254 characters). Values can be entered as a string constant, character type memory variable, or column. Character strings must be enclosed in single (') or double (") quotes.
DATE	Holds a date in the format mm/dd/yy. Values are entered from date memory variables or columns, or date strings converted with the dBASE CTOD( ) function, for example, CTOD("02/15/88").
LOGICAL	Holds a single character, either "T" (for True) or "F" (for False). Values are entered from dBASE logical memory variables or columns, or by the constants .T., .t., .Y.,.y., .F., .f., .N., and .n..

□ *<width>* is the number of character spaces that you want to allow for the data that are to be entered in the designated column. Width must be specified for data types CHARacter, DECIMAL, FLOAT, NUMERIC. You should not specify width for data types SMALLINT, INTEGER, DATE, or LOGICAL.

For example, you may want to set up a table to contain information on all personnel called Employees (abbreviated to Emp). To do so, you might construct it as follows:

```
CREATE TABLE Emp

(id#            SMALLINT,
lastname        CHAR(14),
firstname       CHAR(12),
hiredate        DATE,
salary          DECIMAL(6,2),
commission      DECIMAL(4,1);
```

When you execute the above CREATE TABLE command by pressing Return after the semicolon, *dBASE IV* will return the message:

```
New Table EMP created
```

Unlike *dBASE* commands, SQL statements can be entered on multiple lines as shown above (if you use F9 (Zoom) to edit in a window) and can contain additional spaces or tab characters. The table created above will contain six columns: "id#," "lastname," "firstname," "hiredate," "salary," and "commission."

When you create a SQL table, *dBASE IV* constructs a *dBASE*-format database file and updates the database catalog tables for the definition of the new table. It also enters the table description in the SYSTABLS table and enters descriptions of the column in the SYSCOLS table.

The ALTER TABLE Command

At some time it may be necessary to add one or more columns to a table created earlier. This can be done by using the ALTER TABLE command in either interactive or embedded SQL. The syntax is:

```
ALTER TABLE <table name>
ADD (<column name> <data type> <width>
[,<column name> <data type> <width>, . . . ]);
```

where:

```
(<column name> <data type> <width>
[,<column name> <data type> <width>, . . . ])
```

is the specification for the column or columns you want to add, with each column specification separated from the others by a comma. The rules for adding columns are the same as those for putting columns into the table when it is created.

For example, you may want to add the columns "phone#" and "address" to the Emp table. You can do so by entering:

```
ALTER TABLE Emp
ADD    (phone# CHAR(11),
        address CHAR(30));
```

The ALTER TABLE command can be used only to add one or more columns; it cannot be used to delete a column or to change the definition of an existing column.

When you add a new column to an existing table, *dBASE IV* initializes the new columns to contain a null character string (" "). It sets new NUMERIC columns to zero and new LOGICAL columns to false. The ALTER TABLE command cannot be used to add columns to a view.

The CREATE INDEX Command

Use the CREATE INDEX command to build one or more in-dices. It can be used in both interactive and embedded SQL modes. The syntax is:

```
CREATE [UNIQUE] INDEX <index name>
ON <table name>
(<column name> [[ASC]/DESC]
[,<column name> [[ASC]/DESC], . . . ]);
```

where:

- □ UNIQUE is an optional specification that you may use to force data values in indexed columns to be unique. If the indexed column values are not unique, the index will not be created; instead, *dBASE IV* will return an error message.
- □ *<index name>* is your name for the new index.
- □ *<table name>* is the name of the table containing the column(s) on which the new index will be built.
- □ [,*<column name>* [[ASC]/DESC], . . .]) is the name of the column(s) on which the new index will be built. The optional terms ASC/DESC allow you indicate, if you wish, whether the order of the rows in the index will be ascending or descending; ascending is the default. Each column and its ASC or DESC specification must be separated from preceding column specifications by a comma, and the list of columns to be indexed must be enclosed in parentheses.

For example, if you want to build a UNIQUE index on the "id#" column of the Emp table, enter:

```
CREATE UNIQUE INDEX id#
ON Emp (id# DESC);
```

After the above statement is executed, you will receive the message on your screen:

```
INDEX id# created
```

You should specify ascending or descending according to the order in which you will usually want to retrieve rows. Ascending order indices can be based on all single-column and multicolumn data types except logical. Descending order indices can only be created on single numeric, character, or date data type columns.

dBASE IV uses indices to keep track of the location of rows within a database table. You must specify any indices you want to create, but you cannot specify what indices *dBASE IV* should use in retrieving data. The system will make this decision to select the most efficient index to retrieve data each time you enter a SQL statement.

The column(s) used to create an index are called *index keys* or *tags*, and you can create as many as 48 different keys for any table. You cannot build an index across more than one table, and you cannot build an index on a view.

If you create a UNIQUE index, *dBASE IV* will subsequently check every INSERT or UPDATE statement to make sure that the values of the indexed column remain unique. (All checks to verify unique data values will slow down performance.)

You can only build indices for tables, not for views; but *dBASE IV* may make use of indices based on the underlying table when you use a view. Keep in mind that rows for indices based on character columns are arranged according to the ASCII values of columns, which distinguishes lowercase from uppercase letters. You can see indices that have already been built for tables by displaying columns from the SYSIDXS catalog table.

The CREATE SYNONYM Command

For convenience, you may sometimes want to use a synonym for a table or view name. You can define the synonym and then use it in all statements where you would otherwise use the table or view name. The syntax is:

```
CREATE SYNONYM <synonym name>
FOR <table name>;
```

where:

-   □   <*synonym name*> is a name you want to use instead of the full table or view name. The synonym name must be unique within the current database.
-   □   <*table name*> is the full name of the table or view for which the synonym will be substituted.

For example, you might want to create a synonym "CP" for your Company Policies table. To do so, enter:

```
CREATE SYNONYM CP
FOR CompPol;
```

You can look at the synonym names already created in a database by displaying columns from the SYSSYNS catalog table.

The CREATE VIEW Command

CREATE VIEW is a Data Manipulation Statement rather than a Data Definition Statement because, to employ this command, you must use the SELECT command. Therefore, you will find details on creating views in Chapter 12.

The DROP Command

To eliminate database objects from the database, use the reserved word DROP before the object name. There are slightly different rules connected with the eliminating of each object. Only the creator of a database or the SQL Database Administrator (SQLDBA) can drop a database. The DROP DATABASE command can only be used in interactive SQL mode. To drop a database, the syntax is:

```
DROP DATABASE <database name>;
```

When you eliminate a database with the DROP DATABASE command, the system deletes all .DBF and .MDX files in the database directory and deletes the entry for that database in the catalog table SYSDBS. This command does not delete the directory or any files in the directory with extensions other than .DBF (and its associated memo files) or .MDX.

You cannot drop a database if you or any other user has opened it with the START DATABASE command and has not entered the STOP DATABASE command. Therefore, you must first close it with STOP DATABASE before dropping it.

Only the creator of an index and the SQLDBA can drop an index. To do so, the syntax is:

```
DROP INDEX <index name>;
```

The DROP INDEX command can be executed both in interactive and embedded SQL mode. An index gets dropped automatically when the table on which it is defined is dropped.

The DROP SYNONYM command drops a synonym name defined for a table or view. You can execute this command either in interactive or embedded SQL. To drop a synonym, the syntax is:

```
DROP SYNONYM <synonym name>;
```

A synonym is dropped automatically when the table on which it is defined is dropped.

You can use the DROP TABLE command to eliminate a table from the database in either interactive or embedded SQL mode. Only the creator of a table and the SQLDBA can drop a table. The syntax is:

```
DROP TABLE <table name>;
```

When you execute the DROP TABLE command, the corresponding *dBASE* database file is deleted and all references to the table are removed from the system catalog table. All indices, views, and synonyms based on that table are also dropped.

Once a table is dropped, there is no way you can restore it. To put it back into the database, you must CREATE it again and reINSERT the information into it.

You can eliminate a view by using the DROP VIEW command either interactively or in embedded SQL. Only the creator of a view and the SQLDBA can drop a view. The syntax is:

```
DROP VIEW <view name>;
```

The DROP VIEW command only drops the view definition and the synonyms and views defined on it. The underlying base table is not dropped by the DROP VIEW command. However, if the underlying base table is dropped, any views based on that table are also dropped.

Summary

The use of SQL within *dBASE IV* is introduced, and the use of the SQL Data Definition Statements (DDS) is explained. The syntax for the following DDS commands is shown and their use is illustrated:

CREATE DATABASE

START, STOP and SHOW DATABASE

CREATE and ALTER TABLE

CREATE INDEX

CREATE SYNONYM

CREATE VIEW

DROP commands for database objects.

11

SQL: Inserting, Loading Data, and Querying

When you have set up your database and tables, you will want to INSERT data and query them. The SQL INSERT command for adding records, the LOAD DATA command, the SQL query command SELECT, and the INSERTing by SELECTing from another table are described.

The INSERT Command

The SQL INSERT command is used to put individual rows of data into your tables. The format for INSERT is:

```
INSERT INTO <tablename>
    [(column list)]
    VALUES (<value list>);
```

where:

☐ *<tablename>* names the table into which values are to be inserted.

☐ *<column list>* names the columns, separated from each other by a comma, into which the new values will be inserted.

☐ (*<value list>* is a list of the values, separated by commas and with each character value enclosed in single or double quotes, that are to be inserted into the columns.

To insert more than one row at a time, see the final section in this chapter.

Loading and Unloading Data

Another way to add data to your tables is to use the LOAD DATA FROM command, which is a *dBASE* SQL command that enables you to LOAD DATA FROM foreign files, such as *Lotus 1-2-3* spreadsheet files and *dBASE II* files. The format for the LOAD DATA FROM command is:

```
LOAD DATA FROM [path] <filename>
INTO TABLE <table name>
[TYPE SDF DIF WKS FW2 RPD DBASEII SYLK DELIMITED
[WITH BLANK/WITH <expC>]];
```

where:

☐ *<path>* is the directory path to the file to be loaded. For example, if the file is in the MM subdirectory of the Microsft directory, then the path is \ Microsft \ MM.

☐ *<file name>* is the name of the file you're LOADing from. Thus, if the file is foo in the MM subdirectory of the Microsft directory, the command starts LOAD DATA FROM \ Microsft \ MM \ foo.

☐ [TYPE] is optional, but if it is omitted, it is assumed that the file is a .DBF file. The TYPEs allowed and their meanings are:

SDF: System Data Format.

DIF: DIF spreadsheet format.

WKS: *Lotus 1-2-3* spreadsheet file.

SYLK: Microsoft *Multiplan* spreadsheet file.

FW2:   *Framework 2* file.

RPD: *Rapidfile* database files.

DBASEII: *dBASE II* file.

DELIMITED: Delimited foreign files have variable-length records with the fields separated by a specified character such as a comma, called a *delimiter*. Records are separated by carriage return line feeds.

☐ WITH BLANK are reserved words if the TYPE is DELIMITED with blank.

☐ WITH <*expC*> is required if the TYPE is DELIMITED with other than blank.

dBASE IV also has an UNLOAD DATA command whose purpose is inverse to the LOAD DATA command, namely, to export data to a foreign file. The syntax for the UNLOAD DATA command is almost exactly like the syntax for the LOAD DATA command:

```
UNLOAD DATA TO [path] <filename>
FROM TABLE <table name>
[TYPE SDF DIF WKS FW2 RPD DBASEII SYLK DELIMITED
[WITH BLANK/WITH <expC>]];
```

where <*path*> is the directory path to the export file, <*filename*> is the name of the file to which you're exporting, and [TYPE] is the same as it is for LOAD DATA.

The SELECT Command

In *dBASE IV* SQL, the command you use to perform a query is SELECT. With the SELECT command you designate the information you want out of your tables to give you a "result table.'' The outcome of a SQL query is always a relational table, although it usually won't be exactly the same as one of the tables in your database. The format for SELECT is:

```
SELECT [ALL/DISTINCT] <target list>
[INTO <memvar list>]
FROM <table list [<aliases>]>
[WHERE <conditions>]
[GROUP BY <column list> [HAVING <conditions>]]
[UNION <second SELECT>]
[ORDER BY <column list>/FOR UPDATE OF <column list>]
[SAVE TO TEMP <table> [KEEP]];
```

where:

- ☐ <target list> is a list of table columns and expressions that contain the data you want.

- ☐ [ALL/DISTINCT] are optional reserved words. If you use ALL (which is the default), you will get all the rows satisfying the WHERE clause (see WHERE below). DISTINCT will give you only nonduplicate rows in the result table.

- ☐ [INTO <memvar list>] gives a list of memory variables INTO which the column values are to be selected. The optional INTO can only be used in embedded SQL (see Chapter 13), and then only if the result table contains exactly one row. There must be exactly one memory variable in the <memvar list> for each column in the target list. After successful completion of the query, the memory variables will contain the result of the query.

- ☐ FROM <table list [<aliases>]> lists the tables and/or views from which the columns are to be selected. The optional <aliases> are necessary for some queries and useful for others. For more about views, see Chapter 12.

- ☐ [WHERE <conditions>] gives a list of conditions that must be satisfied by the rows selected out of the tables. The WHERE clause is treated in more detail later in this chapter.

□ [GROUP BY <*column list*> [HAVING <*conditions*>]] is treated in the section entitled "GROUP BY Clause in a SELECT Command."

□ [UNION <*second SELECT*>] is used to combine the rows of two result tables.

□ [ORDER BY <*column list*>] allows you to order the rows of your result table. If your SELECT statement contains ORDER BY, it cannot contain [FOR UPDATE OF].

□ [FOR UPDATE OF <*column list*>] is for use with cursors in embedded SQL (see Chapter 13).

□ [SAVE TO TEMP <*table*> [KEEP]] can be used to save the result table in a temporary table.

Simple SELECTs

The simplest SELECTs are those that pick all the rows and columns from one or more tables. For example, if you want all the rows and columns from a table named Sales, the following SELECT statement will return the Sales Table:

```
SELECT *
FROM Sales;
```

The asterisk (*) after the SELECT here stands for "all the columns." If you want to eliminate any duplicate rows, the SELECT statement is:

```
SELECT DISTINCT *
FROM Sales;
```

To SELECT only the item and price columns from the Sales table, the SELECT statement is:

```
SELECT item, price
FROM Sales;
```

If you want to select all columns from the Sales table and the Salesmen table, the SELECT statement is:

```
SELECT *
FROM Sales, Salesmen;
```

The result table of this SELECT statement will have every row of the Salesmen table concatenated with every row of the Sales table. Thus, the number of rows in the result table will be the number of rows in the Sales table times the number of rows in the Salesmen table.

Since you usually won't want every row of one table concatenated with every row of another table, you will want to use a WHERE clause.

Aliases in the FROM Clause. An alias is another name for a table that you set up in the FROM clause to identify that table or that copy of the table throughout the rest of the SELECT command. You create an alias by leaving a space after the name of the table and then writing the alias in the FROM clause. For example:

```
SELECT name
FROM Salesmen sm
```

where Salesmen is the name of the table and "sm" is the alias to be used for Salesmen in the rest of the query, wherever needed.

As you will see in the section on correlated subqueries and aliases that follows, aliases are sometimes necessary when you have a subquery on the same table as the main query, and the main query is going to be implemented by examining one copy of the table and the subquery is examining another copy of the table. In that situation, the aliases identify the copy of the table being examined. For example, you might have a query and subquery similar to the following:

```
SELECT <target list one>
FROM Salesmen sm1
WHERE . .
            (SELECT <target list two>
            FROM Salesmen sm2
            WHERE sm1.column_name = sm2.column_name);
```

In such a situation, the "sm1" prefixed to the column name identifies the row being examined in the main SELECT and "sm2" prefixed to the column name identifies rows being examined in the subquery.

The WHERE Clause

While the target list allows you to pick out the columns you want from the tables in the FROM clause, the WHERE clause allows you to pick the rows you want. It also enables you to decide which rows should be concatenated with other rows in the case of a SELECT from more than one table. For example, if item is a column in the Sales Table containing the name of the item sold, and you only want those rows WHERE the item is "DESK," then you would use the following SELECT statement:

```
SELECT *
FROM Sales
WHERE item = "DESK";
```

If you want to know which salesman sold the desks, and both the Sales Table and the Salesmen Table have a column "s_id" (salesman ID no.), and the name of the salesman is in a column labeled "name" in the Salesmen Table, then you would use the following SELECT statement:

```
SELECT name, item
FROM Salesmen, Sales
WHERE item = "DESK" AND Salesmen.s_id = Sales.s_id;
```

You can always precede the column name with its table name and a period. In the above WHERE clause, you must use the names of the tables in front of the "s_id" columns in order to make it clear that you want to match the rows from the two tables.

Logical Operators in the WHERE Clause. The AND in the WHERE clause allows you to simultaneously impose two conditions on the result table. You can use any number of ANDs, ORs, and NOTs in a WHERE clause. To determine the order in which the ANDs, ORs, and NOTs are evaluated, you can use parentheses. For example:

```
WHERE NOT(item = "DESK" AND Salesmen.s_id = Sales.s_id);
```

will give a different result table than:

WHERE NOT item = "DESK" AND Salesmen.s_id = Sales.s_id;

which is the same as:

WHERE (NOT (item = "DESK")) AND Salesmen.s_id = Sales.s_id;

because NOT has "higher precedence" than AND.

An operator is said to "have higher precedence" than another operator of the same type if it is applied first in an expression without parentheses. AND has higher precedence than OR. If a sequence of ANDs or a sequence of ORs occurs, then precedence is left to right. For example:

item = "DESK" AND no_sold = 50 AND customer = "Rogers"

gives the same result as:

((item = "DESK" AND no_sold = 50) AND customer = "Rogers")

while

item = "DESK" OR no_sold = 50 AND customer = "Rogers"

gives the same result as:

item = "DESK" OR (no_sold = 50 AND customer = "Rogers"),

and

item = "DESK" OR NOT no_sold = 50 AND customer = "Rogers"

gives the same result as:

item = "DESK" OR ((NOT no_sold = 50) AND customer = "Rogers").

It is always safest to supply your own parentheses in a complicated WHERE clause.

Comparison Operators in the WHERE Clause. The equal (=) sign in the preceding examples is a comparison operator. It is not the only comparison operator you can use. The list of all legal comparison operators in *dBASE IV* is in Table 11-1.

Table 11-1. Comparison Operators.

Symbol	Meaning
>	Greater than
<	Less than
=	Equals
> =	Greater than or equal to
< =	Less than or equal to
< >	Not equal to
! =	Does not equal
!>	Not greater than
!<	Not less than
BETWEEN . . . AND . . .	Specifies a range

For example, if you have a numeric column salary in the Salesmen Table, and you want to find all those salesmen with a salary greater than or equal to $20,000, you can use either of the following WHERE clauses in a SELECT <*target list*> FROM Salesmen command:

```
WHERE salary !< 20000;
```

or

```
WHERE salary > = 20000;
```

You can use BETWEEN . . . AND to specify a range. For example, if you want the names of Salesmen with salaries between $20,000 and $25,000, you can use the following SELECT command:

```
SELECT name
FROM Salesmen
WHERE salary BETWEEN 20000 AND 25000;
```

Arithmetic Operators and Expressions in the WHERE Clause.
The arithmetic operators addition (+), subtraction (–), division
(/), multiplication (*), and exponentiation (** or ^) can be used
to form expressions to be used in the WHERE clause. Expressions
are formed by using one or more column names combined by
arithmetic operators with constants and memory variables. For
example, if ''salary'' and ''COMMISSION'' are both column
names, and ''m_tax'' is a memory variable, then the following
are all expressions:

```
salary * 12
salary – m_tax
"Chicago"
salary * commissn
```

Like the logical operators, the arithmetic operators have an
order of precedence (see Table 11-2). It is best to use parentheses
to make sure that the operations are performed in the order that
you want.

For example, A + B * C ** 2 is computed by squaring C,
multiplying the result times B and adding that to A. If you want
A plus B times C, you must write (A + B) * C, using parentheses
to change the order of precedence. To see that A + B * C yields
a different result from (A + B) * C, assign 2 to A, 3 to B, and 4

Table 11-2. Order of Precedence of Arithmetic Operators.

Highest

Unary + , Unary –
Exponent (** or ^)
Multiply (*), Divide (/)
Add(+), Subtract (–)
Left to Right.

Lowest

to C. With these values A + B * C yields 14 while (A + B) * C yields 20.

Using IN in the WHERE Clause. The reserved word IN can be used in the WHERE clause to select those rows WHERE the value of a certain column is IN a certain set of values. For example, suppose you want the rows where ''salary'' is in the set {20,000, 24,000, 28,000}, then you can use the following WHERE clause:

WHERE salary IN (20000, 24000, 28000)

Using LIKE in the WHERE Clause. LIKE is used in comparisons of character strings with other character strings involving wild cards. Two wild cards, percent (%) and underscore (__), are allowed in SQL. If you are familiar with the use of the wild cards ? and * in DOS or *dBASE,* you should not have much trouble with this concept since percent (%) plays the same role in SQL that asterisk (*) plays in DOS, and underscore (__) plays the same role that question mark (?) plays in DOS and *dBASE.*

To be explicit, % stands for any character string of zero or more characters and __ stands for one unknown character. The wild cards are placed in a character string to create a character string known as a *skeleton.* If the character string to the left of LIKE can be obtained from the skeleton on the right of LIKE by substituting of multiple characters for % and single characters for underscore (__), then the comparison is satisfied; otherwise it fails. For example:

WHERE city LIKE Ch%ag__

will pick out rows having ''city'' equal to Chicago because Chicago can be obtained from Ch%ag__ by substituting ''ic'' for the % and substituting ''o'' for the underscore. It will also pick out rows with city equal to ''Chago,'' ''Chage,'' ''Chimestrago,'' and so forth. But the following:

WHERE city LIKE Ch__ag__

would not pick out rows having ''city'' equal to Chicago because the underscore allows and requires substitution of only one character.

Subqueries in the WHERE Clause. A subquery is a SELECT statement (enclosed in parentheses) that appears in the WHERE clause. A subquery can appear to the right of any comparison operator. The reserved words ANY, ALL, IN, and EXISTS can be used immediately to the left of a subquery. If one of the reserved words—ANY, ALL, IN, and EXISTS—does not occur immediately to the left of the subquery, then the subquery must return exactly one value (datum), or an error condition will occur since a comparison operator expects exactly one value for its comparison. For example, the query:

```
SELECT name
FROM Salesmen
WHERE s_id =    (SELECT s_id
                FROM Sales
                WHERE item = "DESK");
```

will succeed only if there is exactly one salesman who has sold a DESK and will result in an error condition otherwise.

If you want the names of all salesmen who sold DESKs, then you would use the reserved word IN to the left of the subquery as in the following example:

```
SELECT name
FROM Salesmen
TSWHERE s_id IN  (SELECT s_id
                FROM Sales
                WHERE item = "DESK");
```

This query will not result in an error condition even if no salesmen sold desks.

The following query will have the same result table as the previous query:

```
SELECT name
FROM Salesmen
WHERE s_id =    ANY (SELECT s_id
                FROM Sales
                WHERE item = "DESK");
```

Equals ANY, here, means equals any "s_id" in the result

table of the subquery. ANY, ALL, and IN have the same meaning that they have in everyday language. For example, the WHERE clause in the preceding query can be read, WHERE s__id = ANY datum in the result table of the subquery SELECT s__id FROM Sales WHERE ITEM = "desk".

EXISTS with a Subquery. EXISTS preceding a subquery is satisfied if the subquery returns at least one row and is not satisfied otherwise. The rows selected by the main query will be those where EXISTS is satisfied. For example,

```
SELECT name
FROM Salesmen
WHERE EXISTS      (SELECT s__id
                  FROM Sales
                  WHERE Salesmen.s__id = Sales.s__id);
```

will return the names of those salesmen who have at least one row in the Sales table—in other words, those salesmen who have sold something.

You can use NOT in front of EXISTS. For example,

```
SELECT name
FROM Salesmen
WHERE NOT EXISTS   (SELECT s__id
                   FROM Sales
                   WHERE Salesmen.s__id = Sales.s __id);
```

will return the names of those salesmen who have not sold anything.

Correlated Subqueries and Aliases. A subquery is said to be a "correlated" subquery when it is reevaluated for every row examined in the main query. If the main query and the subquery are on the same table, then aliases are frequently required to distinguish the row being examined in the main query from the rows being examined in the subquery.

For example, suppose the Salesmen Table has a column designated "name" for the name of the salesman, a column designated "city" for the city the salesman lives in, and a logical data type column "million," which contains the logical value .T. if the salesman has sold over a million dollars worth of merchandise, and .F. otherwise. Then, if you wish to find all those salesmen who live in the same city with a salesman who has sold over a million dollars worth of merchandise, the following query will return what you want:

```
SELECT name
FROM Salesmen sm1
WHERE EXISTS    (SELECT name
                FROM Salesmen sm2
                WHERE sm1.city = sm2.city
                AND sm2.million = .T.);
```

For example, if you have the simple instance of the Salesmen Table shown in Table 11-3, the above query will return Jones and Rogers but not Smith.

	name	city	million
Table 11-3. Salesmen.	Jones	Chicago	.T.
	Smith	Denver	.F.
	Rogers	Chicago	.F.

If you want the names of those salesmen who have not sold a million dollars worth of merchandise but who live in the same city with a salesman who has, then you would modify the above query as follows:

```
SELECT name
FROM Salesmen sm1
WHERE million = .F. AND EXISTS (SELECT name
                               FROM Salesmen sm2
                               WHERE sm1.city = sm2.city
                               AND sm2.million = .T.);
```

This query would return only Rogers from Table 11-3.

The GROUP BY Clause in a SELECT Command

The GROUP BY clause puts the rows together that have the same values in the columns listed after the GROUP BY. Every column named in the target list following the SELECT must occur in the column list following the GROUP BY unless it is an argument of an aggregate function.

Aggregate Functions. There are five SQL aggregate functions that can be used in the SQL SELECT and HAVING clauses. They are AVG, COUNT, MAX, MIN, and SUM. They are used to obtain summary values over groups of rows. The four aggregate functions—AVG, MAX, MIN, and SUM—have the same format:

FCT ([ALL/DISTINCT] <*column name*>/[ALL] <*expression*>)

where:

- [ ] FCT is to be replaced by one of the required reserved words AVG, MAX, MIN, or SUM.

- [ ] ALL is optional and is the default value and means that the function is to be evaluated over ALL the rows in each group whether or not they are duplicates.

- [ ] DISTINCT is optional and means that the function is to be evaluated only over DISTINCT rows in the group eliminating duplicates.

- [ ] <*column name*> is the name of a column whose values are to be averaged or summed or whose maximum or minimum value is to be found. The column named cannot be of the LOGICAL data type.

- [ ] <*expression*> is an expression that must include a column name and cannot include another aggregate function. For example, SUM(MAX(Salary)) is illegal.

For AVG and SUM, the data type of the column named in <*column name*> must be SMALLINT, INTEGER, DECIMAL, NUMERIC, or FLOAT. For MAX and MIN, the data type can also be CHAR, and the evaluation will be according to the ASCII value. For example, the MAX of "a" and "Z" is "a"; and the MAX of "aa" and "ab" is "ab."

The format for the COUNT function is slightly different:

COUNT ([DISTINCT] <*column name*> / *)

where:

- □ COUNT is a required reserved word.
- □ DISTINCT is optional, meaning COUNT only those rows in the group that have distinct values in the named column.
- □ <*column name*> is the name of the column for which DISTINCT values in the group are to be counted. The column named cannot be of LOGICAL data type.
- □ The asterisk means count all rows in the group satisfying the search conditions in the WHERE clause.

If a GROUP BY clause is not included in a SELECT statement, then there is only one group for the aggregate functions, and it is the set of all rows that satisfy the conditions in the WHERE clause.

For example, if you have a table, Emp, whose columns are "emp_name" (for employee name), "city" (for the city where the employee lives), and "salary" (for the employee's salary), and you want to know the average salary of the employees in each of the cities, you would use the following query:

```
SELECT city, AVG(salary)
FROM Emp
GROUP BY city;
```

If you want to know how many different cities your employees live in, the following query would give you the answer:

```
SELECT COUNT(DISTINCT city)
FROM Emp;
```

If you just want to know how many rows there are in the Emp table, you would use the following query:

```
SELECT COUNT(*)
FROM Emp;
```

The HAVING Clause. The optional HAVING <*clause*> is used just like the WHERE clause except that the properties tested by HAVING must be properties of entire groups. If there is no GROUP BY, the group is taken to be the entire table. Thus, only columns grouped by or aggregate functions can be used in the HAVING clause. For example, if you wanted the average salary for employees who live in Chicago, you could use the following query to get your answer:

```
SELECT city, AVG(salary)
FROM Emp
GROUP BY city HAVING city LIKE "Ch%";
```

But the GROUP BY clause cannot be used if:

☐ The SELECT statement contains an INTO clause.

☐ A VIEW column occurs in the target list where the VIEW definition has a GROUP BY clause in it.

☐ A GROUP BY occurs in a subquery.

A general rule that covers the last two points is that a GROUP BY can occur only once in any complete SELECT statement (i.e., including main query and all subqueries).

The UNION Operation

The reserved word UNION combines the result tables of two or more SELECTs into a single result table. It eliminates duplicate rows. The target lists must have exactly the same number of columns and the same data types and length in each column. For example, suppose you have two tables, Emp (for employees) and Contract (for contractors), and both tables have columns "name," "salary," and "address," with the same data type and length for each column in the two tables, then the following SELECT would produce a result table combining the two:

```
SELECT name, address, salary
FROM Emp
UNION
SELECT name, address, salary
FROM Contract;
```

The following query, however, would result in an error message because the name has character data type, which does not match the numeric data type salary, and the salary numeric data type does not match the character data type address:

```
SELECT name, address, salary
FROM Emp
UNION
SELECT salary, name, address
FROM Contract;
```

The ORDER BY Clause

The ORDER BY clause allows you to order the result table by the values in one or more columns. In effect, it produces a result table sorted on the chosen columns. The order may be ASCending or DESCending, with ascending being the default. If you want descending order, you must insert DESC after the name of the column you want to ORDER BY. For example, if you want employee's names and salaries from the employee table, Emp, ordered in descending order on "salary" first, and ascending order on "name" second, the query would be:

```
SELECT name, salary
FROM Emp
ORDER BY salary DESC, name;
```

The members of the target list may be replaced by the number of the position they occupy in the target list. Thus, the following query will give you the same result table as the preceding query:

```
SELECT name, salary
FROM Emp
ORDER BY 2 DESC, 1;
```

Except for the SAVE TO TEMP clause, the ORDER BY clause must always be the last clause in a SELECT statement.

The SAVE TO TEMP Clause

Use the SAVE TO TEMP clause to save your result table in a temporary table, which you can use during a session in SQL mode. The temporary table will disappear when you leave SQL mode unless you use the optional reserved word KEEP. The full format for SAVE TO TEMP is:

SAVE TO TEMP <*table name*> [<*column list*>] [KEEP]

where:

- □ <*table name*> is the name you wish to give the temporary table.
- □ [<*column list*>] is an optional list of column names for the temporary table.
- □ [KEEP] keeps the table beyond the current SQL session. If you wish to use the resulting table as a SQL table in your SQL database, you will need to use the DBDEFINE <*table name*> command to update your catalog tables to contain data about the new table. (DBDEFINE is discussed in Chapter 9.)

Another way to save a result table is to CREATE a new table and then INSERT your data into it.

Inserting Data Selected from a Different Table

Once you have learned how to use the SQL SELECT command, you can use it in conjunction with the SQL INSERT command to move data from one table to another. The format for this is:

INSERT INTO <*tablename*>
[<*column list*>]
<*select statement*>;

where:

☐ *<tablename>* names the table into which values are to be inserted.

☐ *<column list>* names the columns, separated from each other by a comma, into which the new values will be inserted.

☐ *<SELECT statement>* is a SELECT statement that will select rows to be inserted into the table named after the INSERT INTO command. The data types of the target list of the SELECT statement must match the data types of the optional column list if it is included. If the column list is not included, the data types of the target list of the SELECT statement must match the data types of the columns in the table.

Summary

In this chapter, means for getting data into the database and then getting it out are discussed: the LOAD, UNLOAD, and INSERT commands.

The SQL SELECT command for formulating queries, including subqueries, is discussed in detail as are aggregate functions for obtaining minimum, maximum, and average values as well as counts.

12

SQL: Views, Deleting, Updating, and Joins

SQL VIEWS are a useful tool for setting up tables for special uses. For example, you may have temporary personnel who UPDATE the addresses and phone numbers in your Employee Table. These personnel need to see only the name, address, and phone number columns, not salary or ratings columns, to be able to update the database. A view of the Employee table can be set up that will contain only selected columns.

SQL has the commands UPDATE and DELETE for updating and deleting the rows of tables; both are discussed in this chapter. Transaction processing, which helps you to keep your database in a consistent state, is also discussed.

If you perform a SELECT command, which depends on the relationship between columns in two or more different tables or two or more columns in the same table, the result table is a *join*. Joins have been classified in relational database terminology by type. You will find that an understanding of these types is useful in conceptualizing queries to obtain information from your database.

Views

A view is like a table in that it has rows and columns; it can be selected from; and it can, in special cases, even be updated. However, a view is not stored on disk like a table. Only its definition is stored in the catalog tables. Every time it is referenced by a SQL command, a view is recomputed from its definition, which is a SQL SELECT statement. Thus, what you get when you query a view is completely dependent on the tables and views in the FROM clause of the SELECT statement defining that view.

The format of the CREATE VIEW command is:

```
CREATE VIEW <VIEW name>
[(<column name>, . . . <column name>)]
AS <SELECT statement>
[WITH CHECK OPTION];
```

where:

- □ <VIEW name> must begin with a letter, consist of letters, numbers, and underscores, and be less than nine letters long.

- □ <column name> is an optional column name to be given to a column of the view. If the column names are not included, the names of the columns of the view will be the names in the target list of the defining SELECT statement. Thus, if the target list contains duplicate column names or derived expressions, such as constants, function values, or computed values, you must provide the column names.

- □ <SELECT statement> is any SELECT statement except that (1) it must not contain a UNION clause, (2) it must not contain an ORDER BY clause, and (3) it must not contain a SAVE TO TEMP clause.

- □ WITH CHECK OPTION is an optional clause that causes all updates and inserts to the view to be checked to see that they agree with the view definition.

We will refer to the SELECT statement in the definition of

a VIEW as the "defining SELECT." In *dBASE IV* you cannot UPDATE, INSERT into, or DELETE from a VIEW whose defining SELECT contains more than one table or view.

You cannot use a view whose defining SELECT statement contains a GROUP BY clause in a SELECT statement whose target list contains columns from another table or view. If the target list of the defining SELECT statement of a view contains column names from a table or view that is subsequently dropped, then the view will be dropped.

Views are useful in situations where it is desirable to use only certain columns and rows of tables or combinations of tables. For example, if you do not want your users to be able to look at all the columns of the Employee table (such as salary), but need to give them access to certain other columns, you can create a view (say Pub__emp), which does not include the columns you would prefer to keep private. Then you can GRANT access to Pub__emp instead of the Employee table. For this purpose, the CREATE VIEW command is:

```
CREATE VIEW Pub__emp
AS SELECT name, address, phone
FROM Employee;
```

If you want certain personnel to maintain the information for salesmen only, then you can create a view of salesmen from the Employee table, like the following:

```
CREATE VIEW Salesmn
AS SELECT * FROM Employee
WHERE job__titl = "salesman"
WITH CHECK OPTION;
```

The WITH CHECK OPTION clause can be included to ensure that all of the updates and inserts made to the Salesmn view satisfy the view definition.

You can create a synonym for a view or drop a view just as you can a table. The format for creating a synonym for a view is exactly the same as it is for creating a synonym for a table. The format for dropping a view is:

```
DROP VIEW <view name>;
```

For example, if you wanted to drop the view Salesmn created in the example above, you would type:

```
DROP VIEW Salesmn;
```

Deleting

The format for the DELETE statement is:

```
DELETE FROM <table name> [<alias>]
[WHERE <conditions>];
```

where:

☐ *<table name>* is the name of a table or view from which you intend to delete rows. The table name can be replaced by a synonym. (See CREATE SYNONYM in Chapter 10.)

☐ *[<alias>]* is an optional alias name for the table. (See Chapter 11.)

☐ [WHERE *<conditions>*] is a clause determining the rows to be deleted. (For details on WHERE clauses, see Chapter 11.) **Warning:** If the optional WHERE clause is not included, all of the rows will be deleted from the table. If you start a DELETE statement without a WHERE clause, a warning message will appear on the screen allowing you to abort the DELETE statement by pressing Esc. If the WHERE clause contains a subquery, then the FROM clause in the subquery must not reference the table or view from which the rows are being deleted.

Here are two examples:

```
DELETE FROM Salesmen
WHERE name = "Jones";

DELETE FROM Salesmen
WHERE s_id IN      (SELECT s_id
                    FROM Sales
                    WHERE item = "DESK";
```

Deletes performed during transactions are only *logically* deleted. In order to actually remove logically deleted records, you must use the *dBASE* PACK command.

Updating

The format of the UPDATE command is:

```
UPDATE <table>
SET <column name1> = <value1>
  [,<column name2> = <value2> . . .
  ,<column nameN> = <valueN>]
[WHERE <conditions>];
```

where:

- ☐ *<table>* is the name or synonym for the table or view to be updated.
- ☐ *<column name1>* is the name of a column to be updated.
- ☐ *<value1>* is the value to replace the old value in *column name1*.
- ☐ [WHERE *<conditions>*] is a clause determining the rows to be updated. (For details on WHERE clauses, see Chapter 11.) If the WHERE clause is omitted, every row in the table or view will be updated.

For example:

```
UPDATE Salesmen
SET Salary = Salary * 1.1
WHERE name = "Jones";

UPDATE Salesmen
SET Salary = Salary + 1000
WHERE s_id IN      (SELECT s_id
                    FROM Sales
                    GROUP BY s_id HAVING SUM(Sale_amt)
                    > 50000;
```

Transaction Processing

All SQL statements except CREATE, DROP, ALTER, GRANT, and REVOKE can be included in transactions. The effect is the same as including *dBASE* statements within transactions. In SQL as in *dBASE*, you start a transaction with the command BEGIN TRANSACTION and end it with the END TRANSACTION command. If something goes wrong before the END TRANSACTION command, inserts, updates, and deletes performed after the BEGIN TRANSACTION command can be removed with the ROLLBACK command.

Equijoins

Equijoins are the simplest type of join. The simplest equijoins are formed by choosing two columns, one from each of two tables, where values in the two chosen columns are equal, and concatenating rows of one table with rows of the other table. Frequently there will be a column repeated in each of the two tables primarily for the purpose of performing joins. For example, suppose you have a table, Salesmen, containing a column called "s_id" for salesman's ID number, and another table, Sales, in which you have a column also containing the salesman's ID number to identify the salesman who sold the item in the Sales table. In Figs. 12-1 and 12-2, we give a possible, simple instance of Salesmen and Sales tables. The equijoin of these two tables on the "s_id" column is shown in Table 12-3.

The "s_id" column is repeated twice in the equijoin, Table 12-3. There is no row for Smith in the equijoin table because Smith does not have any matching row in the Sales table. Jones appears in two rows in the equijoin table because there are two matching rows for Jones in the Sales table.

Table 12-3 is a result table for the SELECT statement:

```
SELECT *
FROM Salesmen, Sales
WHERE Salesmen.s_id = Sales.s_id;
```

Table 12-1. Salesmen Table.

s_id	name	address	phone
100	Jones	10 Lake Ave	328 5407
103	Smith	105 Bellaire	540 1616
105	Elliot	1007 Colfax	890 2500

Table 12-2. Sales Table.

s_id	invoice	item	no_sold	price
100	2530	bicycle	5	395.95
105	2531	lawnmower	2	247.50
100	2532	television	4	499.98

Table 12-3. Equijoin of the Salesmen and Sales Tables.

s_id	name	address	phone	s_id	invoice	item	no_sold	price
100	Jones	10 Lake Ave	328 5407	100	2530	bicycle	5	395.95
100	Jones	10 Lake Ave	328 5407	100	2532	television	4	499.98
105	Elliot	1007 Colfax	890 2500	105	2531	lawnmower	2	247.50

Equijoins are always the outcome of SELECT * FROM . . . WHERE statements, which have equality conditions between columns in the WHERE clause. (Equijoins can also be defined in terms of such SELECT statements.)

The Cartesian Product of Two Tables

The cartesian product of two tables is a special case of an equijoin. It is defined as the table you get when you concatenate every row of the second table with every row of the first table. For example, the cartesian product of the Salesmen and the Sales tables is shown in Table 12-4.

Table 12-4. The Cartesian Product of the Salesmen and Sales Tables.

s_id	name	address	phone	s_id	invoice	item	no_sold	price
100	Jones	10 Lake Ave	328 5407	100	2530	bicycle	5	395.95
100	Jones	10 Lake Ave	328 5407	105	2531	lawnmower	2	247.50
100	Jones	10 Lake Ave	328 5407	100	2532	television	4	499.98
103	Smith	105 Bellaire	540 1616	100	2530	bicycle	5	395.95
103	Smith	105 Bellaire	540 1616	105	2531	lawnmower	2	247.50
103	Smith	105 Bellaire	540 1616	100	2532	television	4	499.98
105	Elliot	1007 Colfax	890 2500	100	2530	bicycle	5	395.95
105	Elliot	1007 Colfax	890 2500	105	2531	lawnmower	2	247.50
105	Elliot	1007 Colfax	890 2500	100	2532	television	4	499.98

Notice that the number of rows in the cartesian product of the Salesmen and the Sales tables is the product of the number of rows in the Salesmen table and the number of rows in the Sales table. This fact can be generalized to the cartesian product of any two tables (i.e., the number of rows in the cartesian product of two tables is the product of the number of rows in each of the tables). Thus, if you have one table with 10 rows and another table with 9 rows, the cartesian product will be a table with 90 rows. Clearly, the cartesian product of two tables is never a useful table since it doesn't contain any more information than the two tables alone do. However, it is useful to know about the cartesian product because the equijoin is a subset of the rows of the cartesian product, and *dBASE IV* forms the equijoin from the cartesian product.

The Natural Join

The natural join is obtained from the equijoin by eliminating duplicate columns. For example, the natural join of the Salesmen and the Sales tables is obtained from the equijoin by eliminating the second occurrence of the "s_id" column in Table 12-3. Table 12-5 shows this natural join.

To obtain the natural join by means of a SQL SELECT statement, you must name the columns in the target list rather than just using an asterisk (*). For example, the SELECT statement to obtain the natural join of the Salesmen and the Sales Tables is:

```
SELECT
Salesmen.s_id,name,address,phone,invoice,item,no_sold,price
FROM Salesmen,Sales
WHERE Salesmen.s_id = Sales.s_id;
```

The natural join is more efficient than the equijoin since it eliminates repeated columns.

Elimination of columns from a table is called *projection*. Table 12-5 can be called "the projection of Table 12-3 on Salesmen.s_id, name, address, phone, invoice, item, no_sold, and price."

The natural join is more general than the example above. If you have several tables with columns in common, you can obtain the natural join by performing an equijoin on the common columns followed by a projection eliminating duplicate columns.

In a SELECT statement, you can construct an equijoin by setting columns equal in the WHERE clause. Then you project the equijoin on the columns in the target list following the SELECT. For example, given the three tables I, II, and III in Fig. 12-1, the natural join is table IV. The SELECT statement to obtain the natural join table (IV) is:

```
SELECT I.A,I.B,C,II.D,E,F
FROM I,II,III
WHERE I.A = II.A AND I.B = III.B AND II.D = III.D;
```

Table 12-5. Natural Join of the Salesmen and Sales Tables.

s_id	name	address	phone	invoice	item	no_sold	price
100	Jones	10 Lake Ave	328 5407	2530	bicycle	5	395.95
100	Jones	10 Lake Ave	328 5407	2532	television	4	499.98
105	Elliot	1007 Colfax	890 2500	2531	lawnmower	2	247.50

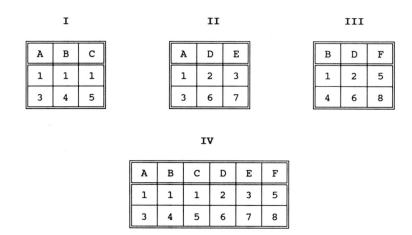

Fig. 12-1. Table IV represents the natural join of tables I, II, and III.

Theta Joins

The term *theta join* is used in the relational database literature to mean joins based on any comparison operator. (See Table 11-1.) Equijoins are just one type of theta join. For example, suppose you have Tables A and B, both having a column named "sex," with column entries either "male" or "female." You want to pair rows that do not have the same sex in the "sex" column. The SELECT statement to obtain the resulting theta join would be:

```
SELECT *
FROM A,B
WHERE A.sex ! = B.sex;
```

Self Joins

Self joins are joins between a table and itself. For example, if you run a dating service and you have a table named Clients with a column named "sex," then you might want a table in which each client is matched with every client of the opposite sex. You could use the following SELECT statement:

```
SELECT *
FROM Clients C1,Clients C2
WHERE C1.sex ! = C2.sex;
```

The C1 and C2 identifiers in the above SELECT statement are aliases (See Chapter 11 for an explanation of aliases) that provide a way of obtaining two copies of the Clients Table. In effect, the FROM Clients C1,Clients C2 provides two copies of the Clients table, one labeled C1 and the other labeled C2.

The above SELECT statement is not very efficient since it would produce a result table in which every client would appear twice, matched with every client of the opposite sex, once at the beginning of the row and once at the end of the row. To eliminate that redundancy, you might want to add the condition C1.sex = "MALE" to the WHERE clause. If you also want to equijoin on age, you would use the following SELECT:

```
SELECT *
FROM Clients C1,Clients C2
WHERE C1.sex = "MALE"
        AND C1.sex ! = C2.sex
        AND C1.age = C2.age;
```

The above SELECT statement will give you a result table where the record of each female client is concatenated with that of a male client of matching age.

Summary

In this chapter the SQL data manipulation commands not discussed in Chapter 11 are examined. These include UPDATE and DELETE. In addition, views and joins are discussed. Views can be used to aid in maintaining database security, while joins aid the user in formulating queries to the database.

13

Embedded SQL

Chapter 8 described how to write programs in *dBASE IV*. This chapter explains how to use SQL in your *dBASE IV* programs. When SQL statements are part of a program, they are said to be "embedded." "Embedded SQL" includes the SQL commands that are specifically for the purpose of using SQL in programs.

When SQL statements are part of your code, the files containing the code must have .PRS file extensions. *dBASE IV* automatically switches to SQL mode when it reads the .PRS file extension; it stays in that mode until returning from the embedded SQL file.

Embedded SQL statements are terminated by a semicolon; *dBASE* commands are not. As noted for *dBASE* commands, the semicolon means that the command is continued on the next line. Since your embedded SQL programs will contain both SQL statements and *dBASE* commands, you must carefully avoid using the semicolon in the wrong place.

In embedded SQL, data definition commands can be used to CREATE your data objects, such as tables and views. You can also use SQL data manipulation commands, such as SELECT, INSERT, UPDATE, and DELETE, to work with the data in these objects.

You can even create result tables and work with the data in the result tables, row by row.

The device for working with result tables is called a *cursor*. This use of the word does not refer to the cursor on your screen. Here, a cursor is like a file for holding a database table. Once a cursor has been declared and opened, it contains a result table determined by a SQL SELECT statement that we call "the defining SELECT." A pointer, called the *cursor pointer*, points at the rows of the result table. By means of an embedded SQL command, FETCH, you can advance the cursor pointer sequentially row by row and transfer the data in the row pointed at by the cursor pointer to memory variables. Under certain conditions, to be explained in this chapter, you can update or delete the row pointed at by the cursor pointer. This will change the underlying table of the defining SELECT. You can have more than one cursor open at a time. The number of cursors open is limited only by the number of work areas available.

You can use the BEGIN TRANSACTION and END TRANSACTION commands with embedded SQL just as in *dBASE* mode.

The DECLARE CURSOR Command

The format for the DECLARE CURSOR command is:

```
DECLARE <cursor name> CURSOR
FOR <SELECT statement>
[FOR UPDATE OF <column list> / <ORDER BY clause>];
```

where:

- □ *<cursor name>* is any name you choose to give the cursor. It must be less than 11 characters long, begin with a letter, and consist of letters, numbers, and underscores.

- □ *<SELECT statement>* is any SELECT statement that defines a result table to be used in the CURSOR program. We will call this SELECT statement the "defining SELECT statement of the cursor."

☐ *<column list>* is a list of columns that can be updated.

☐ *<ORDER BY clause>* is used to order the rows of the CURSOR result table. You cannot use the ORDER BY clause if there is a FOR UPDATE OF clause in the defining SELECT.

A cursor remains declared from the time that the DECLARE CURSOR statement is executed until a SET SQL OFF statement is executed.

You cannot UPDATE the result table if the defining SELECT has any of the following:

☐ Aggregate functions.

☐ UNION, DISTINCT, GROUP BY, or HAVING clauses.

☐ Columns from more than one table or view in the target list.

☐ Columns from a view that is not updateable in the target list.

Opening and Closing a Cursor, SQLCNT

The OPEN CURSOR statement has the following format:

```
OPEN <Cursor name>
```

where:

☐ *<cursor name>* is the name of a cursor from a previously executed DECLARE CURSOR statement.

After a cursor is opened, the memory variable SQLCNT contains the number of rows in the result table. This can be very useful since it gives a value to be used in determining how many times to perform a loop containing a FETCH command, which will follow the OPEN command.

You can open a cursor repeatedly; but after you open it, it must be closed before you can open it again. The format for the CLOSE CURSOR command is:

```
CLOSE <cursor name>;
```

where <cursor name> is the same cursor name used in the OPEN CURSOR statement. You must have opened a cursor before you can close it.

When the OPEN command is successfully executed, a result table is created in a work area and the cursor pointer is associated with the result table. Initially the cursor pointer does not point at any row of the result table. When the FETCH statement is executed the first time, the cursor pointer is made to point at the first row of the result table. After that, the cursor pointer is advanced one row at a time by execution of the FETCH statement, which is discussed in the next section.

FETCH, SQLCODE, and SQLCNT

After FETCH advances the cursor pointer, FETCH transfers the values from the row pointed at into memory variables. If the FETCH advances the cursor pointer beyond the last row of the result table, the cursor is automatically closed, and no values are transferred. The format for FETCH is:

```
FETCH <cursor name>
INTO <variable list>;
```

where:

- ☐ <cursor name> is the name of the cursor being fetched.

- ☐ <variable list> is the list of memory variables into which the values in the row pointed at by the cursor pointer will be transferred.

SQLCODE is a memory variable provided for compatibility with the ANSI standard. It can be used to check the status of operations when running a program (using a .PRS file). SQLCODE has three possible values. Upon successful completion of a SQL command, SQLCODE is set to 0 (zero). If the SQL command results in an error, SQLCODE is set to − 1; and if the last operation didn't affect any rows, SQLCODE is set to + 100. If FETCH causes the cursor pointer to be advanced beyond the last row of the result table, SQLCODE is set to + 100. This can be useful for terminating a DO WHILE loop in a program file. For example, you might have a code like the following:

```
DO WHILE .T.
  FETCH <cursor name>
  INTO <variable list>;
  IF SQLCODE = 100
    EXIT
  ELSE
    * Lines of code
  ENDIF
ENDDO
```

Between two OPEN cursor commands, you must have a CLOSE cursor command. After the OPEN command is executed SQLCNT will contain the number of rows in the result table. You might prefer to use that value to control the number of times you perform a loop containing FETCH. If so, you would need to use a memory variable to count the number of times the FETCH loop is performed. If the memory variable is "m___count," then the code would be like the following:

```
OPEN <cursor name>;
STORE SQLCNT TO m__count
DO WHILE m__count > 0
  FETCH <cursor name>
  INTO <variable list>;
  * Lines of code
  STORE m__count − 1 TO m__count
ENDDO
```

Some Embedded SQL Examples

Posting Sales

The following example achieves the same goal as the posting sales example in Chapter 8. The difference is that the goal is achieved here by doing everything in embedded SQL. You might want to compare what was done in Chapter 8 with what is done here.

Suppose you have tables CREATEd as shown in Fig. 13-1. Now suppose further that you want to post the transactions that you have in the Trnsacts Table. You will need to FETCH the rows of the table, one row at a time, into memory variables, look up the salesman's ID and the price, and enter the result in the Sales table. Then you will reduce inventory accordingly; and finally, you will want to update the Trnsacts table to show that the row has been posted. If an error occurs while processing a row, before the Trnsacts table has been updated, you will want to roll back the changes that have been made until the cause of the error has been determined and you have dealt with it. The program to do this is shown in Fig. 13-2.

Fig. 13-1. Tables for the sales posting example.

```
CREATE TABLE Trnsacts
(type      CHAR(10),      * "SOLD", "RETURNED", "LOST", etc.
 item      CHAR(15),      * "DESK", "CHAIR", "TELEVISION", etc.
 model     CHAR(16),      * like "ZENITH1108YY3".
 invoice   CHAR(8),       * invoice identifier.
 no_units  SMALLINT,      * how many were sold, or returned, etc.
 date      DATE,          * The date of the sale.
 s_first   CHAR(15),      * salesperson's first name.
 s_last    CHAR(15),      * salesperson's last name.
 posted    LOGICAL);      * .T. if it's been posted .F. otherwise.

CREATE TABLE Salesper
(s_id      CHAR(4),       * salesperson's id number as CHAR.
 s_first   CHAR(15),      * salesperson's first name.
 s_last    CHAR(15),      * salesperson's last name.
 address   CHAR(15),      * salesperson's street address.
```

```
city      CHAR(15),      * city salesperson lives in.
phone     CHAR(12));     * salesperson's phone number.

CREATE TABLE Sales
(s_id     CHAR(4),       * salesperson's id number as CHAR.
date      DATE,          * The date of the sale.
item      CHAR(15),      * "DESK", "CHAIR", "TELEVISION", etc.
model     CHAR(16),      * like "ZENITH1108YY3".
invoice   CHAR(8),       * invoice identifier.
no_units  SMALLINT,      * how many were sold, or returned, etc.
tot_amt   NUMERIC(10,2)); * total amount of the sale.

CREATE TABLE Inventry
(item     CHAR(15),      * "DESK", "CHAIR", "TELEVISION", etc.
model     CHAR(16),      * like "ZENITH1108YY3".
price_pu  NUMERIC(10,2), * like 438.99. price per unit.
no_on_hnd SMALLINT);     * number on hand.
```

(Fig. 13-1 ends.)

Fig. 13-2. The posting program (see Fig. 8-2) using embedded SQL.

```
DECLARE Trn CURSOR
FOR SELECT * FROM Trnsacts
FOR UPDATE OF posted;
OPEN Trn;
IF SQLCODE = 0
    STORE SQLCNT TO m_count
    * m_count will be used to count the number of times through
    * the DO WHILE loop.
    DO WHILE m_count > 0

        * Now FETCH the current transaction into memory
        * variables.
        FETCH Trn INTO m_type, m_item, m_model, m_invoice,
        m_no, m_date, m_s_frst, m_s_last, m_posted;

        * Check to see if the transaction has been posted.
        IF .NOT. m_posted

            * Now BEGIN a TRANSACTION doing everything
            * corresponding to this transaction. If no error
            * occurs, the END TRANSACTION command will commit
            * the changes. If an error occurs, the error
            * handler will ROLLBACK the changes.
            ON ERROR DO ERR_PROG
            BEGIN TRANSACTION
            * In other words, if an error occurs, go to a
            * procedure to ROLLBACK changes until the reason
            * for the error can be determined, and corrective
            * action taken.
```

```
        DO CASE
            CASE RTRIM(m_type) = "SOLD"

                    * look up salesperson's id.
                    SELECT s_id INTO m_s_id
                    FROM Salesper
                    WHERE s_first = m_s_frst
                    AND s_last = m_s_last;

                    * look up the unit price.
                    SELECT price_pu INTO m_price
                    FROM Inventry
                    WHERE item = m_item
                    AND model = m_model;

                    * INSERT the sale into the Sales table.
                    INSERT INTO Sales
                    VALUES (m_s_id, m_date, m_item, m_model,
                    m_invoice, m_no,m_no * m_price);

                    * UPDATE the inventory table.
                    UPDATE Inventry
                    SET no_on_hnd = no_on_hnd - m_no
                    WHERE item = m_item
                    AND model = m_model;

                * other CASEs: RTRIM(m_type) = "RETURNED",
                * "LOST", etc.
            ENDCASE
            * set posted = .T. in the transaction table.
            UPDATE Trnsacts
            SET posted = .T.
            WHERE CURRENT OF Trn;
            END TRANSACTION
            ON ERROR
            * Ends the ON ERROR condition because the
            * TRANSACTION has successfully completed.
        ENDIF
        STORE m_count - 1 TO m_count
    ENDDO
    CLOSE Trn;
ENDIF
```

(Fig. 13-2 ends.)

Error Handling

The error handler program in ERR__PROG.PRS must attempt
a ROLLBACK in order to return the database to a consistent
state.Here we give a simple program that you can modify for your

```
@ 1,1 SAY MESSAGE()
WAIT
* Use the WAIT command here so you can see the error message.

ROLLBACK
STORE 1000 TO m_count
* It might take a while for the ROLLBACK to finish.
* So, perform the following loop 1000 times.
DO WHILE .NOT. ROLLBACK() .AND. m_count > 0
    STORE m_count - 1 TO m_count
    @ 5,1 SAY 'ROLLBACK NOT COMPLETED.'
ENDDO
IF .NOT. ROLLBACK()
    @ 5,1 SAY 'ROLLBACK NOT COMPLETED. RETURNING TO MASTER.'
ELSE
    @ 5,1 SAY 'ROLLBACK COMPLETED. RETURNING TO MASTER.'
ENDIF
WAIT
RETURN TO MASTER
```

Fig. 13-3. *Error handling program with embedded SQL.*

own purposes. First you want the error message so you will know what went wrong. Then you want to attempt a ROLLBACK. The code is shown in Fig. 13-3.

Getting a Salesperson's Total Sales

Periodically you may wish to find the total sales of all the salespeople and print them in descending order. The following example uses two cursors so that a value fetched from the first cursor determines the rows selected for the second cursor. This example uses the Salesmen and Sales tables created previously. You may want to compare the code in Fig. 13-4 with the *dBASE* code in Chapter 8, "Getting Salesmen's Total Sales."

Replacing Inventory

To find those inventory items you need to replace, use the code shown in this section. You may want to compare this code

Fig. 13-4. Program to determine total sales in .PRS form.

```
* First CREATE a temporary table to hold the names of the salespeople
* and their total sales.
CREATE TABLE Tot_sale
(s_first  CHAR(15),        * salesperson's first name.
 s_last   CHAR(15),        * salesperson' last name.
 Sum      NUMERIC(10,2));  * salesperson's sales total.

* DECLARE a CURSOR to get the salespeople's names and ids from the
* Salesper table.
DECLARE Men CURSOR
FOR SELECT s_id,s_first,s_last
FROM Salesper;

* DECLARE a CURSOR to get all the sales for a particular salesperson
* from the Sales table
DECLARE Sal CURSOR
FOR SELECT tot_amt
FROM Sales
WHERE s_id = ms_id;

* OPEN the CURSOR for the Salesper table.
OPEN Men;
* Now check that the OPEN didn't result in an error.
IF SQLCODE = 0
    * Set up a memory variable to count the FETCHs in the
    * following DO WHILE loop. SQLCNT contains the number of
    * rows in the result table which equals the number of
    * salespeople.
    STORE SQLCNT TO Men_count
    DO WHILE Men_count > 0

        * Now get a salesperson from Men.
        FETCH Men INTO ms_id,ms_first,ms_last;

        * Now use ms_id to OPEN Sal getting all sales for this
        * salesperson in the result table.
        OPEN Sal;
        IF SQLCODE = 0
            STORE SQLCNT TO Sal_cnt
            STORE 0.00 TO m_sum

            * Now add up the sales for this salesperson in m_sum.
            DO WHILE Sal_cnt > 0

                * Now put the total amount of this sale into
                * the memory variable m_hold.
                FETCH Sal INTO m_hold;
                * Now add m_hold to the sum variable m_sum.
```

(Fig. 13-4 continues.)

```
                              STORE m_sum + m_hold TO m_sum
                              * You are finished adding this sale to m_sum,
                              * so decrement your loop counter Sal_cnt.
                              STORE Sal_cnt - 1 TO Sal_cnt
                    ENDDO
                    * After this DO WHILE loop m_sum contains the sum
                    * of sales for this salesperson.
              ELSE
                    IF SQLCODE = -1
                              * Just in case OPENing Sal produced an error.
                              * Put an error handling routine here and
                              * abort.
                              RETURN
                    ENDIF
              ENDIF

              * Now put the sum of the sales for this salesperson
              * into your temporary table Tot_sale.
              INSERT INTO Tot_sale
              VALUES (ms_first,ms_last,m_sum);

              * CLOSE the Sales table CURSOR so it can be OPENed
              * again for the next salesperson.
              CLOSE Sal;
              * Decrement Men_count since you have finished with this
              * salesperson.
              STORE Men_count - 1 TO Men_count
        ENDDO
              * You are finished getting the sums of sales for all the
              * salespeople.
        ELSE
              IF SQLCODE = -1
                    * Just in case OPENing Men produced an error.
                    * Put an error handling routine here and
                    * abort.
                    RETURN
              ENDIF
        ENDIF
        * CLOSE the Salesper table CURSOR for possible use later.
        CLOSE Men;
        * Now print out the temporary table Tot_sale.
        SET CONSOLE OFF
        SET PRINTER ON
        SELECT * FROM Tot_sale
        ORDER BY sum DESC;
        * The result of this SELECT will be printed out.
        * You can also use the report writer. See Chapter 6.

        * Now you are finished with the Tot_sale table, so drop it.
        DROP TABLE Tot_sale;
        RETURN
```

(Fig. 13-4 ends.)

with the *dBASE* code to do the same thing in Chapter 8, Replacing Inventory.

Suppose you have a supplier's table created as follows:

```
CREATE TABLE Supplier
(item            CHAR(15),
model            CHAR(16),
supplier         CHAR(30),
address          CHAR(15),
city             CHAR(15),
zip              CHAR(15));
```

Now suppose you want to maintain a two-month supply of each item. First you need to find the number of units of each item and model that have been sold in the last two months. Then you need to check inventory to see if there are enough units in stock. If not, you will want to order enough additional units to make up the difference.

It will be useful to also get a list of items and model numbers of those items that are not selling at all. Perhaps you will want to think of a way to dispose of them. First you will need a table to hold the orders, and a table to hold the item and the model number for items that haven't sold. Such a table is shown in Fig. 13-5.

You will want to compute two dates—today's date and the date two months ago—and put them in the date memory variables ml__date and mf__date for use in the program. You can start by declaring a CURSOR for the Inventory Table as shown in Fig. 13-6.

```
CREATE TABLE Orders
(item            CHAR(15),
model            CHAR(16),
number           SMALLINT,          * The number to be ordered.
cost             NUMERIC(10,2),     * The cost of the order.
supplier         CHAR(30),
address          CHAR(15),
city             CHAR(15),
zip              CHAR(15));

CREATE TABLE No_sales
(item            CHAR(15),
model            CHAR(16));
```

Fig. 13-5. Set of tables for orders and "no-sales."

```
DECLARE Inv CURSOR
FOR
SELECT * FROM Inventry;
OPEN Inv;
IF SQLCODE = 0
    STORE SQLCNT TO inv_cnt

    * Now go through the inventory table finding those items and
    * models which sold more units than are left in inventory.
    DO WHILE Inv_cnt > 0
        FETCH Inv INTO m_item, m_model, m_price, m_no;

        * In order to find out how many units were sold,
        * use the aggregate function SUM().
        SELECT SUM(no_units)
        INTO m_comp
        FROM Sales
        WHERE item = m_item AND model = m_model
        AND date BETWEEN mf_date AND ml_date;

        * If the no of units sold in the memory variable m_comp
        * is greater than the number of units on hand, you need
        * to order more.
        IF m_comp > m_no
            STORE m_comp - m_no TO m_diff

            * Since you need to order more, you need the name
            * and address of the supplier.
            SELECT supplier, address, city, zip
            INTO m_splr, m_add, m_city, m_zip
            FROM Supplier
            WHERE item = m_item AND model = m_model;

            * Now INSERT the necessary information into the
            * Orders table.
            INSERT INTO Orders
            VALUES (m_item, m_model, m_diff, m_diff * m_price,
                m_splr, m_add, m_city, m_zip);
        ELSE

            * This is a good place to pick up the items which
            * are not selling.
            IF m_comp = 0

                * INSERT the item and the model number into
                * the No_sales table.
                INSERT INTO No_sales
                VALUES (m_item, m_model);
```

Fig. 13-6. Inventory replacement program (see Fig. 8-4) using embedded SQL.

```
        ENDIF
     ENDIF

     * Decrement the rows counter for the CURSOR Inv.
     STORE inv_cnt - 1 TO inv_cnt
   ENDDO
   CLOSE Inv;
ENDIF
```

(Fig. 13-6 ends.)

Summary

This chapter discusses the methods for embedding SQL commands in *dBASE IV* programs. The use of "cursors" is central to this approach, and several examples are given of excerpts of embedded programs.

These examples can be compared with those in Chapter 8 to see the difference between the use of *dBASE* commands alone and dBASE with embedded SQL.

14

Networking with dBASE IV

dBASE IV can be used in a local area network (LAN) environment. The discussion assumes that your LAN has already been installed. (If not, refer to your Ashton-Tate documentation called *Network Installation Guide*.)

In a networking environment, two or more microcomputers share hardware—such as disk drives, tape storage units, printers, plotters, and scanners—as well as software and data. One microcomputer is designated the *file server*; it manages communication and hardware sharing. The other microcomputers are called *work stations*.

dBASE IV contains a number of features designed especially for the multiuser environment, including:

☐ Logging in
☐ Security
☐ Locking
☐ Errors and error recovery
☐ Customizing *dBASE* at the work station
☐ *dBASE* LAN commands

Logging In to dBASE IV

Your *dBASE IV* system may be protected. (PROTECT is *dBASE IV*'s security system, which is discussed briefly in the following section and in detail in Chapter 9.) If you enter *dBASE* on a protected system, the log-in screen will appear and ask you to fill in your group name, your name, and your password.

Your database administrator (DBA) will have assigned sets of files to different groups within your organization. The group name must be entered on the log-in. If you find you cannot gain access to certain files, it may be because they are not assigned to your group.

The name that you enter on the log-in will be a brief version of your own name. When you fill in your password, it will not appear on the screen. If you make a mistake in entering Group name, Your name, or Your password, you will not be given access, but will have to start over. You can start over three times before *dBASE IV* will return to the operating system. After you successfully fill in the log-in items, the *dBASE IV* copyright notice will appear, followed by the dot prompt.

If you are logging in on a system that is not using PROTECT, the *dBASE IV* copyright notice will appear, and will then be replaced by the dot prompt, signifying that *dBASE IV* is ready for you to use it. If you started by specifying an application program, that program will appear instead of the dot prompt.

Security

In a large, multiuser environment, it may be appropriate to restrict use of certain parts of the database to certain groups or individuals. The PROTECT system within *dBASE IV* accomplishes this with the following three security systems:

☐ *Log-in security* permits log-in only by users with current passwords who are members of groups permitted to use designated files.

☐ *File and field* access security limits the use of specified files and fields to authorized users.

☐ *Data encryption* codes database files so they cannot be read by persons who do not have a data decryption key.

In addition, the SQL portion of *dBASE IV* includes its own system of GRANTing access to specified individuals who only then are able to work with designated tables, views, and columns of data.

Details of these security devices, including how to install a PROTECT system, are described in Chapter 9, which is devoted entirely to database security and integrity.

Locking

When working in the *dBASE IV* LAN environment, you may sometimes encounter the problem of being unable to access a file or record that you are authorized to use. This may be due to the file and record locking system that is imposed to avoid the problem of *collision* (i.e., having one user's changes interfere with another user's work).

Your LAN system protects against simultaneous data access, which might lose data or disrupt the indices. At the same time, it allows multiple use of the database files. It does this by appropriately locking shared files and shared records according to the parameters of the *file-open attribute*.

File-Open and Default File-Open Attributes

A file can be opened in either exclusive or shared mode. If a file is opened in exclusive mode:

☐ Only one user can access the file at a time.

☐ You don't need to lock the file or any record in it.

If a file is opened in shared mode:

☐ Multiple users on the network can access it.
☐ You can lock files and records automatically before updating.

dBASE IV presets or defaults the file-open attribute every time you open a file. You can change this attribute with the SET EXCLUSIVE command. If you SET EXCLUSIVE OFF, all files opened after that will allow shared access. In this case, you will have to be concerned about locking unless the file-access attribute has been set at read-only at the network level. However, the SET EXCLUSIVE OFF command will not affect files already opened.

A file cannot be shared unless it is in a shared directory or you have rights to the directory. Shared directories are established at the network level.

The default file-open attribute is exclusive for most files; therefore, unless the SET EXCLUSIVE OFF command has been issued, you will not have to be concerned about locking. The default settings for the different file types are shown in Table 14-1.

Table 14-1. Default File Open Attributes by File Type.

File Type	Default Open Attribute	Command
Alternate (.TXT)	Exclusive	SET ALTERNATE TO
Catalog (.CAT)	Shared	SET CATALOG TO
Command (.PRG)	Exclusive	MODIFY COMMAND <filename>
	Shared	DO <filename>
Database (.DBF)*	Exclusive	COPY STRUCTURE TO
	Exclusive	COPY TO
	Exclusive	CREATE
	Exclusive	JOIN
	Exclusive	SORT
	Exclusive	TOTAL
	Exclusive**	USE
	Shared	APPEND FROM
	Exclusive <file 1>	CREATE <file 1>

(Table 14-1 Continues.)

File Type	Default Open Attribute	Command
	Shared <*file 2*>	FROM <*file 2*>
	Shared	UPDATE FROM
Format (.FMT)	Shared	SET FORMAT TO
	Exclusive	MODIFY COMMAND <*filename*>
Index (.NDX)*	Exclusive	INDEX ON
	Exclusive†	USE <*file*> INDEX
	Exclusive†	SET INDEX TO
Labels (.LBL)	Exclusive	CREATE LABEL
	Exclusive	MODIFY LABEL
	Shared	LABEL FORM
Memo (.DBT)*	Exclusive†	
Memory (.MEM)	Exclusive	SAVE
	Shared	RESTORE
Procedure (.PRG)	Exclusive	MODIFY COMMAND <*filename*>
	Shared	SET PROCEDURE TO
Query (.QRY)	Exclusive	CREATE QUERY
	Exclusive	MODIFY QUERY
	Shared	SET FILTER TO FILE
Report (.FRM)	Exclusive	CREATE REPORT
	Exclusive	MODIFY REPORT
	Shared	REPORT FORM
View (.VUE)	Exclusive	CREATE VIEW
	Shared	MODIFY VIEW
	Shared	SET VIEW TO

* The default open attribute for index and memo files is always the same as the default for the database file with which they are associated.

† The default is exclusive if SET EXCLUSIVE is ON.

Special cases:

1. Files accessed by the Control Center and the CHANGE and EDIT commands are opened as shared files if SET EXCLUSIVE is OFF.

2. INSERT[BLANK], MODIFY, PACK, PROTECT, REINDEX, RESET IN ALIAS, and ZAP can be used only if the file has been opened for exclusive use. The default for SET EXCLUSIVE is ON. If you try to use one of these commands and the file is not opened for exclusive use, you'll get an error message. You will have to close the file and reopen it for exclusive use.

3. CREATE and SAVE automatically set a file for exclusive use.

(Table 14-1 Ends.)

Locking Features

The following discussion on locking is for programmers whose applications use shared files. All of these measures are designed to prevent *file deadlock,* which is the situation where an infinite loop occurs and no user can access the files necessary to complete a transaction.

If a user opens a shared file for reading only, you don't need to protect it. Problems occur only when a user attempts to update. Locks still permit any user to read the locked file or record even while it is being updated.

The system automatically locks associated files (as well as records); therefore you don't need to consider sharing index or other associated *dBASE* files. In *dBASE IV,* depending on what commands you use, file and/or record locking can be automatic or explicit.

Locking can occur at four levels, with each level more powerful and flexible than the one preceding it. Each level also requires more knowledge of data sharing.

Automatic File Locking. With automatic file locking, users are unaware of the automatic file-locking process. You cannot use commands that operate on an entire file unless the file is locked. When a file is not being used exclusively or is not locked, *dBASE IV* automatically locks the file in use before executing the following commands:

APPEND FROM	LABEL
AVERAGE	PROTECT
CALCULATE	RECALL *<scope>*
COPY	REPLACE *<scope>*
COPY STRUCTURE	REPORT
COUNT	SORT
DELETE *<scope>*	SUM
INDEX	TOTAL
JOIN	UPDATE

If the file can't be locked, you will get an error message. After the command is executed, *dBASE* unlocks the file.

Automatic Record Locking. With automatic record locking, users are unaware of the automatic record locking process. You cannot use commands that work on a record unless the record is locked. When a file is not being used exclusively or is not locked and the record is not locked, *dBASE IV* locks the record automatically before executing the following commands:

APPEND[BLANK]	GET
BROWSE	READ
CHANGE	RECALL
DELETE	REPLACE
EDIT	

When you press any key other than the cursor positioning key, a record is locked automatically. When you press any cursor positioning key that moves to another record, the locked record is automatically unlocked.

Explicit File Locking. With explicit file locking, users can claim and relinquish specified files by using file locking commands and functions. For compatibility with *dBASE III PLUS*, *dBASE IV* supports explicit file locking with the FLOCK( ) function. Explicit file locking is not required because of *dBASE IV*'s automatic file locking facility, but it can be useful when updates might affect many records or index files. Also, with it, you can ensure in advance that a required set of files is available. Since the entire file will be locked, you don't need to lock records. When you use FLOCK( ) to explicitly lock a file, other users can still read that file.

Explicit Record Locking. With explicit record locking, a user can lock a record in a file, thereby preventing access by any other user to that record. For compatibility with *dBASE III PLUS*, *dBASE IV* supports LOCK( ) or RLOCK( ) to explicitly lock a record. If you use either of these two commands, you must use UNLOCK to release the locked record. Other users can read locked records whether they have been locked automatically or explicitly.

The Explicit Locking Process

The locking functions in *dBASE IV*—FLOCK( ), RLOCK( ),

and LOCK( )—operate differently from most *dBASE* functions in that they can execute an action in addition to returning a value (.T. or .F.). They will only lock an unlocked file or record.

The locking functions enable *dBASE IV* to find out whether a file or record has been locked by another user. If the file or record is not locked, the locking function returns a logical true (.T.) and then places the requested lock; otherwise, it returns false (.F.).

You can request explicit file or record locking interactively or you can implement it from within an application program. As with other logical functions, you use lock functions without a comparative operator. For example, do not use an equal sign (=) with the LOCK( ) function. You can use a lock function with the IF and DO WHILE commands. For example:

```
IF LOCK( )
IF .NOT. LOCK( )
 *
 *
 *
DO WHILE LOCK( )
DO WHILE .NOT. LOCK( )
```

Using dBASE Files

How you use *dBASE* files in a LAN environment depends on the file's full opening mode, which consists of a combination of the file-open attribute (exclusive or shared) and the file-access attribute (read-only or read/write).

The File-Open Attribute

Regarding the file-open attribute, a file is opened in one of two modes, either exclusive or shared. If it is opened in exclusive mode:

☐ Only one requesting user can access the file at a time.

☐ There is no need to lock the file or any record in the file.

If a file is opened in share mode:

☐ Multiple users can access the file.

☐ Files and records may be automatically locked before updating.

The file-open attribute is set and maintained from *dBASE IV*, which presets or defaults it every time a file is opened. However, you can change the file-open attribute with the SET EXCLUSIVE command.

File-Access Attributes

The file-access attribute is the permission to read from and write to a file. *dBASE IV* uses the following rules to assign the default file access attribute:

☐ If any *dBASE* file is being created or modified, it is opened for read/write use.

☐ If a command, format, label, query, report, or view file is being used only to obtain information, it is opened for read-only use.

You can override the default with the DOS command ATTRIB to set the file-access attribute to read-only. (For database files, you will have to use the PROTECT program to set the access privilege.)

Some dBASE Networking Commands

If you are a network operator in a LAN environment, the following commands will be useful to you:

☐ DISPLAY/LIST STATUS displays the current status of file locks and tells whether the files are opened for exclusive use. These two commands are identical except that DISPLAY STATUS pauses periodically, whereas LIST STATUS doesn't.

□ DISPLAY USERS displays the network-assigned work-station name of *dBASE* users currently using *dBASE IV* from the shared directory.

□ SET PRINTER redirects print output between a local printer port and the shared network printer.

You can use the RUN/! command only if your work station has enough additional memory to run Command.COM and the called program. If your work station has more than one parallel port, you can use one to access the network printer and another to access a local printer. This way, you won't need to specify the RUN/! command.

Errors and Error Recovery

In *dBASE IV*, how errors are processed depends on the following:

□ If you are at the dot prompt, error processing is up to you. An error message will be displayed.

□ If you issued a full-screen command, error processing will be handled automatically, with error messages displayed in the error box.

□ If you are executing a command file and an ON ERROR command has been issued, *dBASE* will return an error state and an error message will be displayed if an error is not handled immediately by an error procedure.

There are two error functions in *dBASE IV*: ERROR( ) and MESSAGE( ). ON ERROR must be active for these functions to return a value. In the LAN environment, the programmer uses the ERROR function to trap recoverable error conditions, such as an attempt to lock an already locked file.

Customizing dBASE IV at the Work Station

You can customize *dBASE IV* at your own work station, for example, by setting the default word processor you want to use or setting different colors for screen display. You can do this through the Config.DB configuration file described in your *Language Reference* manual.

dBASE LAN Commands

Some *dBASE* commands have additional syntax or enhanced function when they are used for network programming. A summary of such commands is presented in Table 14-2. Each command belongs to a command class, described in the footnote to Table 14-2. Also, some *dBASE* functions are unique to (or are enhanced for use in) the networking environment. These are shown in Table 14-3.

Table 14-2. Summary of Network Programming Commands.

Command	Class*	Environment	Description
BEGIN TRANSACTION	Editing data	Single user and LAN	Alters contents of a record in the active database file.
CHANGE/EDIT	Editing data	Single user and LAN	In network programming, file exclusivity or record lock status is displayed in the Status Bar.
CONVERT	User Assistance	Single user and LAN	Permits use of CHANGE and LKSYS functions.
DISPLAY/LIST STATUS	User Assistance	Single user and LAN	Provides information about currently *dBASE* session.
DISPLAY USERS	User Assistance	LAN	Provides information about currently logged *dBASE* users.
END TRANSACTION	Editing data	Single user and LAN	Ends a transaction to change a record in a database file. Used with BEGIN TRANSACTION.

(Table 14-2 continues.)

Command	Class*	Environment	Description
LOGOUT	Database security	LAN	Forces user to log out and allows new user to log in.
RESET IN ALIAS	Editing data	Single user and LAN	Changes integrity tag in a database file.
RETRY	Programming	Single user and LAN	Executes a command until it can be executed successfully.
ROLLBACK	Manipulating Databases	LAN	Used with BEGIN TRANSACTION to undo changes to a record in a database file.
SET	Parameter Control	Single user and LAN	Displays and changes the current value of SET values.
SET AUTOSAVE	Database Security	Single user and LAN	Automatically updates disk file and directories after I/O operations.
SET ENCRYPTION	Database Security	LAN	Establishes whether a newly created database file is encrypted.
SET EXCLUSIVE	Parameter Control	LAN	Determines file open attribute of all database files during the dBASE session.
SET LOCK	Locking Control	LAN	Enables and disables automatic locking for read-only commands.
SET PRINTER	Parameter Control	Single user and LAN	Redirects printer output to a network or local device.
SET REFRESH	Editing Data	LAN	Updates viewed database information if changed by another user.
SET REPROCESS	Parameter Control	Single user and LAN	Sets the number of times dBASE IV tries a network command or function before producing an error message.
UNLOCK	Locking Control	LAN	Releases record and file locks.
USE EXCLUSIVE	Manipulating Databases	LAN	Opens a database file and related files in the selected work area for exclusive use.

(Table 14-2 continues.)

*Command Class	Meaning
Database Security	Introduces security elements at the programming level.
Editing Data	Allows you to edit data within a database.
Locking Control	Ensures data integrity in network applications.
Parameter Control	Sets a *dBASE* system control parameter.
Programming	Assists in the control and usage of command files.
User Assistance	Provides on-line information.
Manipulating Databases	Specifies .DBF and .NDX files for exclusive use.

(Table 14-2 ends.)

Table 14-3. Summary of Network Programming Functions

Function Name	Description	Data Type
ACCESS( )	Returns a user access level	N
CHANGE( )	Determines whether a record has been changed*	L
COMPLETED( )	Determines if a transaction has been completed	L
ERROR( )	Returns the error number*	N
FLOCK( )	Attempts to lock a database file and returns a success value	L
ISMARKED( )	Determines if a transaction is in progress*	L
LASTKEY( )	Returns the decimal ASCII value of the last key pressed*	N
LKSYS( )	Determines who has locked a record or file and the date and time it was locked*	C
MESSAGE( )	Returns an error message character string*	C
NETWORK( )	Determines the presence of a network	L
RLOCK( )/LOCK( )	Attempts to lock a record and return a success value	L
ROLLBACK( )	Determines whether the last ROLLBACK command was successful*	

*Available in both single-user and network programming. Functions without an asterisk after the description are for use in network programming only.

Summary

This chapter discusses using *dBASE IV* in a local area network (LAN), as well as the *dBASE IV* functionalities that are designed especially for the multi-user environment.

Three types of security systems exist within *dBASE IV*; they are:

Log-in
File and field access security
Data encryption

dBASE IV also provides automatic locking to protect against disruption due to simultaneous data access.

Errors and error processing under different conditions is discussed, and the additional syntax or enhanced functionality of *dBASE LAN* commands when used in the LAN environment is shown in Table 14-2.

A

SQL Error Messages

* allowed for COUNT function only

An asterisk has been used as the argument to a function other than COUNT. The argument for functions AVG, MAX, MIN, and SUM must be a column name.

ADD clause expected in ALTER TABLE

ADD clause missing, misspelled, or misplaced in ALTER TABLE command.

Aggregate function not allowed in WHERE clause

THE SQL aggregate functions AVG, COUNT, MAX, MIN, and SUM are not allowed in a WHERE clause (except as part of the SELECT clause in a subselect). Use two commands: first use a new SELECT command to find the value that would be returned by the function, then use that value as a constant in the WHERE clause of the original SELECT command.

Alias name already exists

You have already applied this alias name to another table at some earlier point in the statement. Use a different alias name.

All SELECT columns must be inside an aggregate function

When HAVING is used without GROUP BY, all SELECT columns must either be constants, or be inside a SQL aggregate function. Place all column names inside an aggregate function, or remove them from the SELECT cause.

All SELECT items must be GROUP BY columns or aggregate functions

A SELECT clause includes both aggregate functions (AVG, COUNT, MAX, MIN, and SUM) and column names not included in functions. All columns not included in functions must be included in GROUP BY clause. Add a GROUP BY clause to the command. If the GROUP BY clause is already part of the command, add the missing SELECT clause column names to it.

Ambiguous column name

A column with the same name appears in two tables, both referenced in the current statement. Prefix ambiguous columns with their table name and a period, as in *<table name>.<column name>*

An illegal table is referenced in a subselect FROM clause

The table upon which the INSERT UPDATE or DELETE command is carried out cannot also be referenced in the FROM clause of a subselect.

Badly formed subquery

Local predicate of an outer query is placed within a nested query. Reformulate query without using a subquery (i.e., use outer predicate to restrict rows retrieved).

Argument too long in CREATE INDEX, GROUP BY, ORDER BY, or SELECT DISTINCT

An index expression of more than 100 characters has caused an error on a CREATE INDEX command, or on a SELECT command including clauses (such as GROUP BY or ORDER BY) which use indices. Specify a shorter index key for a CREATE INDEX command. IF error occurred on a SELECT command, it is an internal error. Remove GROUP BY or ORDER BY clause or DISTINCT keyword.

BY clause is not supported and will be ignored

This is a warning, not an error. *dBASE IV* SQL does not support a BY clause in the GRANT and REVOKE statements. No action needed.

Can't create subdirectory for new database

A SQL table or a non-SQL file or subdirectory has the same name as that used in the CREATE DATABASE statement. Use a different name for the SQL database, or erase and remove the non-SQL file or directory before CREATing the DATABASE.

Cannot ALTER views

Only base tables and their synonyms may be used in an ALTER TABLE statement. You can drop a view, then redefine it to include additional columns.

Cannot CREATE INDEX/GROUP BY/ORDER BY/SELECT DISTINCT on a LOGICAL column

Index cannot be built on a column of LOGICAL data type and all these operations involve either user-defined or internal SQL indexes. Remove the LOGICAL type column

Cannot DROP open database

You tried to drop the active database. First STOP DATABASE, then use the DROP DATABASE command.

Cannot GRANT or REVOKE a privilege to yourself

A GRANT or REVOKE command specifies your own user ID in the TO or FROM clause. You may only grant and revoke privileges of other users. Check the user ID list and make sure it does not contain your own user ID. Make sure you logged in with your own user ID.

Cannot LOAD or UNLOAD DATA for views

LOAD and UNLOAD DATA commands must be used with SQL base tables or their synonyms. You may use a SELECT * statement with SAVE TO TEMP clause on the view and then unload from the temporary table.

Cannot mix ASC and DESC options in index key

If the keyword DESC is specified, it must be specified for all keys in the index.

Catalog table Sysdbs does not exist

The Sysdbs table must be in the SQL Home directory. Make sure that the SQLHOME directive in Config.DB is correct.

Catalog tables are read-only

Direct modification of the catalog tables is not allowed. Only the SYSDBA can directly update the system catalogs.

CHECK OPTION cannot be used with current view

The WITH CHECK OPTION clause cannot be used with a view that cannot be updated. See the UPDATE command entry in Chapter 5 for rules on updating views.

Column is not updatable

A column specified in the SELECT clause cannot be updated. See the UPDATE command entry in Chapter 5 for rules on updating columns.

Column name already exists

A command that names new columns has repeated the same name twice, or has attempted to use a name that already exists for some column in the table. Use a different column name.

Column name longer than 10 characters

SQL column names must contain 10 or fewer characters. They must begin with a letter and contain only letters, digits, and underscores. Check for column names that are too long.

Column name missing in AVG, MAX, MIN, or SUM function.

The SQL aggregate functions AVG, MAX, MIN, and SUM require a column name as their argument. Make sure SQL functions take the form:

< aggregate function> (<column name>).

Column name or number expected in ORDER BY

Only column names or integers can appear in the ORDER BY. After the keywords ORDER BY, either give the column(s) by which you want the result table ordered, or substitute integers indicating the columns according to their place in the SELECT clause.

Column/field names must be specified in SAVE TO TEMP clause

The SELECT returns column derived from functions or constants, so SAVE TO TEMP column/field names must be specified. Add a list of column field names enclosed in parentheses after the filename in the SAVE TO TEMP clause.

Comma or right parenthesis expected

A list has been specified incorrectly. Check for commas between the items and for a right parenthesis at end of list.

Comparison operator or keyword expected

A comparison operator or keyword must follow the first column name or constant in a WHERE clause. The comparison operators are = , > , < , < > , ! = , < = , > = , ! < , and ! > . The comparison keywords are LIKE, IN, and BETWEEN.

Command cannot be executed within a transaction

SQL data definition statements and utility command cannot be used within transactions. Run the command outside of the transaction.

Correlated subquery not allowed in HAVING clause

A subselect in a HAVING clause cannot reference the same table as the outer query. Restructure query into two or more simpler queries, using SAVE TO TEMP clauses if necessary.

Cursor already open

An OPEN command in a .PRS program specifies a cursor that has already been opened. Precede the OPEN command with a CLOSE command.

Cursor declaration does not include the FOR UPDATE OF clause

An error has occurred during execution of an UPDATE WHERE CURRENT OF statement because the DECLARE CURSOR command that defined the cursor used for the UPDATE did not include a FOR UPDATE OF clause. Include the FOR UPDATE OF clause in the DECLARE CURSOR statement of the cursor used for the UPDATE. Note that the ORDER BY clause cannot be used when the FOR UPDATE OF clause is included.

Cursor name previously declared

A DECLARE CURSOR statement contains a cursor name that has already been used in another DECLARE CURSOR statement in the same .PRS program. Choose a new name for the cursor.

Cursor not declared

No DECLARE CURSOR statement defines this cursor. Include a DECLARE CURSOR statement in .PRS program. Make sure the

DECLARE CURSOR statement precedes the first statement that references the cursor.

Cursor not open

A FETCH or CLOSE cursor command in a .PRS program cannot be executed because the specified cursor has not been opened. Precede the FETCH or CLOSE command with an OPEN command.

Cursor not updatable

The DECLARE CURSOR statement that defined the cursor included a SELECT DISTINCT, a UNION, aggregate functions, or included more than one table, or a non-updatable view. Use the cursor only in SELECTs. DECLARE another cursor for use in DELETE/UPDATE WHERE CURRENT OF and INSERT statements.

Data type keyword expected

In a CREATE TABLE or ALTER TABLE command, the data type of a column must be specified after the column name. The SQL data types are: SMALLINT, INTEGER, DECIMAL, NUMERIC, FLOAT, CHAR, LOGICAL, and DATE. If data type is already specified, check for misspelling or misplacement of keyword.

Datatype mismatch of corresponding columns in UNION operation

The corresponding columns of SELECT statements joined by the UNION keyword are not of matching datatypes. Check the datatypes of corresponding columns: SMALLINT, INTEGER, DECIMAL, NUMERIC, and FLOAT types are considered matching for UNION operations. Other datatypes must match exactly.

Database currently open

A command cannot be executed while a database is open. Use a STOP DATABASE statement to close the current database before executing desired command.

Database name already exists

The database name used in a CREATE DATABASE command already exists as a SQL database. Use a different name for the new database.

DBCHECK and RUNSTATS must be used with base tables

A DBCHECK or RUNSTATS command specified a view name or a non-

.DBF filename instead of a base table name. SELECT tablename from SQL catalog table Systabls WHERE table type = T to get a list of non-view tables in the current database directory.

Delimiter must be one character long or keyword BLANK

After the keywords DELIMITED WITH in a LOAD or UNLOAD utility, BLANK or a single character must be specified as delimiter.

Different table name is specified in cursor declaration

The table specified in the DECLARE CURSOR statement is not the same as the table specified by the UPDATE/DELETE WHERE CURRENT OF statement using that cursor. Check table and cursor names to make sure both are identified correctly in both the DECLARE CURSOR and UPDATE/DELETE WHERE CURRENT OF statements.

DISTINCT must be followed by a column name

When the keyword DISTINCT is used with the SQL aggregate functions, it must be followed by a column name.

Duplicate userid

The GRANT or REVOKE command user ID list contains duplicate user IDs. Remove duplicate user IDs.

Equals sign expected

Equals sign missing or misplaced after the keyword SET in an UPDATE statement.

Expression not allowed in GROUP BY/ORDER BY

Only column names are allowed in GROUP BY lists. Only column names or integers are allowed in ORDER BY lists. Remove all expressions from the clause.

File encryption error

Check file encryption. You can SET ENCRYPTION OFF and use a SQL UNLOAD, or dBASE COPY TO command to create an unencrypted file copy.

File has invalid SQL encryption

DBCHECK or RUNSTATS has encountered a file that has an invalid SQL encryption. Try to copy an unencrypted version of the file by using the SQL UNLOAD command.

File is encrypted

DBDEFINE cannot be used with an encrypted file. If the file is dBASE encrypted, SET SQL OFF, SET ENCRYPTION OFF and use the dBASE COPY TO command to create an unencrypted copy of the file. Erase the encrypted version before re-executing DBDEFINE. If file is SQL encrypted, use SQL UNLOAD command to create an unencrypted copy. Erase the encrypted version before re-executing DBDEFINE.

File is not legal dBASE SQL

An error has occurred on DBCHECK, DBDEFINE, or RUNSTATS because the header of a file indicates that it is not a dBASE or SQL file. Make sure you have not copied a non-dBASE/SQL file with a .DBF extension. Remove the bad file from the DQL database before re-executing the utility command.

File is not SQL encrypted

DBCHECK or RUNSTATS has encountered an encrypted file not under SQL encryption key. File must be decrypted and/or removed before re-executing command. If successful, erase encrypted version, use DBDEFINE <*filename*> and re-execute DBCHECK or RUNSTATS. If UNLOAD is not successful, table must be dropped in SQL before DBCHECK or RUNSTATS will execute.

File not found in current database

Error occurred on a DBCHECK, DBDEFINE or RUNSTATS command because filename following the command keyword does not name a file in the active database directory. Check for mispelled filename. Check active database directory to be sure the .DBF in question is there.

File open error

File read error

File seek error

File write error

Filename is same as existing synonym

Error occurs on DBDEFINE when the .DBF file specified in command has the same name as existing SQL synonym. Rename the .DBF before re-executing DBDEFINE *<filename>*.

First argument of LIKE clause must be a CHAR column

The column name preceding the keyword LIKE in a WHERE clause does not identify a CHARACTER type column. Do not use LIKE with a non-CHARACTER type column.

Float value out of range

A float value greater than 10^{308} or smaller than 10^{-309} cannot be entered.

GRANT OPTION ignored for UPDATE with column list specified

This is a warning, not an error. The grantee will not be able to GRANT the UPDATE privilege to others because the UPDATE privilege was granted only for certain columns. No action needed. If the UPDATE privilege is granted without a column list, then the WITH GRANT OPTION will become effective.

GRANT OPTION ignored when GRANT is TO PUBLIC

This is a warning, not an error. The GRANT OPTION is ignored because the privileges are being granted to PUBLIC and so no further grants will be necessary. No action needed.

GROUP BY clause needed

The SELECT clause includes both SQL aggregate functions (AVG, COUNT, MAX, MIN, or SUM) and column names. All column names that are not part of the aggregate functions must be included in a GROUP BY clause.

GROUP BY column(s) not specified in the SELECT clause

A column has been specified in the GROUP BY clause that is not included in the SELECT clause. Include the GROUP BY column(s) in the SELECT clause. All non-GROUP BY columns in the SELECT clause must be columns derived from aggregate functions.

GROUP BY, HAVING, ORDER BY, UNION, or FOR UPDATE OF not allowed with INTO clause

A SELECT statement in a .PRS program includes both the INTO clause and one of the disallowed clauses. A SELECT with INTO clause should return only one row and cannot include these clauses.

HAVING clause must include aggregate functions

The HAVING clause is used after a GROUP BY clause to specify a search condition. Since rows are already aggregated by the GROUP BY clause, the HAVING condition must also be based on aggregated data. Use the aggregate function(s) AVG, COUNT, MAX, MIN, or SUM in the HAVING clause.

Host variable count in INTO clause is not equal to number of SELECT items

A SELECT statement in a .PRS program contains an INTO clause with a number of variables that does not match the number of columns in the SELECT clause.

In UNION, ORDER BY column(s) must be specified by integers

You may use an ORDER BY clause to order the result table of two SELECTs joined by a UNION, but you must use integers instead of column names since column names may differ in the two SELECT clauses. Replace column names with integers (for example, to ORDER BY the first column, use 1, the second column use 2, and so on.

Incompatible data types in comparison

The data types of columns, constant, or expressions in a comparison do not match. Check the data types of columns used. Check for missing quotes on string constants.

Incompatible data types in expression

Columns or constants with incompatible data types have been used in an expression. CHAR., LOGICAL, and DATE types cannot be mixed with the data types that hold numeric values or with each other. Check the data types of columns used in the expression to make sure they are compatible with other columns, constants, or functions used in it.

Incomplete SQL statement

A name, keyword, operator, comma, or semicolon is missing or misspelled. Check the correct syntax of command. Check for a missing semicolon at end of the SQL command.

Incorrect data type for arguments in dBASE function

Refers to a *dBASE* function used in a SQL statement. Check the *dBASE* manual for the correct data types in the function.

Incorrect number of INSERT items

The number of values from the VALUES clause or the subselect doesn't match the number of columns specified in the column list (or in the table if no column list was given). Check that the column list includes the exact columns for which data are to be inserted. Check the VALUES list or subselect SELECT clause to make sure the correct number of values are provided.

Incorrect number of arguments in dBASE function

Refers to a *dBASE* function used in a SQL statement. For example, this error might occur when the CTOD() function is used with an invalid value for the date, as in CTOD (99/99/99). Check *dBASE* manual for correct syntax and usage of the function.

Index column cannot be logical type

Index cannot be built on a column of LOGICAL data type.

Index name already exists

The index name used in a CREATE INDEX command already exists as a SQL index. Use a different index name for the new index.

Insufficient memory

Insufficient memory available for allocation. Simplify queries by breaking long statements into several short ones.

Insufficient privilege

You do not have the privilege to perform the requested operation on the table or view specified. Have the creator of the table/view grant you privileges on it. Anyone who received the privileges WITH GRANT OPTION may also GRANT them to you.

Insufficient privilege to CREATE VIEW

To create a view, you must have SELECT privileges for every table on which the view is based. Delete the table for which you lack SE-LECT privileges from the view definition. Or have someone grant you SELECT privileges on the table.

Integer expected

A noninteger value was encountered.

Internal SQL error #1

Undefined nodename.

Internal SQL error #2

String table overflow. Simplify your query.

Internal SQL error #3

Illegal SQL statement.

Internal SQL error #4

Internal relation table overflows. Simplify your query.

Internal SQL error #5

Error in parse tree. Simplify your query.

Internal SQL error #6

A unique index has been used and more than 10 unique indexes all use the same column as part of their unique key. Drop some unique indexes.

Internal SQL error #7

Internal file open error.

Internal SQL error #8

Internal relation table overflow. Simplify your query.

Internal SQL error #9

Too many columns created in temporary relations. Simplify your query.

Internal SQL error #10

Optimizer join class error. Simplify your query.

Internal SQL error #11

Temporary SYSTABL overflows in optimizer. Simplify your query.

Internal SQL error #12
Temporary SYSCOLUMNS overflows in optimizer. Simplify your query.

Internal SQL error #13
Error in temporary system catalogs in optimizer. Simplify your query.

Internal SQL error #14
Invalid pointer to free allocated memory.

Internal SQL error #15
Insufficient memory available for allocation. Simplify queries by breaking long statements into several shorter ones.

Internal SQL error #16
File seek error.

Internal SQL error #17
File read error.

Internal SQL error #18
File write error.

Internal SQL error #19
Internal hash table for system catalogs overflow. Simplify your query.

Internal SQL error #20
File open error.

Internal SQL error #24
Query array overflow.

Internal SQL error #25
Internal error during default optimization.

Internal SQL error #26
Internal error during default optimization.

Internal SQL error #27
Internal error during default optimization.

Internal SQL error #28

Internal error during default optimization.

Internal SQL error #29

The emitted dBASE source line is longer than 1024 bytes. Check for an * in a SELECT clause that stands for many columns, or for a complex WHERE predicate, especially IN, ANY, and ALL predicates. Reformulate query.

Internal SQL utility error #1

Error in dBASE routine that returns information to DBCHECK, DBDEFINE or RUNSTATS.

Internal SQL utility error #2

Bad file pointer encountered during execution of DBCHECK, DBDEFINE, or RUNSTATS.

Internal SQL utility error #3

Bad structure pointer encountered during execution of DBCHECK, DBDEFINE, or RUNSTATS.

Internal SQL utility error #4

Bad index pointer encountered during execution of DBCHECK, DBDEFINE, or RUNSTATS.

Internal SQL utility error #5

Bad column pointer encountered during execution of DBCHECK, DBDEFINE, or RUNSTATS.

INTO clause not allowed in cursor declaration

The SELECT in a DECLARE CURSOR statement cannot include the INTO clause. Delete the INTO clause.

Invalid argument for aggregate function

You have used an asterisk (*) or a column of a disallowed data type in the AVG, MAX, MIN or SUM function. Columns of data type Logical cannot be used in SQL functions. The argument of SUM and AVG functions must be a column or expression that yields a numeric value.

Invalid COUNT argument

COUNT argument must be (*) or (DISTINCT/ALL <column name>).

Invalid SQL statement

In the stand-alone version, the first word in a statement is not recognized as a SQL keyword. This message will probably be superseded by the PI parser, which will check all non-*dBASE* first tokens against a table of legal SQL first tokens.

Invalid arithmetic expression

An arithmetic expression was expected.

Invalid character

Only letters, digits, and underscores are allowed in object and column names. Numbers may contain only digits and decimal points. Delete any disallowed characters.

Invalid column number in ORDER BY clause

Column number is not an integer, or is greater than the number of columns returned by the SELECT clause. Make sure the column number corresponds to the column's placement in the SELECT clause. For example, the first column is designated by the number 1, the second by 2, and so on.

Invalid constant

A SQL statement is expecting a constant, but no value is specified. Check for empty parentheses in values lists.

Invalid decimal length

CREATE TABLE command specifies the length of a Numeric or Decimal type column incorrectly. The width and scale of Numeric and Decimal type columns is specified as (x,y) where y is not greater than $x - 2$ for Numerics, or $x - 1$ for Decimals. For both types, y may not exceed 18.

Invalid file type specified

In the LOAD and UNLOAD statements, file type may be specified as SDF, DIF, WKS, SYLK, or DELIMITED. Check file type. If the file loaded from or unloaded to is a *dBASE* .DBF file, type need not be specified.

Invalid filename

An invalid file name appears in the LOAD or UNLOAD statement. Check that the file name (and path) are correctly specified. When the file is a *dBASE* .DBF, the extension need not be specified.

Invalid INSERT item

Items in the value list following the keyword VALUES cannot be column names or compound expressions involving arithmetic operators. Check value list to be sure it contains only the following: constants, dBASE functions, memory variables, or USER.

Invalid logical predicate

Comparison operators or keywords other than equal (=) or not equal (! = , < >, or #) cannot be used with column of datatype LOGICAL in a WHERE predicate.

Invalid password

Invalid password in file header.

Invalid string operator

Operators other than plus and minus cannot be used with strings. Remove disallowed operator. Also check that you have not mistakenly identified something as a string by inadvertently starting a name with a quotation mark.

Invalid SYSTIME.MEM

The SYSTIME.MEM time stamp in the active database directly is invalid. Make sure you have not accidentally overwritten SYSTIME.MEM. Try copying it from a backup of the database.

Invalid unary operator

An operator has been inappropriately applied to a non-numeric value. Check for typographical errors or operators in front of CHAR, LOGICAL, or DATE columns.

Keyword AND expected

Keyword AND expected after first argument in BETWEEN clause. Check that keyword AND is not missing, misspelled, or misplaced.

Keyword AS expected

Keyword AS missing, misspelled, or misplaced in CREATE VIEW command. AS follows the view name (and optional column list) and precedes the subselect.

Keyword ASC or DESC, comma, or right parenthesis expected

The CREATE INDEX command is incomplete. Add ASC or DESC option if desired after the column name(s) in the column list (use commas to separate items in the list) and be sure a right parenthesis ends the column list.

Keyword ASC or DESC, comma, or semicolon expected

An ORDER BY clause is incomplete. Ascending, or descending order may be specified after the column name(s) in the ORDER BY clause. ASC is the default. The statement must be terminated with a semicolon (;).

Keyword BY expected

The keyword ORDER must be followed by the keyword BY. Check that BY is not missing, misspelled, or misplaced.

Keyword CHECK expected

Keyword CHECK missing, misspelled, or misplaced in WITH CHECK OPTION clause of CREATE VIEW command.

Keyword CURSOR expected

The keyword CURSOR is missing or misspelled in the DECLARE CURSOR statement in a .PRS program.

Keyword DATA expected

Missing keyword DATA in LOAD or UNLOAD statement. Check that the word DATA is directly after the word LOAD or UNLOAD and that it is spelled correctly.

Keyword DATABASE expected

Keyword DATABASE missing, misplaced, or misspelled in START, STOP, or SHOW DATABASE command.

Keyword DATABASE, TABLE, INDEX, SYNONYM, or VIEW expected

Keyword missing or misspelled after DROP keyword. Use DATABASE, TABLE, INDEX, SYNONYM, or VIEW depending on the kind of object to be dropped.

Keyword DATABASE, TABLE, INDEX, SYNONYM, or VIEW expected

Keyword missing, misplaced, or misspelled in a CREATE statement.

Keyword FOR expected

The Keyword FOR is missing, misplaced, or misspelled in the CREATE SYNONYM or DECLARE CURSOR command.

Keyword FROM expected

Keyword FROM missing, misplaced, or misspelled in LOAD, UNLOAD, SELECT, REVOKE, or DELETE command.

Keyword GRANT expected

Keyword GRANT missing, misplaced, or misspelled in the WITH GRANT OPTION clause of a GRANT statement.

Keyword INDEX expected

The keywords CREATE UNIQUE must be followed by the word INDEX. Check that the keyword INDEX is not missing, misspelled, or misplaced.

Keyword INTO expected

Keyword INTO missing, misplaced, or misspelled in FETCH, INSERT, or LOAD DATA statement.

Keyword not allowed in interactive mode

A keyword used during an interactive SQL session can only be used in a .PRS program. All keywords related to the use of SQL cursors are used only in programs. Replace the keyword with an interactive SQL command.

Keyword OF expected

Keyword OF missing, misplaced, or misspelled in FOR UPDATE OF or WHERE CURRENT OF clause.

Keyword ON expected

Keyword ON missing, misspelled, or misplaced in CREATE INDEX, GRANT or REVOKE command.

Keyword OPTION expected

Keyword OPTION missing, misspelled, or misplaced in the WITH GRANT OPTION clause of a GRANT command.

Keyword SELECT expected

The keyword SELECT is missing, misplaced, or misspelled after the keyword UNION or in a CREATE VIEW command after the keyword AS. The missing SELECT keyword is the first word of the required subselect used in these statements.

Keyword SELECT missing in DECLARE CURSOR statement

Keyword SELECT missing, misplaced, or misspelled in DECLARE CURSOR statement. A SELECT statement must follow the keyword FOR.

Keyword SET expected

Keyword SET missing, misplaced, or misspelled in UPDATE statement.

Keyword TABLE expected

Keyword TABLE missing, misspelled, or misplaced in ALTER TABLE, LOAD, or UNLOAD command.

Keyword TEMP expected

Keyword TEMP missing, misplaced, or misspelled in the SAVE TO TEMP clause of a SELECT statement.

Keyword TO expected

Keyword TO missing, misspelled, or misplaced in GRANT or UNLOAD command or the SAVE TO TEMP clause of a SELECT command.

Keyword UPDATE expected

Keyword UPDATE missing, misspelled, or misplaced in the FOR UPDATE OF clause in the DECLARE CURSOR statement.

Keyword VALUES or SELECT expected

The INSERT statement must include either a VALUES clause or a subselect. Check that one of the keywords is included and that it is not misspelled or misplaced.

Keyword WITH expected

Keyword WITH missing, misplaced, or misspelled in LOAD or UNLOAD utility where delimiters are specified. When data are loaded to or unloaded from *dBASE* files, the TYPE and WIDTH clauses need not be specified.

Keywords BETWEEN, LIKE, or IN expected

A WHERE clause is incorrectly specified. Check correct syntax of the desired form of the WHERE clause.

Left parenthesis missing

A left parenthesis is missing before the beginning of a list. Check syntax of command for required parenthesis.

Memory variable and dBASE fct. not allowed in SELECT with UNION

All SELECT columns must be named columns or constants when UNION is used. Remove memory variables, dBASE functions, and array references from SELECT clauses.

Missing end quotes for string

Strings must be enclosed in quotes. Add missing quote ('). Check to make sure that you mean to be specifying a string and that you have not inadvertently used a quote which has been interpreted as a begin string marker.

Name already exists

The name used in a CREATE TABLE, CREATE SYNONYM, or CREATE VIEW command already names an existing SQL table, synonym, or view. Use a different name for the new table, synonym, or view.

Name, constant, or expression expected

A scalar value was expected. Check that a column name, constant, or expression has not been omitted from the statement.

Name expected

An object name is missing, misplaced, or misspelled. Check that database, table, view, synonym, or column names are correctly specified.

Name longer than 10 characters

All SQL names must contain 10 or fewer characters. (Database and table names must contain 8 or fewer.) They must begin with a letter and contain only letters, digits, and underscores.

Name longer than 8 characters not allowed

The name for a database or table exceeds eight characters in length. Use a name of eight characters or less (beginning with a letter and containing only letters, digits, and underscores.)

Nested function not allowed

An aggregate function contains another function nested within it. Remove the nested function.

No alias defined for self-join

When a self-join form of the WHERE clause is used, an alias must be defined in the FROM clause. The table name cannot be referenced twice, nor may a synonym name be used in place of an alias. Use a FROM clause of the form: FROM <tablename> <alias name>. Then prefix column names in the SELECT and WHERE clauses as necessary.

No ALTER or INDEX privileges for views

These privileges cannot be granted or revoked because views cannot be altered or indexed. You cannot GRANT ALL PRIVILEGES on views because ALL includes the ALTER and INDEX privileges. Do not use the keyword ALL. Do specify a privilege list that can contain the following privileges: DELETE, INSERT, SELECT, or UPDATE.

No current row available for UPDATE or DELETE

This error occurs only in .PRS programs where UPDATEs and DELETEs are being performed under SQL cursor control. Make sure a FETCH has been executed before the UPDATE or DELETE is attempted.

No database open

The command requested can only be executed when a database is open. If you have entered SQL with all databases closed, or if you used the STOP DATABASE command, the current command cannot be executed. Use a START DATABASE command before retrieving information.

No .DBF file in the current database

No .DBF files (other than the SQL catalog tables) were found during execution of DBDEFINE command. Make sure that the .DBF files you want to define as SQL tables have been copied into the current database directory before executing the DBDEFINE command.

No GROUP BY or HAVING in subquery

The GROUP BY and HAVING clauses are not allowed in subqueries of a basic WHERE predicate. Remove GROUP BY or HAVING or change the form of the predicate.

Non-numeric array subscript

All array subscripts must evaluate to integers. If columns or functions are used, check that the data type of the expression is numeric.

Number of column must be the same in UNION operation

The SELECT statements joined by the UNION keyword do not generate the same number of columns. Change the SELECT clauses of the SELECT statements so that they return the same number of columns. Columns must also be of matching data type and length.

Number of SAVE TO TEMP columns does not match number of SELECT columns

The SAVE TO TEMP column list must contain the same number of columns as the SELECT statement results being saved. If all the columns in the result table are named columns (not derived from functions, constants, and so on), then no column list need be specified in the SAVE TO TEMP clause.

Number of view columns does not match number of SELECT columns

In a CREATE VIEW command, the number of columns specified in the view column list is not the same as the number of columns generated in the SELECT clause. If all the columns in the view are named columns (not the result of aggregate functions, expressions, and so on), then the column list may be omitted and the view column will inherit SELECT column names.

Numeric value too large

A value exceeds *dBASE* limits on numeric values.

Numeric value too small

A value is smaller than the smallest allowable *dBASE* numeric value.

ORDER BY clause not allowed in CREATE VIEW

An ORDER BY clause was included as part of the AS SELECT in a CREATE VIEW statement. The ORDER BY clause may only be used in a full SELECT, with UNION and in the DECLARE CURSOR statement. Remove the ORDER BY clause. You may use an ORDER BY clause when you SELECT from the view.

ORDER BY column(s) not specified in the SELECT clause

A column has been specified in the ORDER BY clause that is not included in the SELECT clause. Include the ORDER BY column(s) in the SELECT clause.

Only one DISTINCT allowed in any SELECT clause

The keyword DISTINCT has appeared more than once in a SELECT clause.

Path too long

A path name may not exceed 64 characters.

Right bracket missing

A left bracket appears without a matching right bracket. Check array references to make sure brackets match. Square brackets are not used elsewhere in SQL.

Right parenthesis missing

A left parenthesis is present without a matching right parenthesis. Check for missing right parenthesis in subselects, aggregate functions, and so on.

SAVE TO TEMP clause not allowed

SAVE TO TEMP clause not allowed as part of a DECLARE CURSOR statement or when an INTO clause is used in a SELECT statement. Reexecute the statement as a SELECT without an INTO clause.

SELECT cannot include both FOR UPDATE OF and ORDER BY clauses

A SELECT or DECLARE CURSOR statement includes both the FOR UPDATE OF and ORDER BY clauses. If a cursor defined in a DECLARE CURSOR statement is to be used in an UPDATE WHERE CURRENT OF statement, then the FOR UPDATE OF clause must be chosen; otherwise, drop it and keep the ORDER BY clause.

Second argument of LIKE clause must be a character string

A column name or other noncharacter string item follows the keyword LIKE in a WHERE clause. LIKE must be followed by a character string. Replace disallowed item with a character string. Check that you have not inadvertently forgotten the beginning quote of the character string.

SELECT column names must be in aggregate functions

When HAVING is used without GROUP BY, all column names in the SELECT clause must be in SQL aggregate functions. Add a GROUP BY clause with all SELECT clause column names included in it, or use aggregate function in SELECT clause.

Systimes error

Systimes error.

Table already exists

The filename following the DBDEFINE keyword already exists as a SQL table. No new entries can be made in the SQL catalog tables for this file. If you need to redefine this table (because of DBCHECK errors, or for any other readon) you must copy the .DBF to another directory, DROP it in SQL, copy the .DBF back then use DBDEFINE <filename>.

Table not found in the SQL catalog tables

Table name specified in DBCHECK or RUNSTATS command does not exist in the SQL catalog tables. Verify correct table name with a SELECT from Systabls catalog table.

Table not included in current statement

A column prefixed with the table name from which it comes is referenced, but its table is not included in a FROM clause. Add the missing table name to the FROM clause.

Too many indexes for a table

Table already has 47 indexes. A SQL table cannot have more than 47 indexes (i.e., no more than 47 .NDX tags in its production .MDX).

Too many columns in a table

A CREATE TABLE or ALTER TABLE command would result in a table of more than 255 columns. Use the following query to see how many columns a table already has: SELECT Colcount FROM Systabls WHERE Tbname = "<table name>";

Too many unique indexes

A unique index has been used and more than 10 unique indexes all use the same column as part of their unique key. Drop some unique indexes.

Too many values specified in INSERT

A column list was specified that contained more columns than exist in the table. Check the column list for duplicate column names and remove extra columns.

Too many work areas open

Either more than 10 tables are referenced in one SQL statement or the user left some work areas open before issuing the SET SQL ON command, and the total number of work areas open is greater than 10. Reference fewer tables in the FROM clause or return to *dBASE* and close work areas.

Undefined column name

The column name that caused the error is not a column of any of the tables referenced in the command. You have referenced the wrong table, forgotten to include a table in the FROM clause, misspelled the column name, or used a column name that doesn't exist.

Undefined database name

There is no entry in the SQL system catalog table Sysdbs.DBF for this database. Check that you have not given an incorrect database name or use a CREATE DATABASE statement to create the database. If you already have a non-SQL subdirectory with the same name, you must first erase and remove this directory outside of SQL.

Undefined index name

The index named in a DROP INDEX command does not exist as a SQL index. (The index name is not entered in the SQL catalog table SYSIDXS.) Do a SELECT from the system catalog table Sysidxs to verify the correct name of the index.

Undefined privilege in GRANT or REVOKE statement

You may grant and revoke the following privileges: SELECT, INSERT, DELETE, UPDATE, INDEX, ALATER. Check for misspellings or keywords (such as CREATE) that cannot be granted.

Undefined symbol

An unrecognized or inappropriate symbol has been accidentally included in the statement. Check for and delete any symbols such as $ or & or arithmetic comparison or operator symbols accidentally included in names or keywords.

Undefined synonym name

The synonym named in a DROP SYNONYM command does not exist as a SQL synonym. (The synonym name is not entered in the catalog table Syssyns.) Check that you have not given a table or view name by mistake. Use a SELECT from the catalog table Syssyns to get a listing of all existing synonym names.

Undefined table name

The table, synonym, or view requested is not entered in the relevant SQL catalog table. Either the name is misspelled or a CREATE (or DBDEFINE) command was never used. Check that you have not put a column name or other item where a table name was expected. Do a SELECT from the appropriate catalog table (Systabls, Syssyns, or Sysviews) to list correct names.

Undefined view name

The view named in a DROP VIEW command is not a SQL view. (The view name is not entered in the catalog table Sysviews). Do a SELECT from the catalog table Sysviews to verify existing view names.

UNION is not allowed in a view definition

The UNION keyword has been included in a CREATE VIEW command. You may select columns from more than one table to create a single view, but the UNION operation is not allowed.

UPDATE column list is ignored in REVOKE statement

This is a warning, not an error. REVOKE of an UPDATE privilege applies to all columns in a table after revoking the UPDATE privilege, GRANT is again specifying the columns to which it applies.

UPDATE column(s) not defined in cursor declaration

The UPDATE WHERE CURRENT OF statement in a .PRS program UPDATEs columns that were not included in the column list of the FOR UPDATE OF clause of the associated DECLARE CURSOR statement. Add all columns to be UPDATEd to the column list in the FOR UPDATE OF clause of the DECLARE CURSOR statement.

Value exceeds column length

A value is longer than the column into which it is to be entered. SE-

LECT FROM SYSCOLS to determine the length of the column into which you are entering values.

Value must match column data type

An UPDATE or INSERT value doesn't match the data type of the column into which it is to be placed. Check the data type of the column. Be sure dates are correctly entered in the form CTOD('*dd/mm/yy*'). Check for missing beginning quotes on character strings.

View column names must be specified

The SELECT clause of the CREATE VIEW statement includes columns derived from aggregate functions or from two different tables, and view column names cannot simply be inherited from the SELECT. Add a list of column names enclosed in parentheses after the keywords CREATE VIEW.

View defined with GROUP BY cannot be used in a join

A view referenced in the FROM clause of a statement joining views (and tables) has a GROUP BY clause as part of its definition. This view cannot be used in a join.

View defined with GROUP BY cannot be used in a query including a GROUP BY clause

A SELECT statement including a GROUP BY clause references a view that has a GROUP BY clause as part of its definition. Remove the GROUP BY clause in the current SELECT or do not use this view in this query.

View is not updatable

A DELETE, INSERT, or UPDATE was attempted on a view that cannot be updated. Views with definitions referencing more than one table, or including GROUP BY, SELECT DISTINCT, or aggregate functions are not updatable.

Views cannot be INDEXed

A CREATE INDEX command included a view name instead of a table or synonym name. Views cannot be INDEXed.

B

dBASE IV Commands

This appendix consists of a complete listing of the available commands in *dBASE IV*.

dBASE Command	*Allowed in SQL*	*New or Modified*	*Description*
! or RUN	Yes	No	Runs a DOS-level system command
?, ??	Yes	Yes	Now support AT, FUNCTION, PICTURE and STYLE for printer output
??? <expression list>	Yes	Yes	Outputs <expression list> to printer
&&	Yes	No	Indicates a program comment
*	Yes	No	Comment indicator in programs
@CLEAR...	Yes	No	Draws and erases boxes and lines
@DOUBLE/PANEL/ NONE/	Yes	Yes	Allows character selection for boxes
@FILL TO	Yes	Yes	Rapidly changes display color
@SAY . . . GET	Yes	Yes	Displays/gets user data. Provides extended data validation, help, and custom prompts
ACCEPT	Yes	No	Enters a character string into a memory variable

dBASE Command	Allowed in SQL	New or Modified	Description
ACTIVATE MENU	Yes	Yes	Activates/locates a menu into memory
ACTIVATE POPUP	Yes	Yes	Activates/locates a popup into memory
ACTIVATE SCREEN	Yes	Yes	Transfers output from active window to global screen
ACTIVATE WINDOW	Yes	Yes	Activates one or all defined windows
APPEND [BLANK]	No	No	Appends records
APPEND FROM	No	Yes	Appends/imports records from other files or arrays
APPEND MEMO	No	No	Appends a memo field from an existing field
ASSIST	No	Yes	Invokes Control Center
AVERAGE	No	Yes	Computes the arithmetic average of expressions and saves to a memory variable or an array
BEGIN TRANSACTION	Yes	Yes	Opens a log file for transaction processing
BROWSE	No	Yes	Invokes menu-assisted, 17-record screen display
BUILD	No	Yes	Stand-alone utility. See *RunTime* manual
CALCULATE	No	Yes	Calculates financial and statistical functions
CALL	Yes	No	Executes a binary program module
CANCEL	Yes	No	Stops program execution
CHANGE	No	No	Changes specified fields and records
CLEAR	Yes	Yes	Clears specified parameters from memory (all allowed except ALL, FIELDS, MEMORY)
CLOSE	Yes	No	Closes specified files (all allowed except ALL, DATABASES, and INDEX)
COMPILE	Yes	Yes	Generates *dBASE* object code for *dBASE* programs
CONVERT TO	No	Yes	Adds a field for multiuser lock detection
CONTINUE	No	No	Continues to next located record
COPY FILE	Yes	No	Duplicates a file
COPY INDEXES	No	Yes	Creates .MDX tags

dBASE Command	Allowed in SQL	New or Modified	Description
COPY MEMO	No	Yes	Copies specified memo to field
COPY STRUCTURE	No	Yes	Duplicates a structure in a new file
COPY TAG	No	Yes	Creates a new .NDX file
COPY TO	No	No	Copies/exports records to a new file
COPY TO ARRAY	No	Yes	Copies records to an array
COUNT	No	No	Counts records in a file
CREATE FROM	No	Yes	Creates a new file from a file created with COPY STRUCTURE EXTENDED
CREATE TAG FROM	No	No	Creates index tag from .NDX file
CREATE/MODIFY	No	No	Creates or modifies a database file
CREATE/MODIFY APPLICATION	No	Yes	Accesses the application generator
CREATE/MODIFY CATALOGUE	No	No	Creates or modifies a catalog file
CREATE/MODIFY LABEL	No	No	Creates or modifies a label form file
CREATE/MODIFY QUERY	No	No	Creates or edits a view file
CREATE/MODIFY REPORT	No	No	Creates or modifies a report file
CREATE/MODIFY SCREEN	No	No	Creates or modifies a screen form file
CREATE STRUCTURE	No	Yes	Accepts F and N data types and all new database field attributes
CREATE/MODIFY VIEW	No	Yes	Accesses QBE
DEACTIVATE MENU	Yes	Yes	Removes an active menu from memory
DEACTIVATE POPUP	Yes	Yes	Removes an active popup from memory
DEACTIVATE WINDOW	Yes	Yes	Removes windows from memory
DEBUG	Yes	Yes	Calls the debugger program
DECLARE	Yes	Yes	Creates memory variable array
DEFINE BAR	Yes	Yes	Defines a menu bar
DEFINE BOX	No	Yes	Establishes parameters for graphic box
DEFINE MENU	Yes	Yes	Defines a menu
DEFINE PAD	Yes	Yes	Defines a menu pad in defined menu
DEFINE POPUP	Yes	Yes	Defines a popup window
DEFINE WINDOW	Yes	Yes	Defines a window
DELETE	No	No	Deletes records from a file

dBASE Command	Allowed in SQL	New or Modified	Description
DELETE FILE	Yes	No	Deletes a file
DELETE TAG	No	Yes	Deletes an index tag
DIRECTORY	Yes	No	Displays a drive directory
DISPLAY FILES	Yes	No	Displays/prints files
DISPLAY HISTORY	Yes	No	Displays/prints previously executed commands from history
DISPLAY MEMORY	Yes	Yes	Displays/prints current memory variables
DISPLAY STATUS	Yes	Yes	Displays/prints system status
DISPLAY STRUCTURE	No	Yes	Displays/prints current file structure
DISPLAY USERS	Yes	No	Displays user name list on a network
DO	Yes	No	Executes a program
DO CASE	Yes	No	Starts block of CASE statements
DO WHILE	Yes	No	Executes conditional loop in a program
EDIT	No	Edit	Displays records one at a time
EJECT	Yes	No	Sends a form feed to a printer
ENDPRINTJOB	Yes	Yes	Defines end of print job
END TRANSACTION	Yes	Yes	Closes a transaction processing log file
ERASE	Yes	No	Deletes a specified file
EXIT	Yes	No	Exits program execution
EXPORT TO	No	Yes	Converts/exports a .DBF file
FIND	No	No	Finds a record
FUNCTION	Yes	Yes	Declares a user-defined function
GO/GOTO	No	No	Positions the record pointer in a file
[GOTO] <exp>	No	No	Positions the record pointer in a file
HELP	Yes	No	Displays context-sensitive help
IF-ELSE-ENDIF	Yes	No	Provides conditional branching in program
IMPORT FROM	No	Yes	Imports a file
INDEX	No	Yes	Creates an index file (.NDX or .MDX)
INPUT	Yes	No	Enters an expression into a memory variable
INSERT	No	No	Inserts a record into a file

dBASE Command	Allowed in SQL	New or Modified	Description
JOIN	No	No	Combines records from two database files
LABEL FORM	No	No	Prints labels
LINK <*filename*>	No	Yes	Stand-alone program for joining up to 256 related program object files
LIST	No	Yes	Lists/prints specified fields and records
LIST FILES	Yes	Yes	Lists/prints matching files
LIST HISTORY	Yes	Yes	Lists/prints commands in history (in chronological order)
LIST MEMORY	Yes	Yes	Lists/prints memory variables
LIST STATUS	Yes	No	Lists/prints system status and parameters
LIST STRUCTURE	No	Yes	Lists/prints a database file structure
LIST USERS	Yes	No	Lists/prints network user names
LOAD	Yes	No	Loads a binary program module
LOCATE	No	No	Locates a record and positions the record pointer
LOGOUT	Yes	No	Logs a user out of *dBASE IV* on a LAN
LOOP	Yes	Yes	
MODIFY COMMAND/FILE	Yes	Yes	Starts text editor for editing program files
MODIFY STRUCTURE	No	Yes	Changes a database file structure
MOVE	Yes	No	Saves/prints a screen image in memory
MOVE WINDOW TO	Yes	Yes	Moves a predefined window
NOTE	Yes	No	Indicates comments in a program file
ON ERROR/ESCAPE/KEY	Yes	Yes	Executes specified command on condition or key
ON PAD	Yes	Yes	Activates an associated menu-pad popup
ON PAGE	No	Yes	Allows you to specify action at page break
ON READERROR	Yes	Yes	Executes specified command on incorrect entry
ON SELECTION PAD	Yes	Yes	Specifies the execution of a command for selection of a menu pad
ON SELECTION POPUP	Yes	Yes	Specifies the execution of a command for selection of a popup menu
PACK	No	No	Removes records marked for deletion

dBASE Command	Allowed in SQL	New or Modified	Description
PARAMETERS	Yes	No	Specifies memory variables used with DO command
PLAY MACRO	Yes	Yes	Plays back a macro
PRINTJOB	Yes	Yes	Defines start of print job
PRIVATE	Yes	No	Defines memory variables as private
PROCEDURE	Yes	No	Identifies the beginning of a procedure file
PROTECT	Yes	No	Menu-driven command that assigns user log-in names and access privileges
PUBLIC	Yes	Yes	Defines memory variables as public
QUIT	Yes	No	Closes all files and exits to DOS
READ[SAVE]	Yes	No	Reads current fields of a record
RECALL	No	No	Unmarks records marked for deletion
REINDEX	No	Yes	Rebuilds open index files
RELEASE	Yes	No	Erases memory variables from RAM (all options supported except RELEASE ALL)
RELEASE MENUS	Yes	Yes	Erases menus from the screen and RAM
RELEASE MODULE	Yes	No	Erases a program module loaded in RAM
RELEASE POPUPS	Yes	Yes	Erases popup menus from the screen and RAM
RELEASE WINDOWS	Yes	Yes	Erases windows from the screen and RAM
RENAME	Yes	No	Assigns a new name to an existing file
REPLACE	No	Yes	Changes the contents of fields in a record
REPORT FORM	No	No	Displays/prints tabular reports of data
RESET	Yes	Yes	Resets tag of transaction in log file
RESTORE	Yes	No	Restores named memory variables to RAM
RESTORE MACROS	Yes	Yes	Restores macros to RAM from disk file
RESTORE WINDOW	Yes	Yes	Restores windows from a disk file
RESUME	Yes	No	Resumes execution of a suspended program
RETRY	Yes	No	Retries a command after its previous execution from a program

dBASE Command	Allowed in SQL	New or Modified	Description
RETURN	Yes	No	Returns to a point from which a program call was made
ROLLBACK	Yes	Yes	Restores a file to a pretransaction status
RUN	Yes	No	Runs a DOS-level file from within dBASE IV
SAVE MACROS	Yes	Yes	Saves macros to a disk file
SAVE TO	Yes	No	Copies memory variables to a disk file
SAVE WINDOW	Yes	Yes	Saves windows to a disk file
SCAN	No	Yes	Finds the next record of a search
SEEK	No	No	Positions the record pointer to the first record
SELECT	No	No	Activates the specified work area
SET	Yes	No	Displays a menu for setting parameters
SET ALTERNATE ON/OFF	Yes	No	Controls recording of dBASE commands and output in a text file
SET ALTERNATE TO	Yes	Yes	Sends screen output to a text file
SET AUTOSAVE ON/OFF	Yes	Yes	Controls automatic storage of open files
SET BELL ON/OFF	Yes	Yes	Sets the audible prompt on or off
SET BELL TO	Yes	Yes	Sets the tone and duration of the audible prompt
SET BLOCKSIZE	Yes	Yes	Sets memo field size
SET BORDER	Yes	Yes	Sets menu, window, or popup border
SET CARRY ON/OFF	No	No	Sets carryover of fields to next record
SET CARRY TO	No	Yes	Specifies fields updated with carry
SET CATALOG ON/OFF	No	No	Controls addition of open files to catalog
SET CATALOG TO	No	No	Opens a catalog file
SET CENTURY ON/OFF	Yes	No	Controls display of century in a date field
SET CLOCK ON/OFF	Yes	Yes	Controls display of the system clock
SET CLOCK TO	Yes	Yes	Controls position of clock display
SET COLOR OF	Yes	No	Sets color of special screen areas
SET COLOR ON/OFF	Yes	No	Specifies monochrome or color display
SET COLOR TO	Yes	Yes	Sets overall color

dBASE Command	Allowed in SQL	New or Modified	Description
SET CONFIRM ON/OFF	Yes	No	Controls advance of cursor from field to field
SET CONSOLE ON/OFF	Yes	No	Controls output of display to screen
SET CURRENCY LEFT/RIGHT	Yes	Yes	Controls display of currency symbols
SET CURRENCY TO	Yes	Yes	Specifies the currency symbol used
SET DATE TO	Yes	Yes	Sets date format
SET DEBUG ON/OFF	Yes	No	Controls the output of SET ECHO ON to the printer
SET DECIMALS TO	Yes	No	Specifies the number of decimal places displayed with SET FIXED off
SET DEFAULT TO	Yes	No	Specifies the default drive
SET DELETED ON/OFF	No	No	Controls use of records marked for deletion
SET DELIMITERS ON/OFF	No	No	Controls the use of entry form delimiters
SET DELIMITERS TO	Yes	No	Specifies delimiters for field and variable displays
SET DESIGN ON/OFF	No	No	Restricts transfers to design mode
SET DEVELOPMENT	Yes	Yes	
SET DEVICE TO	Yes	Yes	Controls output of the @...SAY command to the screen, a printer, or a file
SET DISPLAY TO	Yes	No	Sets display mode of monochrome or color displays
SET DOHISTORY ON/OFF	Yes	Yes	(This command had been deleted. It is no longer necessary.
SET ECHO ON/OFF	Yes	No	Controls output of executed commands to screen or printer
SET ENCRYPTION ON/OFF	Yes	No	Controls encryption of protected files
SET ESCAPE ON/OFF	No	No	Controls interruption of program with Esc key
SET EXACT ON/OFF	Yes	No	Controls exactness of matches in character-string comparisons
SET EXCLUSIVE ON/OFF	Yes	No	Controls whether files are accessed exclusively on a network

dBASE Command	Allowed in SQL	New or Modified	Description
SET FIELDS ON/OFF	No	No	Controls use of fields list
SET FIELDS TO	No	Yes	Specifies a fields list
SET FILTER TO	No	Yes	Specifies select conditions that fields in records must meet
SET FIXED ON/OFF	Yes	Yes	Controls whether a fixed number of decimal places is displayed in calculations
SET FORMAT TO	Yes	No	Opens a format file for data entry
SET FULLPATH	Yes	Yes	Shows full path for MDX( ) and NDX( )
SET FUNCTION	Yes	Yes	Sets operation of function keys
SET HEADING ON/OFF	Yes	No	Controls display of headings over the display of fields in LIST or DISPLAY
SET HELP ON/OFF	Yes	No	Controls the display of help prompts
SET HISTORY ON/OFF	Yes	No	Controls whether commands are saved in the history buffer
SET HISTORY TO	Yes	No	Specifies the number of commands saved in the history buffer
SET HOURS TO	Yes	Yes	Specifies a 12- or 24-hour clock
SET INDEX TO	No	Yes	Opens index files
SET INSTRUCT ON/OFF	Yes	No	Controls display of instruction boxes in menus
SET INTENSITY ON/OFF	Yes	No	Controls whether screens include enhanced display
SET LOCK ON/OFF	Yes	No	Controls use of automatic record locking
SET MARGIN TO	Yes	No	Controls setting of left printer margin
SET MARK TO	Yes	Yes	Specifies the date separator character
SET MEMOWIDTH TO	Yes	No	Specifies setting of memo field columns
SET MENUS ON/OFF	Yes	Yes	Controls whether memo fields are displayed in full-screen displays
SET MESSAGE TO	Yes	No	Specifies messages displayed at the bottom of the screen.
SET NEAR ON/OFF	No	Yes	Specifies whether a seek is satisfied by a *nearmatch*

dBASE Command	Allowed in SQL	New or Modified	Description
SET ODOMETER TO	Yes	No	Controls the update interval for the record interval
SET ORDER TO	No	Yes	Specifies a controlling index
SET PATH TO	Yes	No	Specifies a directory path for file searches
SET PAUSE ON/OFF	Yes	Yes	Controls scrolling of SQL results
SET POINT TO	Yes	Yes	Specifies the character used for decimal point displays
SET PRECISION TO	Yes	Yes	Specifies the precision of fixed point arithmetic
SET PRINTER ON/OFF	Yes	No	Controls output sent to a printer
SET PRINTER TO	Yes	No	Redirects print output
SET PROCEDURE TO	Yes	No	Opens a procedure file
SET REFRESH TO	Yes	Yes	Set time to check for record change
SET RELATION TO	No	Yes	Links specified database files
SET REPROCESS TO	Yes	Yes	Sets command retry count
SET SAFETY ON/OFF	No	No	Prompts for confirmation before overwriting file
SET SCOREBOARD ON/OFF	Yes	No	Enables message line display on line 0
SET SEPARATOR TO	Yes	Yes	Specifies a numeric value separator
SET SKIP TO	No	Yes	Specifies a file in a relation
SET SPACE	Yes	Yes	
SET SQL ON/OFF	Yes	Yes	Starts/stops SQL mode in interactive mode
SET STATUS ON/OFF	Yes	No	Enables display of status bar
SET STEP ON/OFF	No	No	Specifies whether commands are executed one at a time in a program
SET TALK ON/OFF	No	No	Enables display of command execution on the screen
SET TITLE ON/OFF	No	No	Specifies whether files are titled when added to a *dBASE* catalog

dBASE Command	*Allowed in SQL*	*New or Modified*	*Description*
SET TRAP ON/OFF	Yes	Yes	Controls whether debugger is invoked when an error occurs or Esc is pressed during program execution; also directs DO command
SET TYPEAHEAD TO	Yes	No	Specifies the size of the type-ahead buffer
SET UNIQUE ON/OFF	No	No	Determines if only unique records are displayed
SET VIEW TO	No	Yes	Activates a *dBASE* view
SHOW MENU	Yes	Yes	Displays a menu without activating it
SHOW POPUP	Yes	Yes	Displays a popup without activating it
SKIP	No	No	Moves the record pointer forward or backward
SORT	No	No	Creates a new copy of a database file, arranging the records in specified order
STORE	Yes	No	Stores an expression to a memory variable
SUM	No	Yes	Computes an arithmetic sum
SUSPEND	Yes	No	Interrupts program execution without terminating
TEXT-ENDTEXT	Yes	No	Displays a block of text from a program file
TOTAL ON	No	Yes	Creates a summary database of numeric totals
TYPE	Yes	Yes	Displays contents of a file to the screen or printer
UNLOCK	No	No	Unlocks files or records in a specified work area
UPDATE	No	Yes	Makes batch changes to a database file
USE	No	Yes	Activates a database file
WAIT	Yes	No	Pauses program execution and waits for user response
ZAP	No	No	Removes all records from an active database file

C

dBASE IV Functions

This appendix contains a complete listing of *dBASE IV* functions, new and old, as well as their applicability to both interactive and procedural (program) modes.

Function	Description	Allowed in SQL Mode	Allowed in SQL Statement	New or Changed in dBASE IV
&	Performs macro substitution	Yes	No	Yes
ABS( )	Returns absolute value	Yes	Yes	Yes
ACCESS( )	Returns access level of current user	Yes	No	Yes
ACOS( )	Returns angle with trigonometric cosine matching specified value	Yes	Yes	Yes
ALIAS( )	Returns alias name of specified work area	No	No	Yes
ASC( )	Does character-to-ASCII conversion	Yes	Yes	No
ASIN( )	Returns angle with trigonometric sine matching specified value	Yes	Yes	Yes

Function	Description	Allowed in SQL Mode	Allowed in SQL Statement	New or Changed in dBASE IV
AT( )	May now take memo field name as its second argument	Yes	Yes	Yes
ATAN( )	Returns angle with trigonometric tangent matching specified value	Yes	Yes	Yes
ATN2( )	Returns angle with trigonometric cosine and sine matching specified values	Yes	Yes	Yes
BAR( )	Returns bar name of last selected prompt bar	Yes	No	Yes
BOF( )	Indicates beginning of file	No	No	No
CALL( )	Executes a binary module	Yes	Yes	Yes
CDOW( )	Returns day of week	Yes	Yes	No
CEILING( )	Returns ceiling of an expression	Yes	Yes	Yes
CHANGE( )	Tests whether current record has been changed	No	No	Yes
CHR( )	Does ASCII decimal-to-character conversions	Yes	Yes	No
CMONTH( )	Returns name of month from a date	Yes	Yes	No
COL( )	Returns cursor column on screen	Yes	No	No
COMPLETED( )	Indicates whether transaction is completed	Yes	No	Yes
COS	Returns cosine from angle in radians	Yes	Yes	Yes
CTOD( )	Does character-to-date conversions	Yes	Yes	No

Function	Description	Allowed in SQL Mode	Allowed in SQL Statement	New or Changed in dBASE IV
DATE( )	Returns system date	Yes	Yes	No
DAY( )	Returns number of the day of month	Yes	Yes	No
DBF( )	Returns name of database file in use	No	No	No
DELETED( )	Determines whether record is marked for deletion	No	No	No
DIFFERENCE( )	Indicates difference between two Soundex codes	Yes	Yes	Yes
DISKSPACE( )	Returns number of free bytes on default drive	Yes	No	No
DMY( )	Does date format conversion	Yes	Yes	Yes
DOW( )	Returns number of day of week	Yes	Yes	No
DTOC( )	Converts date to character string	Yes	Yes	No
DTOR( )	Converts degrees to radians	Yes	Yes	Yes
DTOS( )	Returns the ANSI date	Yes	Yes	Yes
EOF( )	Indicates end of file	No	No	No
ERROR( )	Returns error number causing ON ERROR condition	Yes	Yes	No
EXP( )	Determines number from its natural logarithm	Yes	Yes	No
FIELD( )	Determines names of fields from their numbers	No	No	No
FILE( )	Verifies the existence of a file	Yes	No	No
FIXED( )	Does floating-point to fixed-point decimal number conversion	Yes	Yes	Yes
FKLABEL( )	Determines name of function key from its label	Yes	No	No
FKMAX( )	Indicates maximum number of programmable function keys	Yes	No	No
FLOAT( )	Converts data type N fixed-point into data type F floating-point			Yes

Function	Description	Allowed in SQL Mode	Allowed in SQL Statement	New or Changed in dBASE IV
FLOCK( )	Locks all records in a database file	No	No	No
FLOOR( )	Returns largest integer < = value	Yes	Yes	Yes
FOUND( )	Indicates if record found	No	No	No
FV( )	Future value of investment	No	No	Yes
GETENV( )	Returns DOS environment parameters (SET *parm* =)	Yes	No	No
IIF( )	Performs immediate IF operation	No	No	No
INKEY( )	Returns decimal ASCII value of last key pressed	Yes	No	No
INT( )	Does conversion to integer by truncating decimals	Yes	Yes	No
ISALPHA( )	Determines if first character is alphabetic	Yes	No	No
ISCOLOR( )	Determines if color graphics board is installed	Yes	No	No
ISLOWER( )	Determines if first character is lowercase	Yes	No	No
ISMARKED( )	Indicates if changes exist in current database file	No	No	Yes
ISUPPER( )	Determines if first character is uppercase	Yes	No	No
KEY( )	Key expression of index file or MDX tag	No	No	Yes
LASTKEY( )	Returns ASCII code of key pressed to exit full-screen command	Yes	No	Yes
LEFT( )	Returns a specified number of characters counting from left of string	Yes	Yes	No
LEN( )	Returns number of characters in a string or memo field	Yes	Yes	Yes

Function	Description	Allowed in SQL Mode	Allowed in SQL Statement	New or Changed in dBASE IV
LIKE( )	QBE function that compares strings using wild cards	Yes	No	Yes
LINENO( )	Returns the file relative line number of current command			Yes
LKSYS( )	Returns time or date of lock or ID of user who last locked record or file			Yes
LOCK( )	Used in networking to lock a database record. Will remain in effect until UNLOCK( ) is issued.	No	No	Yes
LOG( )	Returns natural (base-e) logarithm	Yes	Yes	No
LOG10( )	Returns base-10 logarithm	Yes	Yes	No
LOOKUP( )	Looks up record from another database file	No	No	Yes
LOWER( )	Indicates whether letter is upper- or lowercase	Yes	Yes	No
LTRIM( )	Removes leading blanks from field	Yes	Yes	No
LUPDATE( )	Returns last file update date	No	No	No
MAX( )	Maximum of two numbers	Yes	No	No
MDX( )	Returns tag names of an .MDX file			Yes
MDY( )	Converts date to format Mon DD YY	Yes	Yes	Yes
MEMLINES( )	Returns the number of word-wrapped lines in memo field	No	No	Yes
MEMORY( )	Returns RAM in K bytes	Yes	No	Yes
MENU( )	Returns name of active menu	Yes	No	Yes
MESSAGE( )	Returns the error message string of last error causing ON ERROR condition	Yes	No	No
MIN( )	Minimum of two values	Yes	No	No

Function	Description	Allowed in SQL Mode	Allowed in SQL Statement	New or Changed in dBASE IV
MLINE( )	Indicates line of memo field	No	No	Yes
MOD( )	Does modulo arithmetic (remainder of a division)	Yes	Yes	No
MONTH( )	Returns month number in a date	Yes	Yes	No
NDX( )	Returns name of an index file	No	No	Yes
NETWORK( )	Returns .T. if system on a network	Yes	No	Yes
ORDER( )	Name of primary order index file	No	No	Yes
OS( )	Operating system	Yes	No	No
PAD( )	Prompt pad name of active menu	Yes	No	Yes
PAYMENT( )	Amount of periodic payment on loan	No	No	Yes
PCOL( )	Printer column position	Yes	No	No
PI( )	Provides constant for ratio of circumference to diameter	Yes	Yes	Yes
POPUP( )	Returns name of active popup menu	Yes	No	Yes
PRINTSTATUS( )	Returns printer status	Yes	No	Yes
PROGRAM( )	Returns current executing program	Yes	No	Yes
PROMPT( )	Returns prompt of last selected option	Yes	No	Yes
PROW( )	Printer row	Yes	No	No
PV( )	Present value of payments	No	No	Yes
RAND( )	Provides random number	Yes	Yes	Yes
READKEY( )	Integer value of key pressed	Yes	No	No
RECCOUNT( )	Number of records in current database	No	No	No

Function	Description	Allowed in SQL Mode	Allowed in SQL Statement	New or Changed in dBASE IV
RECNO( )	Current record number	No	No	No
RECSIZE( )	Size of record	No	No	No
REPLICATE( )	Repeats a character expression a given number of times	Yes	Yes	No
RIGHT( )	Returns a specified number of characters from the right of string	Yes	Yes	No
RLOCK( )	Locks a database file	No	No	No
ROLLBACK( )	Determines if ROLLBACK is successful	Yes	No	Yes
ROUND( )	Rounds off numbers to specified number of decimals	Yes	Yes	No
ROW( )	Row number of screen cursor	Yes	No	No
RTOD( )	Does radians-to-degrees conversa-tion	Yes	Yes	Yes
RTRIM( )	Removes trailing blanks	Yes	Yes	No
SEEK( )	Returns .T. if index key found	No	No	Yes
SELECT( )	Returns number representing an unused work area	No	No	Yes
SET( )	Returns parameters of SET commands	Yes	No	Yes
SIGN( )	Returns mathematical sign of number	Yes	Yes	Yes
SIN( )	Returns sine value from an angle in radians	Yes	Yes	No
SOUNDEX( )	Returns Soundex codes	Yes	Yes	Yes
SPACE( )	Provides character string made of blank spaces	Yes	Yes	No
SQRT( )	Calculates square root of a number	Yes	Yes	No
STR( )	Does number-to-character string conversion	Yes	Yes	No

Function	Description	Allowed in SQL Mode	Allowed in SQL Statement	New or Changed in dBASE IV
STUFF( )	Replaces part of a string with another	Yes	Yes	No
SUBSTR( )	Extracts specified number of characters from a string or memo field	Yes	Yes	Yes
TAG( )	Name of specified tag	No	No	Yes
TAN( )	Returns tangent value in radians from an angle	Yes	Yes	Yes
TIME( )	Provides system clock value	Yes	Yes	No
TRANSFORM( )	Performs PICTURE formatting	Yes	No	No
TRIM( )	Removes trailing blanks	Yes	Yes	No
TYPE( )	Returns data type of an expression	Yes	No	No
UPPER( )	Does uppercase conversion	Yes	Yes	No
VAL( )	Does character-string to number conversion	Yes	Yes	No
VARREAD( )	Name of field or memory variable currently being edited	Yes	No	Yes
VERSION( )	Returns dBASE IV version number	Yes	No	No
YEAR( )	Returns year from date expression	Yes	Yes	No

Glossary

aggregate function—A group function. A function operating on the values in one column of a table and producing a single value as its result. Same as "built-in" function.

argument—An expression inside the parentheses of a function, supplying a value for the function to operate on.

ASCII—A standard for using digital data to represent printable characters. An acronym for American Standard Code for Information Exchange.

attribute—A column heading in a table.

base table—Any "real" table in the database, as opposed to a "virtual table."

candidate row—A row selected by a main query, the field values of which are used in the execution of a correlated subquery.

cartesian product—An equijoin where the set of conditions is empty.

case sensitivity—Ability to distinguish between upper- and lowercase letters.

catalog—In *dBASE* mode, a file containing information about all the files in a particular database. The catalog is necessary to work from the Control Center. In SQL mode, the catalog is a set of system-controlled tables maintained by SQL for statistical and data definition purposes.

CHAR—A data type that stores character strings.

character string—A sequence of characters.

concatenated index—An index created on more than one column of a table. Used to guarantee that those columns are unique for every row in the table.

DBA—See *database administrator*.

DCL—See *Data Control Language*.

DDL—See *Data Definition Language*.

DML—See *Data Manipulation Language*.

database administrator—The DBA, a user authorized to grant and revoke other users' access to the system, modify options affecting all users, and perform other administrative functions.

Data Control Language (DCL)—One category of SQL statements. These statements control access to the data and to the database. Examples are GRANT CONNECT, GRANT SELECT, UPDATE ON, REVOKE DBA.

Data Definition Language (DDL)— One category of SQL statements. These statements define (CREATE) or delete (DROP) database objects. Examples are CREATE VIEW, CREATE TABLE, CREATE INDEX, DROP TABLE.

data dictionary—A comprehensive set of tables and views usually owned by the DBA. Also contains information available to DBA only about users, privileges, and auditing. A central source of information for the database itself and for all users. In *dBASE IV* the catalog tables replace the data dictionary.

Data Manipulation Language (DML)— One category of SQL statements. These statements query and update the actual data. Examples are SELECT, INSERT, DELETE, UPDATE.

data type—Any one of the forms of data stored and manipulated. Data types supported by *dBASE IV* are CHAR, DATE, LOGICAL, NUMERIC, FLOAT, SMALLINT, INTEGER, and DECIMAL.

date field—A field whose value is a date. Sometimes applied to a field whose value is a number representing a date.

datum—a single unit of data.

DBA—See *database administrator*.

deadlock—A situation where two users are each vying for resources locked by the other; and therefore, neither user can obtain the necessary resource to complete the work.

default—The value of any option built into the system that will be used by the system if the user fails to specify a value for that option.

distinct—Unique.

dummy table—A table containing fictitious or temporary data. Useful as the object of a SELECT command intended to copy the value of one field to another field.

embedded SQL—An application program consisting of programming language text and SQL text.

equijoin—A join condition specifying the relationship "equals" (=).

export—Transfer database files into some other storage area.

expression—A combination of constants, variables, and operators producing a result of a single data type, usually used as the arguments to commands.

field—A part of a table that holds one piece of data. The intersection of a row and a column.

form feed—A control character that causes the printer to skip to the top of a new sheet of paper.

function—An operation that may be performed by placing the function's name in an expression. Most functions take one or more arguments within the parentheses and use the value(s) of the argument(s) in the operation.

group function—A function operating on a column or expression in all of the rows selected by a query and computing a single value from them. For example, AVG computes an average. Same as Aggregate Function and "built-in" function.

index—A data structure used primarily to speed searching for data. In the case of a table, an index provides faster access than doing a full table scan.

initialization—The initial preparing of a database, always done when installing a database system for the first time.

interactive SQL—An operating environment in which SQL commands can be executed one at a time. Commands are entered at the SQL. prompt (similar to the environment provided at the *dBASE* dot prompt) with results immediately displayed.

join—An operation on two or more tables resulting in a single table, depending on test conditions among some of the columns in the tables.

macro—In *dBASE IV*, a macro is a substitution method whereby a value is substituted for a memory variable or a function key, which can then be used as a command or part of a command.

main query—The outermost query in a query containing a subquery. The query containing the first SELECT command in a series of SELECT commands. Also called the "outer query" as opposed to a subquery which is called the "inner query."

memory variable—A *dBASE* variable that allows you to specify a value in expressions, search conditions and with SQL predicates such as

IN or LIKE. Also can be used in commands to transfer data to columns in tables with the INSERT command. When used with the FETCH command, will return values from columns.

natural join—An equijoin taken on the common column(s) of two or more tables with the duplicate(s) of the common column(s) removed.

nested SELECT—See *subquery*.

nesting—An arrangement of two processing steps in which one invokes the other.

non-equijoin—A join condition specifying a relationship other than "equals", e.g. $<$, $>$, $>=$, $>=$.

NUMBER data type—A data type for numeric data.

object—Something stored in a database. Examples are tables, views, synonyms, indexes, columns, reports, stored procedures, stored programs.

outer join—The rows that do not match the join condition.

parameter—A memory variable whose value is passed to a subprogram.

precedence—The order in which the system performs operations on an expression.

propagation—The process of copying a value from one field to another, logically related field, or computing a value to be stored in a related field. For example, when an employee's social security number is entered in a block of a salary record form, it may be propagated to a block of a withholding tax form.

public synonym—A synonym for a database object that the DBA has created for use by all users.

QBE—Query By Example, a user-friendly query language.

query—An instruction to SQL or QBE that will retrieve information from one or more tables or views.

read consistency—Feature whereby a SQL query always sees a snapshot of a table as it existed at the start of query execution even while others may be modifying the table.

record—One row of a table.

relational database—A database that appears to the user to be just a collection of tables.

reserved word—A word with a special meaning in *dBASE IV* and therefore not available to users in naming tables, views, or columns.

self-join—A join operation in which rows of the same table are joined to each other.

semijoin—The rows of one table that are linked with the rows of another table in a join.

SQL—Structured Query Language.

Structured Query Language (SQL)— A particular formal language for storing and retrieving information in a database.

subquery—A query used as a clause in a SQL command. Also called an "inner query" as opposed to the main query, which is called the "outer query," a "nested SELECT," or a subSELECT. The result of a subquery is to provide information needed to complete the main query.

syntax—The linear order of words or symbols.

target list—The list of columns appearing directly after the SELECT in a query or subquery.

temporary tables—Frequently required to order data and to execute SQL statements, including DISTINCT, ORDER BY, or GROUP BY clauses.

theta join—A join based on any comparison operator.

transaction—A logical unit of work as defined by the user. In *dBASE IV*, a transaction is the set of tasks to be performed by the commands between a BEGIN TRANSACTION command and an END TRANSACTION command.

transaction processing—The processing of logical units of work, rather than individual entries, to keep the database consistent.

unique index—An index that imposes uniqueness on each value it indexes. May be a single column or concatenated columns.

unit of work—A logical unit of work is equivalent to a transaction. Includes all SQL statements since you either logged on, last committed, or last rolled back your work. A transaction can encompass one SQL statement or many SQL statements.

view—A table that does not physically exist as such in storage, but looks to the user as though it does. A part of a table that does exist in the database. A "virtual" table.

virtual column—A column in a query result, the value of which was calculated from the value(s) of other column(s).

virtual table—A table that does not actually exist in the database but looks to the user as though it does. Contrast with "base table." See *view*.

wrapping—Moving the end of a heading or field to a new line when it is too long to fit on one line.

Index

Index

Index

blackboard, 68
boldface, 105
borders, 32
BOTTOM, 131
boxes, 121
BROWSE, 11, 13, 27, 59, 63-66,
127, 141, 238
Browse a Database or View Dialog,
127
buttons, 56

C

CALCULATE, 21, 35, 237
calculated fields, 68, 71
CANCEL, 142, 143
capitalization, 65
Cartesian product, SQL, 213
catalog, 43
Catalog File, 2
Catalog Menu, 46
choices in, 47
operation of, 46
CHANGE, 13, 28, 29, 141, 238
CHAR, 179, 180, 201
CLEAR ALL, 141
CLEAR MENU, 26
CLEAR POPUP, 27
CLEAR WINDOW, 25
clock, 54
CLOSE ALL/DATABASE/INDEX,
142
CNT, 21, 81
commands
new and modified, 7-41
popup, 23
summary of dBASE, 268-278
uppercase notation for, 5
comparison operators, WHERE
clause and, 195
compiler, 38
COMPLETED function, 143
COMPRESS, 127
condition boxes, 68, 71
Condition menu, Query By
Example (QBE), 88
Control Center, 2, 42-57
Application panel in, 113
ASSIST to enter, 42
Data panel in, 58-66
Exit Menu for, 52
function keys for, 44
getting help in, 55
main menus for, 45
panel submenus for, 53
quitting dBASE iv with, 57
screen display of, 43
CONVERT, 28
COPY, 35, 38, 141, 237
COPY INDEXES/TAG, 28

COPY MEMO, 40
COPY STRUCTURE, 237
correlated subqueries, 199
COUNT, 35, 201, 237
CREATE, 141, 142, 185, 212, 218
CREATE APPLICATION, 113
CREATE DATABASE, 172, 176
CREATE INDEX, 129, 163, 172, 182
CREATE SYNONYM, 183, 210
CREATE TABLE, 172, 180
CREATE VIEW, 173, 184, 208
CREATE/MODIFY, 13
CREATE/MODIFY STRUCTURE,
178
CRP extension, 155
Ctrl-N, 60

D

data control statements, 173
data definition statements, 172
data encryption, 155
SQL mode, 165
data encryption security level, 153
data manipulation statements, 173
Data panel, 58-66
Append Menu in, 61
creating a new file in, 59
Exit menu in, 62
five menus in, 60
Go To menu in, 62
Organize menu in, 61
data submenu, 53
data types, SQL, 179
Database File Design, 59
database objects, 6
using SQL to create, 172-186
databases, 58-66
adding existing files to, 62
Append menu for, 61
BROWSE command for, 63-66
creating a new file for, 59
EDIT for, 66
Exit menu for, 62
Fields Menu for, 64
Go To menu for, 62, 65
Layout menu for, 60
opening and closing files in, 62
Organize menu for, 61
Records Menu for, 63
relational, 1
DATE, 179, 180
dBASE IV
command summary, 268-278
conventions for, 4
dBASE III Plus vs., 3
features of, 2
function summary for, 278-286
introduction to, 1-6
key names and key labels, 19

networking with, 232-245
procedural interface for, 139-151
quitting, 57
security levels in, 153
DBCHECK, 152, 162, 167, 169, 173
DBDEFINE, 152, 162, 167, 169, 173
DBLINK, 38
Dbsystem.DB file, 153
DEACTIVATE MENU, 26
DEACTIVATE POPUP, 27
DEACTIVATE WINDOW, 25
DEBUG, 39
debugger, 39
DECIMAL, 168, 179, 180, 201
DECLARE CURSOR, 219
default file-open attributes, 234
DEFINE BAR, 24, 131
DEFINE MENU, 25
DEFINE PAD, 25
DEFINE POPUP, 24
DEFINE WINDOW, 11, 13, 24
DELETE, 127, 141, 159, 163, 168,
173, 218
DELETE FILE, 142
DELETE TAG, 15
deleting, Query By Example (QBE),
79
Design menu, APGEN, 118
destination, 61
DISPLAY, 129
setting color for, 30
DISPLAY MEMORY, 16
Display Menu, 52
DISPLAY STATUS, 15
DISPLAY STRUCTURE, 15
DO, 26, 27
DO WHILE, 21
Document.MAC, 112
DOS menus, 51
DOS utilities submenu, 47, 49
dot prompt, 2, 42
function key values at, 45
DROP, 212
DROP DATABASE, 172, 184, 185
DROP INDEX, 173, 185
DROP SYNONYM, 185
DROP TABLE, 172, 185
DROP VIEW, 186
DTOS, 32

E

EDIT, 12, 13, 27, 29, 59, 63, 66,
127, 141
Edit Database Description Dialog,
61
ellipses, command definition of, 5
embedded code, 124
embedded SQL, 175, 218-231
DECLARE CURSOR, 219

300

Index

Other Bestsellers From TAB

☐ **INCREASING PRODUCTIVITY WITH PFS® AND THE IBM® ASSISTANT SERIES—2NED EDITION—Burton**

If you use any or all of the popular PFS software modules . . . if you're thinking of investing in this highly versatile business tool . . . or if you're interested in discovering an exclusive source for practical, problem-solving "templates" to help you access maximum productivity power from each and ever PFS module . . . You can't afford to miss this completely revised, updated, and expanded new second edition of *Increasing Productivity with PFS and the IBM Assistant Series*! 256 pp., 240 illus., 7" × 10".

Paper $21.95   **Hard $22.95**
Book No. 2729

☐ **SUPERCALC® 3: LEARNING, USING AND MASTERING—Willis and Pasewark**

Whether you're a first-time spreadsheet user who wants a thorough introduction to SuperCalc 3 . . . a SuperCalc user who is upgrading to Version 3 . . . or an experienced business programmer who is switching from another spreadsheet program . . . you will find this an essential guide to mastering all the powerful, updated, multifaceted features offered by this amazing business tool! In no time at all you'll be putting your IBM® PC, PCjr, Apple® IIe, or TI Professional to work in dozens of number-crunching ways using SuperCalc 3—the powerful electronic spreadsheet that lets you custom design your own microcomputer program for organizing, arranging, and manipulating all types of information. 256 pp., 125 illus., 7" × 10".

Paper $16.95   **Hard $22.95**
Book No. 2694

☐ **WORKING WITH DISPLAYWRITE 3—Krumm**

At last, a thorough, hands-on guide that shows you how to make documents that look exactly as you want them to . . . precise, professional, attractive, and eye-catching. This first, easy-to-follow handbook on mastering IBM's state-of-the-art word-processing program, DisplayWrite 3, will help you present an image of your company or business that clearly demands respect. 320 pp., 7" × 10".

Paper $17.95   **Hard $24.95**
Book No. 2664

☐ **PROGRAMMING WITH dBASE III® PLUS—Prague and Hammitt**

Packed with expert programming techniques and shortcuts, this is an essential guide to Ashton Tate's newest version of it dBASE relational database manager for the IBM® PC™. It includes all the practical, use-it-now advice and guidance beginning PC users are looking for . . . as well as power programming techniques that will allow more advanced users to increase productivity while sharply reducing application development time. 384 pp., 150 illus., 7" × 10".

Paper $21.95   **Hard $29.95**
Book No. 2726

☐ **HARVARD PROJECT MANAGER/TOTAL PROJECT MANAGER: CONTROLLING YOUR RESOURCES—Kasevich**

Whether involved in engineering, manufacturing, publishing, agriculture, retailing, or government, today's "smart" managers are discovering that a desk-top or personal computer and the right software are essential ingredients for success. And nowhere is this more important than in project management—the defining and organizing of all aspects of a project so that time and resources can be put to most productive use. 240 pp., 180 illus., 7" × 10".

Paper $16.95   **Hard $21.95**
Book No. 2678

☐ **MULTIMATE® USER'S GUIDE—Spear and Ritchie**

Unlike the user's manuals that come with MultiMate or other books that simply restate what's already in those user's manuals, *MultiMate® User's Guide* provides a wealth of "inside" information on MultiMate's special utilities and shows you how to create a wide range of business documents successfully. Authors Barbara Spead and Deborah Ritchie also include handy "from experience" tips and hints that eliminate the frustration of trying to figure out MultiMate's more elusive applications potential and makes it possible for you to write professional-quality documents right from the start. 192 pp., 7" × 10".

Paper $14.95   **Hard $21.95**
Book No. 2623

Other Bestsellers From TAB

Other Bestsellers From TAB